How Debuggers Work

Algorithms, Data Structures, and Architecture

Jonathan B. Rosenberg

WILEY COMPUTER PUBLISHING

JOHN WILEY & SONS, INC.

New York • Chichester • Brisbane • Toronto • Singapore • Weinheim

Executive Publisher: Katherine Schowalter

Editor: Marjorie Spencer

Managing Editor: Susan Curtin

Text Design & Composition: Pronto Design & Production Inc.

Library of Congress Cataloging-in-Publication Data:

Rosenberg, Jonathan B., 1956-
       How Debuggers work: algorithms, data structure, and architecture
      / Jonathan B. Rosenberg.
             p. cm.
      Includes bibliographical references and index.
      ISBN 0-471-14966-7 (alk. paper)
      1. Debugging in computer science. 2. Computer algorithms.
      3. Data structures (Computer science) 4. Computer architecture
    I. Title.
QA76.9.D43R67   1996   96-9195
005.1'4—dc20   CIP

Printed in the United States of America
10 9 8 7 6 5 4 3 2

About the Authors

Jonathan B. Rosenberg, author

Jonathan B. Rosenberg is the Vice President of C++ and Internet Products Development at Borland International. He is responsible for C++ and related products including teams building the Integrated Development Environment, Compilers, Linkers and related tools, the ObjectWindows Library, as well as Companion Products such as CodeGuard, TASM and Tools, and more. His C++ team also builds components used in many other Borland products including the editor, debugger, compiler backend, and linker for Delphi. His initial role at Borland was Project Manager for Debuggers where he was responsible for debugger technology used in C++ and Pascal products on Windows and OS/2. He was also responsible for Internet product development including the Java tool Latte currently under development.

Prior to Borland, he was Manager of Tools for MasPar Computer Corporation from 1988 to 1992. An initial founder of MasPar, he was the architect of the MasPar Programming Environment built in Smalltalk and C++. Prior to MasPar he was a professor of Computer Science at Duke University from 1986 to 1988. From 1982 to 1986 he was Director of Design Research and Technology at the Microelectronics Center of North Carolina in Research Triangle Park. MCNC was a 100 person research consortium focused on Very Large Scale Integrated chip design. Jonathan completed his Ph.D. in computer science from Duke University in Durham, NC in May 1983. His BA was in Mathematics from Kalamazoo College in 1978. Jonathan is originally from Birmingham, Michigan.

Steven Correll, contributor

Steven Correll has developed compilers, debuggers, and runtime systems in research environments and commercial environments, including Lawrence Livermore National Laboratory, Borland International, and several startup companies, including Mips Computer Systems.

P r e f a c e

Who Should Read This Book?

This book is for people who are curious about how debuggers work. It is also for those brave individuals who are embarking on the creation of a new debugger or a tool similar to a debugger. Even for developers who are not building a debugger, this book has a lot to offer. Every developer has spent—and will spend—an enormous time in front of one debugger or another. And if you understand a complex tool—which debuggers most certainly are—you can use it and understand what it is telling you and why much better. Debuggers, very complex beasts, have direct interactions with the CPU and intimate dealings with the operating system; they must be built closely in conjunction with the compiler, linker, and other application development tools. People interested in systems technology will find a lot to dig into in this book. Finally, anyone interested in algorithms will find a lot of unique and interesting algorithms that debuggers use to perform their normal functions.

What Will You Get Out of This Book?

You will see how hardware has evolved to support debugging. This dimension is important because debugging keeps getting more and more essential and the requirements on debuggers and the functionality they offer keep rising. Similar to the hardware evolution, the operating systems and their support and understanding of debuggers have grown enormously in the past ten years. But it is clear—and I will show why—that operating systems have a long way to go to provide what debuggers really need to develop outstanding functionality for debugging the kinds of applications now in demand. I will give you a much better understanding of how these vital and very complex tools work—I will give you a detailed look "under the hood." If you should ever need to build a debugger—from a simple, specialized debugging tool to be used only, by you, all the way up to a battle-hardened, production-quality, mass market debugger—I try to document here the collective knowledge of a broad array of debugger technology. And finally, you will learn about some very interesting and sometimes very clever algorithms employed in debuggers. Wherever possible, I will call out, in a stylized fashion, the most interesting, most important debugger algorithms.

Layout of This Book

- Chapter 1 is introductory and covers basic principals of debuggers and the environments in which they operate.

- Chapter 2 gives an overview of debugger architecture—what the user interface and paradigms are, how a debugger is put together, and how the various components interact.

- Chapters 3 and 4 cover basic underlying infrastructure: hardware and operating system support needed by debuggers to be able to provide the most basic functionality.

- Chapter 5 delves into the details of how a debugger controls the execution of a child process (which we will usually call the *debuggee*).

- Chapter 6 then explores the algorithms and data structures behind breakpoints and single-stepping—the two most important ways in which a debugger controls the execution of the debuggee. Breakpoints are like probes placed into a running program to observe it during operation (and without changing the program beforehand). Single-stepping is a way to carefully "walk through" a program to watch its behavior step-by-step and observe its control flow.

- Chapters 7 and 8 focus on three aspects of observing a program's context. First, I examine stack back traces. Next I explore the why's and wherefore's of disassembling hardware instructions and relating them back to the user's original source code. And finally, I explore in detail the very large topic of inspecting program variables in the debuggee. This includes symbol table lookup, scope resolution, address mappings, expression evaluation, function evaluation and more.

- Chapter 9 covers the complex and vitally important issues of multithreaded debugging. The modern operating systems provide "just enough rope..." to start using threads and to quickly run into serious programming—and debugging—issues with threads. Debuggers are still supposed to help you solve the resulting difficult multithreaded bugs.

- Chapter 10 addresses the special circumstances of debugging GUI (graphical user interface) applications. Because almost all applications have a major user interface component and because almost all modern GUI systems are event-based, there are a lot of important common issues to cover.

- Chapter 11 focuses on special uses of debuggers (or debugger-related tools) such as memory corruption debugging, reverse execution, hooking debuggers, remote debugging, debugging on parallel architecture machines, and the debugging of distributed objects.

- Chapter 12 covers the very complex issues surrounding debugging optimized code. The microprocessor industry trend is toward more and more RISC processors (even Intel is moving in this direction), and RISC demands better and better compiler optimization work to meet its performance goals. This will put more and more pressure on debuggers to handle these optimizations, without having to pull out all optimizations just to debug an application.

A c k n o w l e d g m e n t s

Steve Correll wrote the first version of Chapters 7 and 8 on variable inspection and symbol tables and contributed some sections on stack crawling, reverse disassembly, and debugging optimized code. He is extremely knowledgeable about the interface between debuggers and compilers, and I could not have developed those portions of the book without his contributions.

Steve Bird came up with the book title and pushed me in all those ocean swims that kept me sharp and focused.

Paul Gross gave me the encouragement to complete this even when there was no time to do so. He also allowed me to include screen shots from Borland products as concrete user interface examples.

Melissa Avilla, my assistant, is someone without whom I would not be able to keep things organized and on track.

Nan Borreson helped me get me connected to a publisher in the first place.

Alastair Fyfe, Borland's resident debugger guru, was a great resource. He has worked on debuggers for UNIX `ptrace()`, UNIX /proc, Windows 3.1 using TOOLHELP, and Win 32 for Windows 95 and Windows NT. He has worked around all the weirdness of those systems and has gained a wealth of valuable knowledge about debuggers. He reviewed the technical content in several chapters in this book, thereby improving the accuracy immensely.

Simon Field has worked on numerous debuggers and profilers over a span of a decade. He is one of the smartest people I have ever worked with, and also one of the most strong-willed.

David Williams is one of a new breed of fanatic Java enthusiasts. And they *will* take over the programming world, so he's a good one to keep as a friend. He and his partner, Jean-Paul Buu-Sau, can probably take credit for writing the first-ever native Java debugger.

Peter Christy, Kevin Redden, and others at Apple agreed to divulge debugger APIs for Mac OS so they could be included in this book.

The Borland C++ team taught me much about high-quality programmer tools and about how good (and how fun, and how trying) a development team can be.

My wife, Carole, is the best partner a person could have. In spite of her lack of detailed interest in this topic, she was interested in me and my completion of this work. My kids, Zachary and Joanna, were curious and supportive, but they could not figure out who would want to read about debuggers.

C o n t e n t s

1

Introduction

Debuggers are critical tools for the development of software. They are studied very little, as compared, for example, to compilers. But more hours are typically spent debugging programs than compiling them. Debuggers are very difficult tools to build robustly because they depend heavily on relatively weak portions of operating systems and because they tend to stress the underlying operating system's capabilities. More sophisticated operating system features and the relentless trend toward more advanced graphical programs put increased demands on debugger capabilities. This book is an introduction to how debuggers operate, and it discusses algorithms used by production debuggers.

Basic Concepts of Debuggers

The term *debugger* is something of a misnomer. Strictly speaking, a debugger is a tool to help track down, isolate, and remove *bugs* from software programs. Bugs are software defects that have been affectionately known as "bugs"[1] since the infamous moth of the Harvard Mark I days (ROCHESTER 1983). In truth, debuggers are tools to illuminate the dynamic nature of a program—they are used to understand a program as well as find and fix defects. Debuggers are the magnifying glass, the microscope, the logic analyzer, the profiler, and the browser with which a program can be examined. In spite of the limited scope of the term *debugger*, I will still use this term to describe these software analyzers.

---

[1]According to a possibly apocryphal story told by Grace Hopper, the moth that caused the erroneous program behavior in the Harvard Mark I that day is now enshrined in a log book housed in a Navy museum in Virginia, forever to be known as the first computer "bug."

Debuggers are quite complex pieces of software. Their inner workings require a suite of sophisticated algorithms and data structures to accomplish their tasks. Debuggers also require an exceptionally close cooperation with and intimate knowledge of the operating system. These algorithms and interfaces are one of the subjects of this book. To discuss debuggers adequately, I must first cover some background information and terminology. Here are some basic questions about debuggers I will answer to provide the necessary background from which to start:

- What are they?

- Who uses them?

- How are they used?

- Why are they used?

- When are they used?

- How do they work?

What Are They?

Debuggers are software tools that help determine why the program does not behave correctly. They aid a programmer in understanding a program and then in finding the cause of the discrepancy. The programmer can then repair the defect and so allow the program to work according to its original intent. A debugger is a tool that controls the application being debugged so as to allow the programmer to follow the flow of program execution and, at any desired point, stop the program and inspect the state of the program to verify its correctness.

Who Uses Them?

Typically, the original developer uses a debugger, but later a maintainer, a tester, or an adapter may. In any case, it is a programmer. A debugger can be a useful way for someone new to a piece of code to get up to speed on that code in preparation for maintenance or continued expansion of the code.

How Are They Used?

Debuggers are used by rerunning the application, sometimes after a special compilation that prepares them for debugging, in conjunction with the debugger tool itself. The debugger carefully controls the application using special facilities provided by the underlying operating system to give the user very fine control over the program under test (much the way a piece of electronic test equipment gives control over a circuit under test). The user controls execution using commonly found debugger features such as *breakpoints* and *single-step*. The state of the program is examined until the cause of the defect is detected; then the programmer can attempt a fix and begin to search for any other defects.

Why Are They Used?

Debuggers are a necessary part of the engineering process when dealing with something as complex as software systems. All interactions cannot be predicted, specifications usually are not written to the level of programming details, and implementation is an inherently difficult and error-prone process. As software gets continuously more complex, debuggers become more and more important in tracking down problems.

When Are They Used?

First, debuggers are used at program inception time, when only part of the implementation of a design is complete. Second, when an identifiable module or subsystem is completed and ready for use, a debugger can help make sure this component is ready for integration with other components. Third, as testing progresses on a completed program and uncovers new defects, the debugger becomes increasingly important because the program's bugs tend to get more difficult to detect and isolate over time. Fourth, debuggers are used as changes and adaptations are made to existing programs that introduce new complexities and therefore destabilize previously working code.

How Do They Work?

How debuggers work and how they will change over time are the primary subjects of this book. First, to present a complete overview, the various types of debuggers, the variety of approaches used to accomplish debugging, and a brief history of debugging are covered.

There are numerous approaches to debugging—perhaps as many as there are bugs. A few of the techniques used include using print statements, printing to log files, sprinkling the code with assertions, using post-mortem dumps, having programs that provide function call stacks on termination (i.e. crash), profiling, heap checking, automated data flow analysis, reverse execution, system call tracing tools, and, of course, interactive source-level debugging.

Interactive debugging tools also come in assorted flavors. One type is a kernel debugger for dealing with problems with an OS kernel on its own (only for OS developers) or for interactions between heavily OS-dependent applications and the OS. Another type is a basic machine-level debugger for debugging the actual running code (that is, machine instructions) as they are processed by the CPU. Similar to this is an in-circuit emulator (ICE), which emulates the system services so all interactions between an application and the system can be monitored and traced. Interpretive programming environments, such as those available for Basic, Smalltalk, and Java as well as other high-level languages, provide very effective debugging solutions (LALONDE 1990) because the debugger is well integrated into the run-time interpreter and has very tight control over the running application.

A very important class of debugging is source-level symbolic debugging—the primary emphasis of this book. The model presented to the user is that the user's high-level language source code is executed directly by the CPU. Source-level symbolic debugging proves to be the most effective and most frequently used technique for debugging end-user applications.

The historical progression of debugging tools has gone from static post-mortem dumps, to more interactive dump analyzers, to machine-level debuggers, to basic symbolic debuggers, to command-line symbolic debuggers, to full-screen text mode debuggers, to graphical user interface (GUI) debuggers, to the current state-of-the-art, full-fledged programming environments that integrate editor, compiler, debugger, browser, profiler, and more.

Programmers typically spend large quantities of time using debuggers. Debugging is both analytic and intuitive, and these disparate approaches direct the way debuggers must work. It must be easy for the user to switch very rapidly from one mode to the other as progress is made in the investigation phase of a perceived problem. When the programmer's program manifests a bug, the major problem is the difficulty of determining which of the user's assumptions about the program's behavior have been violated. Frequently, the programmer has trouble accepting that some assumption is being violated (GRAMLICH 1983). Thus, debuggers must be very reliable, feature rich, high performance, and adaptive. Remember, unlike many other software systems, the focus of a debugger is a broken application. Garbage-in garbage-out is not an acceptable guiding principle for debuggers. In short, tremendous demands are placed on debuggers so they must exhibit all the very best attributes of any software and be ready for any way in which an application may be broken. This is why the examination of debuggers is so important— they need to be well-designed, efficient, robust, and highly usable.

Current State-of-the-Art

In this section I will establish the sort of debugger we will study. The current state-of-the-art is a graphical user interface (GUI) debugger with a rich set of windows (or views), each of which supports a different aspect of debugging. This debugger may be a stand-alone tool, or it may be integrated into a more general programming environment that also includes compilers, linkers, editors, and more (LAZZERINI 1992). The state-of-the-art "debugger" covers a lot more functionality than its name implies. For example, it may log all calls to certain APIs, and it may provide sophisticated profiling capabilities as well as other capabilities that stretch the traditional view of "debugging."

Current debuggers can all control the execution of the program under scrutiny by using breakpoints (available in a wide variety) and instruction-level single-step. A breakpoint is a special code placed in the executing code stream that, when executed, causes a special trap to occur that the processor and the operating system report to the debugger. Most CPUs have special instructions for this purpose, provided explicitly for use by a debugger. Single-step allows the debugger to control the processor executing the subject program at such a fine-grained level that only a single machine instruction may be executed. Again, most modern processors have a special mode that can be set by a debugger that causes the processor, when told to commence execution, to execute only a single instruction before stopping and giving control back to the debugger program.

Debuggers report back to the user how, why, and where the application stopped. The application may have hit a user-inserted breakpoint, or it may have caused an exception condition, or it may have stopped for some other reason. Once stopped it is possible to examine the state of the application, which includes the current stack back trace (a list of all the functions called in order), the values in the hardware registers, the contents of all the application's accessible memory, and any other state that may be pertinent to the debugging process. Also while stopped, functions contained in the application under test can be executed *in situ* to allow you to determine the behavior that particular function will have at the current time.

In spite of how much can be gained by building debugging tools that model the high-level source being directly executed, it is also important that debuggers show the underlying implementation (CARGILL 1986). This is why debuggers provide disassembly views and direct access to hardware registers. The user gains a lot of confidence from these views because, when chasing a bug, the user must believe that some aspects of the program or its environment are acting as expected and can be counted on. Users typically keep trying out theories that explain a bug by checking all the things that must be true in order to support that theory.

The applications being debugged may be much more complex than the debugger itself (this clearly is the trend) and are most often themselves GUI-type applications. This means the debugger must take special care to remain non-invasive, especially on platforms that provide, at best, very fragile windowing systems.

A number of debuggers have provided modes where mixed interpreted and compiled code can be handled (CARLE 1987). This approach allows for much better control over the portion of the application being interpreted. This can be important when dealing with high levels of compiler optimization or sophisticated reverse execution schemes as well. If the compiler has so distorted the final instruction stream through optimizations that the programmer cannot easily map this back onto the original source code, switching to a mode where the actual source code is interpreted may remove a major source of confusion for the programmer.

Another important debugging technology is called "fix-and-run." The goal of this approach is to minimize the turnaround time between creating a fix to test and the ability to actually test the system with the modification in place. This technique consists of modifying fragments of code and adding them to or merging them into a running image. In larger applications, and for doing exploratory investigations before a fix is merged into the source code, this technique is very advantageous.

It is starting to become clear that performance analysis should not be considered completely distinct from the correct operation of a program—for one thing, it is a bug if an application runs too slowly. Therefore, debuggers are emerging that fully embrace performance analysis, but this additional capability is not yet the accepted state-of-the-art. It is also becoming clear that program browsing cannot be disjoint from the debugging process. **Browsing** is the process of examining the content and meaning of the source code text to better understand the program. Program understanding on the part of the developer is essential to effective debugging. However, profiling (and other sorts of analysis) and browsing deserve separate treatment and are not discussed in detail in this book.

Debugger Basic Principles

In this section, I present four key principles of debugger design and development. First, the Heisenberg principle that says the debugger must intrude on the debuggee in a minimal way. Second, at all costs, the debugger must be truthful so the programmer always trusts it. Third, the debugger's most important role is the presentation of content information so the user always knows where he is and how he got there in the debuggee. And fourth, unfortunately, the debugger you have to use is almost always behind technologically where you need it to be.

The Heisenberg Principle

It is important to any sort of in-process testing or monitoring that the test procedure does not unduly affect the normal operation of the system being tested. Hardware or chip testers go to a lot of trouble to make sure that the insertion of the probe into the circuit being tested does not affect that circuit. Similarly, the act of debugging an application should not change the behavior of the application. If this is not the case, the usefulness of the debugger falls into question. Non-intrusiveness in these and other sorts of systems being measured or tested has been formally defined by Heisenberg and is called the Heisenberg Principle (GRAMLICH 1983).

In software debugging, a debugger violates the pure Heisenberg Principle in a lot of ways. The simple fact that the debugger is in memory and is controlled by the same operating system as the application being debugged can affect the application. Depending on the operating system, adding a new process to the mix can change the addresses in the debugged application and the sequencing of when the process gets access to the CPU as determined by the operating system's scheduling algorithm. Bugs that are affected by this sort of thing are rare but extremely challenging and time-consuming because they are now so elusive. Bugs of this sort may also disappear when print statements are added to the source code of the debugged application and compiled in because the addition of the print statement may shift objects around in memory just enough to move the elusive bug somewhere else (or to mask it for now).

On windowing systems that depend fundamentally on event-based programming, the intrusiveness of the debugger can be even more problematic, especially if the debugger is also a GUI application that depends on events flowing into and out of the operating system. With Windows 3.1 and the Mac OS, the debugger is in the same address space as the debuggee and, even worse, the message queue is shared by all applications so messages for the application and for the debugger are intermixed in the single input queue. This puts a large burden on the debugger in attempting to minimize intrusiveness. On newer and more robust operating systems a running application is better protected. On these systems the debugger cannot directly manipulate the process—instead, it must use the debug API to affect the debuggee in any way.

Operating system designers as well as debugger designers worry a lot about the Heisenberg Principle. Their effort is worthwhile because the better they are able to keep the debugger from being intrusive and from impacting the behavior of the debuggee, the fewer bugs will disappear and become elusive only when run under the auspices of a debugger, leaving the application developer with no effective way to proceed.

Truthful Debugging

The second critical debugging principle is to always provide truthful information during debugging. Polle Zellweger, in her Ph.D. dissertation on debugging optimized code (ZELLWEGER 1984), developed this theme and defended its importance eloquently. This principle states that the debugger must never mislead the user because the user is frequently testing out theories of how the observed failure (bug) may be caused. Any misinformation will devastate the user, send the user off in the wrong direction potentially, and cause a general lack of trust to develop between the user and the debugging tool that will put into question everything reported by the debugger and will dramatically hamper effective progress. Zellweger focused on this principle with respect to debugging optimized code. An **optimizing compiler** performs some transformation on the code over-and-above the code produced for the un-optimized version that must now be unwound by the debugger. It is very difficult for the compiler and debugger to communicate effectively and completely enough to allow the debugger to give the user accurate information about how the optimized code maps back to the original source code.

There is more to truthful behavior than just reporting the effects of optimization accurately. When a stack back-trace gets corrupted, the debugger may try to work around the problem and unwind the stack in spite of the memory corruption. But if the debugger attempts to do this, any information that is not known with certainty must be presented honestly so as to maintain a high degree of trust between the user and the debugger.

Another common way a debugger could stumble and not be truthful to the user occurs when reporting the values of variables. After the location in the source and the stack back-trace, the values of variables are the most important information the user needs to determine the state of the debuggee. If the debugger does not report a value correctly, the user is badly misled and may spend countless hours tracking down the wrong bug. This can easily happen with modern compilers; even when not doing a high degree of optimization, they always do a certain amount of register allocation optimization. This is especially true with RISC chips and other processors that have lots of registers and for whom memory access is relatively expensive. The debugger may be fooled that the variable the user wishes to inspect is in memory when it actually is in a register. The result is that the debugger lies. In some cases, the compiler eliminates a variable because it is never needed throughout the remainder of the current function. In this case the debugger must show that the variable is actually "dead."

Context Is the Torch in a Dark Cave

This principle refers to the most important information the programmer needs during debugging: program context information. Context can include several different types of information such as source code, stack back-trace, variable values, thread information, and more. The first and most important question the application developer asks is "Where did the bug manifest itself and how did this happen?" To answer this question, the user wants the debugger to show the line in the source code where the fault occurred. When the application crashed, if the debugger has control over the application or can attach to the process while it is still maintained by the operating system, the debugger can determine this information and actually show the source code and highlight the line that actually had the fault. The program counter stops advancing when the fault occurs, and the debugger can use this stop point to determine the source location that corresponds. However, this may not point to the actual cause of the bug. Many bugs occur in one place but their effect (a crash) does not show up until much later.

After source code location the next most important component of context is the stack back-trace. This tells the user "How did the program get here?" This is done by showing the list of functions that the program passed through on the way to the current location (and will have to pass back through on the way back to the program's origin point). Specifically, the current function the program has stopped in is shown on the top of the stack listing. Next is the function that called this function, and so on, back to the original function that initiated the program's startup.

In multithreaded and multiprocess systems, the debugger must also be able to clearly and simply show the threads in the process as well as other processes with which debuggee process interacts. This information is crucial because multiprocess applications exist in the context of all the processes working together toward a certain end; if a bug shows up in one process, it may actually be caused by a problem with another cooperating process or by some communication problem between the processes. The same interactions also hold for multithreaded applications. The thread of execution that actually displays the fault may or may not be the source of the actual bug, and information about all the threads in the process is needed as part of the context information.

The values of variables, both global and local, are the next most critical component of the context picture presented to the application developer. If the values of variables are wrong, that can certainly point directly to the cause of the bug. Off-by-one is the most common programming error, and it frequently shows up as a bug, such as memory corruption if an array is accessed one element past its declared limit. That bug would be an illegal memory reference, and the programmer might find this by inspecting the loop variable, quickly seeing that the variable's current value is one too large to be correct.

Finally, the ultimate context authority is the information presented in what is commonly called a CPU view. Here information about the actual machine instructions currently about to be executed, the current register values, and the current hardware stack (from which the software stack previously discussed is derived) is presented.

All of these topics as well as many more will be discussed as we proceed through this book.

Debugging Trails Systems Developments

The final principle I wish to present is the principle that system developments occur long before any corresponding strong debugging support for the new systems developments is available. This is important because the systems vendors respond to the mass market, and the mass market requires certain technologies; the mass market also needs to debug applications as it tries to employ these new technologies. However, there is almost no pressure from the market to force vendors to build the necessary debugging support. For example, it was not until Win 32 (the basis for Windows NT and Windows 95) that there was sufficient OS support for debugging Windows GUI applications. Previously, the mass market operating system was Windows 3.1, which initially had no debugging support. Microsoft provided a Dynamic Link Library (DLL) that offered marginal support for debugging Windows applications. There are numerous examples like this one. Debugger developers need to push the systems vendors to provide the necessary infrastructure to enable support of the latest technologies. Application developers need to push not only for the technologies they need for the next great feature and their next chance for competitive advantage but also for the debuggers they will need to debug these ever increasingly complicated applications.

Debugger Classification

This section extends the introduction to debuggers by examining some of the different classes of debuggers. Debugging is a very general activity, but each specific application and bug require a special use of a debugger to locate and eliminate the fault quickly and decisively. To address all the different types of applications and bugs that application developers attack, several different types of debuggers have been built for fairly specialized uses.

Source-level (Symbolic) versus Machine-level

The developer of an application who is using a debugger has a lot to gain if the original source code is mapped directly to the application's machine code executing within the debugger. The compiler's job is to transform the source text into machine instructions that execute directly on the hardware platform. Mapping the machine instructions back to the original source text is not trivial for the debugger to do. But the benefits are enormous because it is not the machine instructions that are meaningful to the application developer—it is the original, high-level language source code. Early debuggers were not able to make the reverse mapping back from machine instructions to the original source code. But as applications grew in complexity this became more and more essential. The goal is to have the debugger give the illusion that the source code is being directly executed as if the underlying machine is not an Intel, SPARC, PowerPC, or whatever CPU, but is a C/C++, Pascal, COBOL, Basic, or Java execution engine. The trick to doing this is to have the compiler provide extensive debug information about the source code and how it was mapped into machine code. The nature of this information is discussed in detail later in Chapter 8. Even with this illusion that the debugger is directly executing the source code for you, there are times when you still need to dip down into the low-level, machine-specific details of how the program is actually running on the hardware. Therefore, every source-level debugger also needs to provide the low-level information. This is usually done by providing a *CPU view* that includes disassembly information, register values, a memory dump facility, and perhaps other machine-specific information.

Stand-alone versus Integrated Development Environments

A **stand-alone debugger** is a program dedicated solely to debugging and is separate from compiling and editing. A very established stand-alone debugger known as Turbo Debugger is shown in Figure 1.1.

The reason to move from stand-alone debuggers to integrated development environments that include debuggers is programmer productivity. It is much

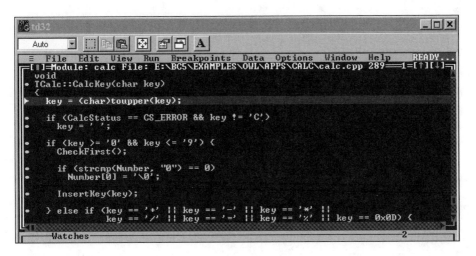

Figure 1.1

A stand-alone debugger. *Using Turbo Debugger 32 as an example, this figure shows a character-mode stand-alone debugger that works on Win 32 systems. This example shows the source code annotated with which lines correspond to executable code, and it shows where the instruction pointer stopped (near the top of the screen).*

better for developers to have a single tool on which to do development. At the developer's fingertips are all the tools needed, integrated for consistency, easier use, and higher levels of functionality.

In these integrated development environments (IDE), the developer quickly goes from editing to compiling to debugging in that typical cycle that repeats itself hundreds or thousands of times in large projects. In the editor view, you can set breakpoints as well as make changes to the source code via normal editing functions. From here you can also get feedback about where execution stopped and why. In the past, many developers have raised serious concerns about intrusiveness of a GUI debugger integrated into an IDE itself debugging a GUI application. On unprotected operating systems, especially ones with a single shared input queue for messages from devices such as mouse and keyboard, this was more of an issue than it is today. But there are occasions when the GUI debugger is more intrusive than a simpler, character mode debugger. However, the advantages overwhelmingly outweigh the disadvantages. GUI debuggers offer a more natural user environment: they operate just like all the other applications running on this platform. Further,

GUI debuggers integrated into a single environment offer a much higher level of functionality than possible with stand-alone debuggers.

The integrated debugger has access directly to the same compiler that is used to compile the application being debugged. While a stand-alone debugger can be effectively integrated with the run-time library (for example, for C++ exception support), the major limitation of a stand-alone debugger is the lack of access to the persistent compiler symbol tables and to the compiler itself. Direct access to the compiler means that when it is necessary for the debugger to evaluate an expression, that expression will be interpreted (that is, parsed) in exactly the same way and with the exact same resulting behavior as if that same code were part of the compiled application. The ability to directly manipulate the debuggee from the editor is a huge win: The shift is only in the user's mind, from looking at the source to edit it to looking at the debugger's view of the source being executed.

The integrated GUI debugger uses a variety of views to show different "slices" of the debuggee program. The editor view is also the source view. In addition, the stack view shows the function call stack, the CPU view shows the state of the low-level machine during execution, and the project manager shows all the files used to build the debuggee that are also available to the debugger for setting breakpoints and inspecting variables.

In terms of features offered, modern integrated debuggers have the same basic set as that offered by stand-alone debuggers. In addition, some features are not possible in stand-alone debuggers, such as integration with run-time library support for memory allocation error detection and integrated breakpoint-based profiling.

4GL versus 3GL

Fourth-generation languages (4GL) are used primarily in high-productivity, business-oriented application-generation tools with an emphasis on database-based applications. Examples of 4GL tools include PowerBuilder, Delphi, Visual Basic, and many others. Smalltalk is used as both a 3GL and a 4GL; I will treat it in this section. One characteristic of most 4GL tools is that they are based on an interpreted language such as Basic or Smalltalk. Being based on an interpreter offers distinct advantages. It enhances ease-of-use because it can give direct and immediate feedback about what effect a change the user makes will have. Debugging is made dramatically simpler because the interpreter provides a safe, protected environment in which both the target application and the debugger can run. Some cases of truly compiled 4GL development tools are now counteracting the advantages of interpreted systems with something much more compelling: productivity and performance. Delphi is a recent good example of this approach, which I will discuss in this section. The granddaddy of these 4GL tools is Visual Basic, which I cover first.

Visual Basic

BASIC is a simple language invented at Dartmouth in 1964 by Kemeney and Kurtz (KEMENEY 1985) to "make it easy and pleasant for Dartmouth students to learn programming." Several commercial tools have been developed based on Basic over the past three decades. The only one that really became entrenched and reached into the business applications arena was Visual Basic. The key to its success has been "visual" programming paradigm for ease of use. The approach it uses to debugging also has made this a very high productivity system.

The heart of Visual Basic is a Basic language interpreter. Each change made in the source code is checked by the interpreter for correctness before running. For the new change to become part of the running program requires the interpreter to re-generate a small amount of new p-code to be inserted into the interpreted stream for the entire application.

Most of the necessary debugger functionality is available in an interpreted system like Visual Basic. For example, Visual Basic 3.0 offers the debugging capabilities listed in Table 1.1.

Figure 1.2 shows Visual Basic's standard screen layout. The debug menu contents are shown to give a feel for the debugger features provided.

Implementation of standard debugger functionality is much simpler in this interpreted environment than in a native mode debugger. Breakpoints are just special p-code entries inserted into the stream of codes being scanned by the interpreter. When the special breakpoint code is seen, the interpreter stops and interacts with the user. No special interactions with the operating system or underlying hardware need take place.

Smalltalk

Smalltalk is a highly object-oriented language with a strong notion of class, inheritance, and events (LEWIS 1995) and yet is also implemented as an interpreted system.

TABLE 1.1 *Visual BASIC 3.0's Features*

Breakpoints	halt execution at certain points to look for problems, such as incorrect variable types, mixups in variable names, flaws in logical comparisons, endless loops, garbled output, problems with arrays, and so on
Watch expressions	at code creation/editing time or while in break mode to allow you to monitor the value of a particular expression as your code execution progresses
Single step	watches execution proceed one statement at a time
Procedure step	traces execution proceeding through the application one procedure at a time
Out-of-line interpreter	tests out new lines of code in a mini-interpreter; can have side effects that change variable values
Procedure call stack	views the current execution context

Smalltalk is based on a virtual machine that executes p-code. Most Smalltalk systems can also compile down to native machine code on a function-by-function basis. To set a breakpoint, you modify the source code to contain the **halt** keyword and re-execute that function. This debugging approach is the same one used in Basic interpreted systems. Smalltalk systems are very smart about incrementally executing a function at a time. Inspecting variables is done by inserting code that displays the values desired and re-executing. Several commercial Smalltalk systems have become very popular in business application development, especially within the financial community. Smalltalk's object-oriented power, combined with its ease-of-use (including debugging) and the cross-platform nature of interpreted Smalltalk, has driven its success.

Delphi

Delphi is a Visual Rapid Application Development environment based on a dialect of Pascal called ObjectPascal. Delphi fully compiles (not interprets) ObjectPascal down to the native Intel machine code. It has an IDE (similar to Visual Basic's) and a debugger with the same capabilities as those we will examine in more detail for C and C++. Figure 1.3 is a screen capture showing Delphi in debugging mode. The source view (which is also the programmer's editor) shows the execution being stopped. A separate call stack view shows the history of functions called to get to the current stopping point. And a breakpoint view shows the list of all currently active breakpoints.

OS Kernel versus Application-level

Kernel debugging is a necessary part of developing device drivers. Modern operating systems have a robust set of APIs and tools to allow the modification of OS behavior via the addition of specialized device drivers. Device

```
' Click event procedure for operator keys (+, -, x, /, =).
' If the immediately preceeding keypress was part of a
' number, increment NumOps. If one operand is present,
' set Op1. If two are present, set Op1 equal to the
' result of the operation on Op1 and the current
' input string, and display the result.
'
Sub Operator_Click (Index As Integer)
    TempReadout = ReadOut
    If LastInput = "NUMS" Then
        NumOps = NumOps + 1
    End If
    Select Case NumOps
        Case 0
        If Operator(Index).Caption = "-" And LastInput <> "NEG" Then
            ReadOut = "-" & ReadOut
            LastInput = "NEG"
        End If
        Case 1
        Op1 = ReadOut
        If Operator(Index).Caption = "-" And LastInput <> "NUMS" And OpFlag
            ReadOut = "-"
            LastInput = "NEG"
        End If
        Case 2
        Op2 = TempReadout
        Select Case OpFlag
            Case "+"
                Op1 = Val(Op1) + Val(Op2)
```

Debug Window [CALC.FRM:Operator_Click]

```
[CALC.FRM:Operator_Click] LastInput: "NONE"
[CALC.FRM:Operator_Click] Index: 2
[CALC.FRM:Operator_Click] NumOps: 0
```

Figure 1.2

Visual Basic debugger. *Using Visual Basic 3.0 as an example of a 4GL system, shown here is a screen showing an application stopped after a single-step operation with a watch window open on three variables being watched as the program runs.*

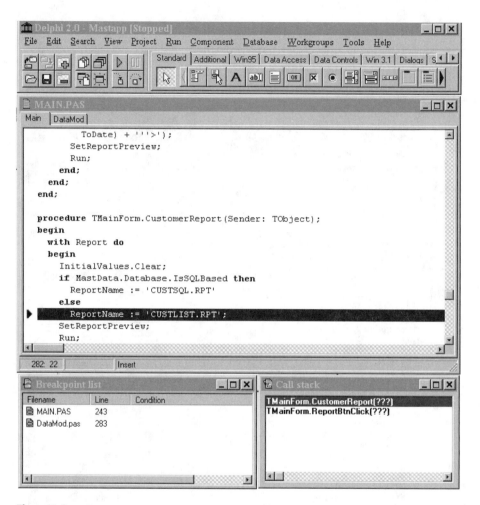

Figure 1.3

Delphi 2.0 debugger. *Using Delphi 2.0, we show here several debugger views with the application being debugged stopped at a breakpoint.*

drivers can be anything from a special timer module to aid a profiler to a sophisticated driver for a specialized real-time hardware data collection device. Kernel debugging is normally set up in such a way that two machines are involved: the host machine and the target machine being debugged. This gets the debugger completely out of the picture during debugging, which is critical when debugging OS components such as device drivers. As the machine crashes, there would be no way for a debugger on the crashing machine to report the scenario, whereas the remote machine can capture this critical information. Vendors such as Microsoft provide two versions of an operating system to developers of device drivers. One is the retail version, which is built with full optimization and without debug symbol information. The other, which Microsoft calls the "checked" build, has optimizations turned off or down and is built with full debugging symbols, which allows for detailed stack traces and inspection of key variables during debugging.

The setup for **WinDbg**, the Microsoft NT kernel debugger, is to have two NT machines connect via a serial cable. The target machine will have the checked build (with full debug symbols), and the host machine will use the standard retail version of NT. With the target machine enabling kernel debugging, the host machine running **WinDbg** can completely control the target machine. The checked build of NT running on the target machine has numerous ASSERTS that will check various values, any of which evaluating to false will cause a trap to the debugger. When an exception such as that caused by an ASSERT occurs, all threads halt except a special thread that communicates with **WinDbg**.

Another way in which kernel debugging is used is to catch user application problems in the way they deal with OS resources. If an application running on the debugging version of the OS kernel makes illegal calls to the OS APIs, the OS will log an error. Furthermore, as a process exits, the kernel will report about resource leaks such as window or file handles not returned (freed) back to the system.

Application-specific versus In-circuit Emulation

Application-specific debuggers are general-purpose, high-level debuggers that control one or just a few applications at one time. They notify the OS of their intentions and thereby get notifications from the OS when important events occur within one specific application.

In-circuit emulators sit between the operating system and the bare hardware and can watch and monitor all processes and all interactions between applications and the operating system. Typically these kinds of debuggers are lower-level and are used for development of add-on hardware or for very special types of heavily system-interacting applications (such as debuggers themselves).

At this point, I have completed the overview of debuggers and will now focus on one particular type of debugger—the source-level symbolic GUI debugger.

2

Debugger Architecture

Architecture Overview

Having presented some of the possible varieties of debuggers in Chapter 1, I will focus the rest of this book on the algorithms, data structures, architecture, and inner workings of the most commonly used type of debugger: the symbolic (maps underlying machine representation back to user-created source code), graphical user-interface-based (presents windows or views of different aspects of the underlying application to the user in an interactive, windows-based fashion), application-oriented debugger (focused on user-written applications, not operating system components).

In this chapter I discuss a generic architecture for the state-of-the-art debugger of our target type. No specific brand of debugger is assumed[1] but I have found that most debuggers match the architecture presented here fairly closely. Differences between debuggers are based more on what views they present to the user and what features are exposed in those views than on basic underlying architectural differences. First I present, in Figure 2.1, a diagram that shows that a debugger must, at its core, be closely tied to the underlying operating system; from there, it is built out to present a set of features to users through some sort of user interface.

---

[1]However, with permission, I use screen shots from a current commercial debugger, Borland International's Borland C++ 5.0 integrated debugger, to show how various views look during a debugging session.

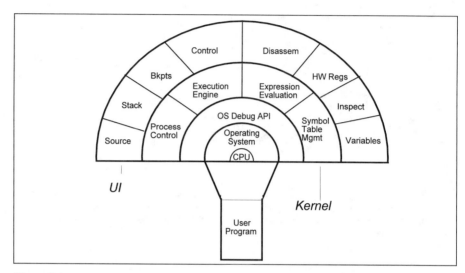

Figure 2.1

Typical debugger architecture.   *Graphical representation of basic debugger architecture. Outer-most ring represents user interface presented to user. Inner-most circle represents the core of the debugger interfacing to the underlying operating system.*

User Interface

This section describes the state-of-the-art graphical debugger user interface. Following the diagram above, I will work from the outer-most circle inward in my discussion of the debugger's architecture. The user interface for this graphical debugger consists of a series of views (or windows). Each view represents a different "picture" of the program being debugged. At any point in time, when the application is stopped, these "pictures" represent some state the application is in. A control view may provide a centralized locus of control for all debugger functions and a place for status presentation, as shown in Figure 2.2.

Relating this screen shot to the architecture diagram (Figure 2.1), we have here a source view that is also the program editor, where changes are made to the source code for the application. Below the source view is general feedback to the user about modules loaded during execution, errors encountered, and any other valuable information to aid the user in program understanding. Finally, the bottom-most view is not directly related to debugging—it is the *project view* that shows the user the major components (source files, object modules, dynamically loaded libraries, executables, etc.) that comprise the currently active application.

The next screen shot, shown in Figure 2.3, shows two additional, important control areas of the debugger: the main debug menu and the thread and process view. The thread and process view allows monitoring of the various processes that constitute a single working application. More and more in modern applications, more than one process is involved in the correct execution of an application. And those processes may include multiple threads of execution that require debugger visibility into their inner workings. Chapter 9 discusses issues of multiprocess and multithread debugging.

Figure 2.2

Debugger jumping-off points.   *Sample screen from Borland C++ IDE showing the surrounding control structures for the debugger. The source view is the same as the editor and breakpoints, and other debugger annotations appear in the left margin. Messages from the compiler, the operating system, and the debugger are maintained and give the user context for what is happening to the program shown in the message view. The project view gives both a graphical "make" facility and direct access to debugging of all parts of a project.*

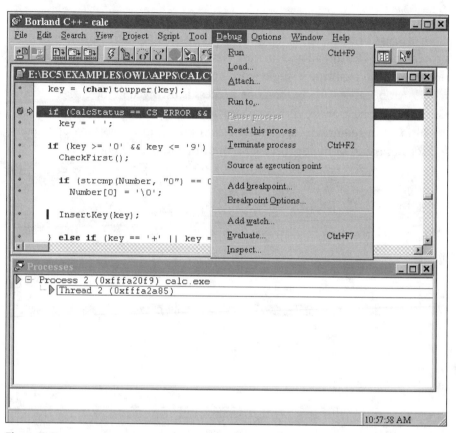

Figure 2.3

Debugger control structures. *A second sample screen from Borland C++ IDE showing the more direct debugger controls, such as the process and threads view that shows all processes and their respective threads that are under the debugger's control. Also the menu used to control the debugger is shown in its pulled-down state.*

Source View

The source view, shown in Figure 2.4, is the most critical focal point for the programmer during debugging. This is the view that gives the user the *illusion* that the debugger is actually executing the originally typed source code directly. In this view—which is also the programmer's editor—the user is presented with information about which statements are executable. The color syntax highlighting editor is set up to show programming language keywords in bold, comments in blue italic, and other program elements in standard black type. Executable statements show a small red dot in the gutter, indicating where breakpoints may be set. Active breakpoints show larger red stop signs. Breakpoints are *probe points* placed into the executable via the debugger where the programmer wishes execution to halt so that more information about the program can be ascertained. Breakpoints will be discussed in detail in Chapter 6. Finally, the current location of the program counter (or instruction pointer) is shown with a green arrow. It is the debugger's responsibility to map the underlying machine execution back to this source view so that the illusion of direct execution of source code is maintained for the user. When this is not possible, an alternate view must be

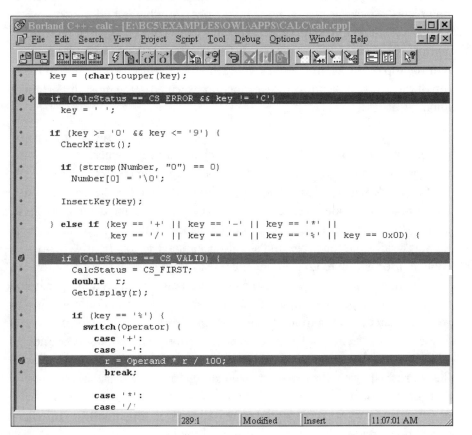

Figure 2.4

Source code with breakpoints. *This view shows the source code annotated in this case with darker color to show the type of language syntax used in each language expression. It also shows breakpoint locations and currently active breakpoints in the left margin. The current program counter location is also shown with the arrow and full-width dark highlight bar.*

shown that represents the machine-level execution directly. This is the CPU or disassembly view, which I will show later.

Stack View

Probably the second-most important view during debugging is the stack view. The stack view gives a representation of the function or procedure stack trace. This view is thread-specific as there is a stack maintained for each active thread in a process. A stack trace consists of a series of stack frames. Each frame represents a single function call, also known as an activation record. Stacks *grow* downward typically (from highest address to lowest), so some debuggers mimic this and show the stack growing downward textually as well. However, the user is better served if the most recent frame is at the top of the list in the stack view; the user naturally looks first at the top of the list, and the most recent function executed is the most important initial feedback.

Wherever possible, a stack frame is presented symbolically, showing the name of the procedure called and its parameters. In cases where no symbolic information is available (because it's an operating system entry point or because no debugging information is available) the entry is shown simply as an address in the code space. Stack traces are critical during debugging. Frequently the error in the program can immediately be discerned by noticing in the stack view that the program "should never have gotten here"—that is enough information to go examine the most recent stack frame's function to see how the logic is wrong. Or, if the program halted with an unhandled fatal exception, the top frame on the stack tells exactly what function it was in when it faulted; examination of that function clearly shows the logic error. These stack views should have a direct connection back to the source and CPU views so that selecting a specific stack frame allows navigation back to the appropriate view for more detailed examination of either the source for that function or the machine-level context for it. Figure 2.5 shows a stack view where the most recent stack frame is always on top and the point where execution started is always at the bottom of the list.

Breakpoints View

The breakpoints view gives an overview of all the breakpoints set by the user anywhere in the currently active processes. Breakpoints are critical tools that

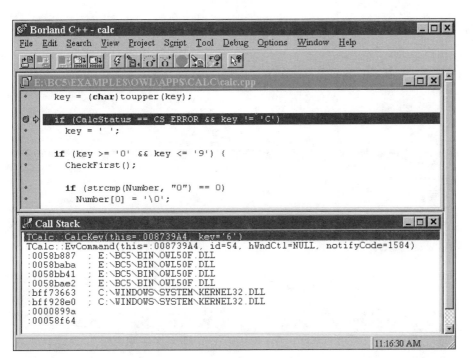

Figure 2.5

Call Stack view.   *The Call Stack view shows the function trace back as mapped onto the hardware stack. Wherever possible, the debugger shows the symbolic name of the function and its arguments to help give context. The Stack View is also a way to get to a specific point in the source code, usually by directly following a specific entry in this stack view.*

allow the programmer to control execution of the program and specify how and where the application will stop to allow further examination. Breakpoints displayed in this view show the source location of each breakpoint as well as its status. The status of a breakpoint may be active, inactive, or unverified. Active breakpoints will cause execution to stop if they are reached. Inactive breakpoints are place holders that the user can turn active but currently will not cause execution to stop if reached. Unverified breakpoints have been set in code that has not yet been loaded into the process's address space. This might occur if the program source has been edited since last execution and the location of existing or new breakpoints is no longer known to map to a specific location in memory. These will become verified when the code is recompiled to accommodate programmer changes and the compiler-generated debug information is once again available to the

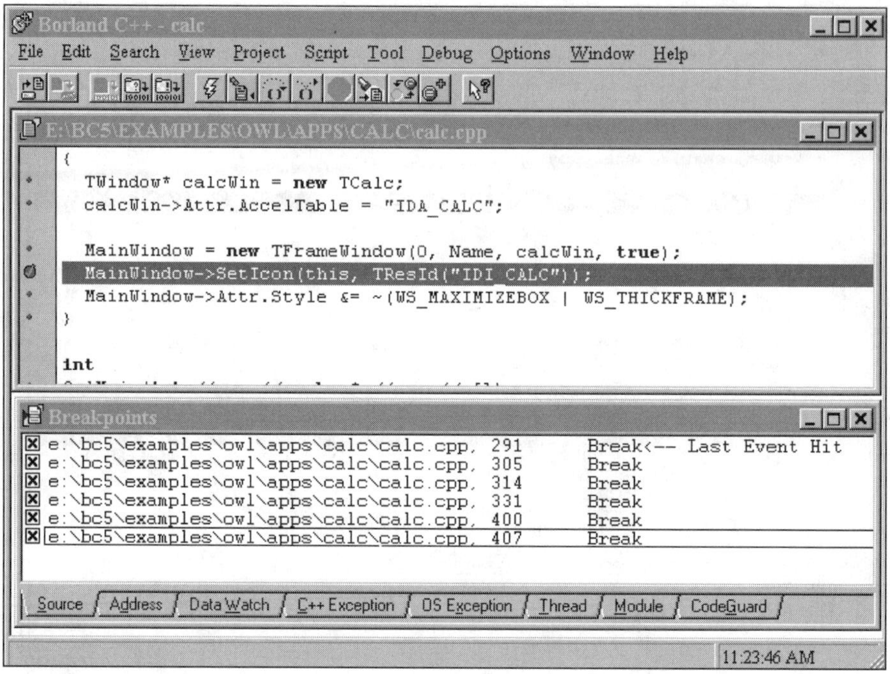

Figure 2.6

Breakpoint dialog. *The breakpoint dialog allows details about a particular breakpoint to be viewed and modified. Attributes associated with a breakpoint include its location in memory, whether an expression should be triggered when this breakpoint is activated, and if so what is that expression, if the breakpoint when hit should actually allow control to proceed a certain number of times, whether control should stop at all when this breakpoint is hit or should some expression be evaluated instead (to cause side effects) or if the result of some expression should just be logged.*

debugger. This view, shown in Figure 2.6, also shows that there are numerous types of breakpoints including source, address, data watch, exception, thread, and module. These types of breakpoints and many other features of breakpoints will be discussed in detail in Chapter 6.

CPU View

The CPU or machine-level view is critical to most debugging situations because while the source view gives an excellent mapping of the machine representation back to the source code, it is rarely enough to completely understand how the program is behaving. Almost any non-trivial program will have issues in how it interacts with the operating system, and this requires looking at and stepping through low-level machine instructions. Even with logic errors in strictly user-created code, frequently the quickest way to uncover the problem is by examining the generated assembly-level code and the current state of the hardware registers.

The CPU view contains several subviews or panes, as typified by Figure 2.7. Typical among these are the disassembly pane, the registers pane, the memory dump pane, the flags pane, and the hardware stack pane. The disassembly pane is where the currently selected range of code address machine instructions are *disassembled* back into their textual assembly-language representation. Here both the actual hex machine codes as well as the symbolic assembly codes are shown, with the green arrow showing the current location of the program counter. To help the programmer further discern the

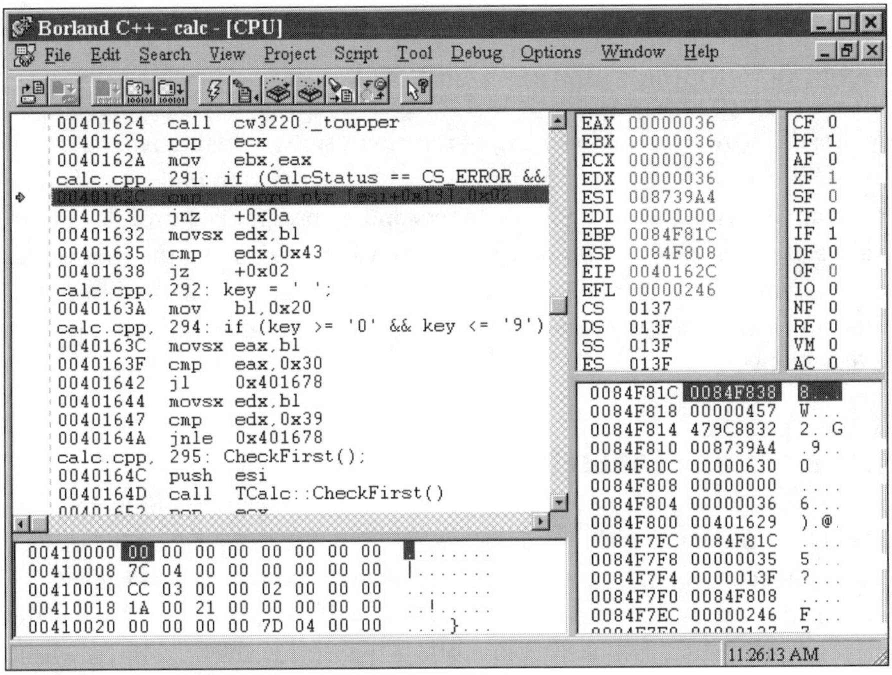

Figure 2.7

CPU view. *The disassembly view shows machine-specific information as well as the actual assembly-level instructions for a given region of code segment memory. Several panes are put together to make up this disassembly or CPU view: the disassembled listing, stack, and registers are shown here. Other panes might be included as well. The disassembled code pane shows the source code, if available, from which these instructions were generated.*

mapping between the executing code and the source code, wherever a symbol or source code line is shown, it is interwoven into the listing. The registers pane shows the symbolic name (here using the Intel x86 standard names) and their current values. These values can be changed by the programmer directly through this pane. Next to this is the flags plane, which shows the symbolic x86 names for the CPU flags and their current values. Below these panes is the stack pane, which is actually just a specialized memory viewer looking at the memory occupied by the stack. This shows the hex addresses and the current values stored at those addresses. Finally, below the disassembly pane is the memory dump pane. This is a general memory dumper that shows the addresses of the memory being examined and the byte values of the data stored at those locations.

Variables View

Returning to the symbolic level, the variables view is closely tied to the *browser*, which in turn is closely tied to the compiler-generated symbol tables; the browser allows viewing of functions, types, variables, and classes in a C++ source program. Examining variables is critical to understanding program behavior. Second only to understanding program control flow, the values of the program's variables are critical to understanding the root causes of program defects. Browsing, shown in Figure 2.8, gives a single view onto lots of program data while the inspector (shown next) gives focus onto a specific variable.

Inspector and Evaluator

An inspector allows the user to examine the structure of complex program objects. An evaluator, as shown in Figure 2.9, is similar to an inspector, but it allows the entry of any legal programming language expression that will be evaluated by the debugger in the current running program context. The way this view is typically used is to inspect or evaluate specific variables or objects when the program has stopped at some point, such as a breakpoint or after a single-step. The evaluator allows virtual "programming-on-the-fly" because additional code that was not placed into the executing program can now be executed as if it were in the executable. The evaluator also allows debuggee functions to be called so very complex expressions that involve calls to functions can be entered. I will go into more details on this complex debugger feature in Chapter 8.

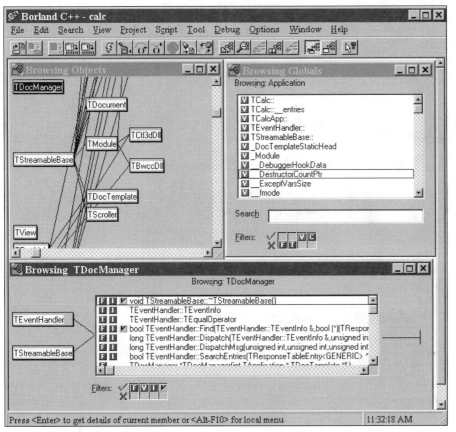

Figure 2.8

Variables view. *Browser views are shown looking at objects, and global variables, with a more detailed view of a particular object where methods and instance variables are shown as well.*

Other views might exist as well. In later sections of the book, the views shown here as well as others will be discussed in more detail as we delve into the inner workings behind them.

Debugger Kernel

The next layer in our abstract architectural description can best be labeled the debugger kernel. This is the part of the debugger that services all the views we just examined. It is here that process control takes place. The application we wish to debug is, to the operating system, a process. The debugger

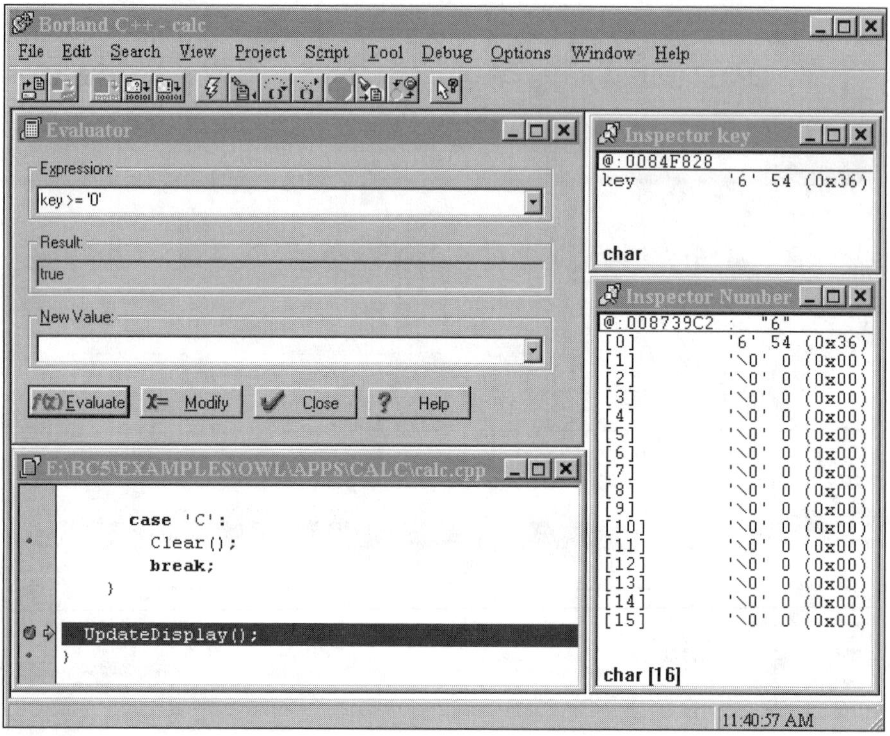

Figure 2.9

Inspector. *The inspector shows the value of some variable. It may also show some useful type information and its physical location in memory. In many cases this view also allows the current value of this variable to be modified.*

may initiate process creation, or it may attach to an already running process, but in either case, that process then becomes the debuggee. At the end of a debug session, the debugger kernel must terminate the process being debugged and disentangle the debugger from it. The kernel is also responsible for symbol table access. The symbol table is usually part of the file that contains the executable code for the program the user wants to debug. The symbol table must be consulted to determine a mapping between source statements and byte addresses of executable instructions. This "statement" information provides necessary guidance for setting breakpoints. The symbol table also contains information about program variables so that the debugger can map a source-level variable or data structure to a specific location or locations in the data memory of the debuggee. Associated with this will be type information provided by the compiler that gives the debugger guidance on how to interpret the raw bits in debuggee memory correctly.

Using the statement information portion of the symbol table as a guide, the execution control section of the debugger kernel can control the debuggee in such a way that the user seems to actually watch the source code being executed. Execution control includes running the debuggee to the next breakpoint, single-stepping by instruction or by statement, dealing with debuggee-generated exceptions, evaluating functions by executing them in situ, and a few other ancillary operations.

Expression evaluation is the process of using the debugger to evaluate variables and to apply operators and call functions as specified by the user-entered expressions. The user is "experimenting" by typing in short code fragments that should be evaluated in the context of the current execution location in the debuggee. These expressions should act as if they actually were in the program being debugged even though they are actually typed in to the debugger. The debugger evaluator must access a compiler parser (or have the equivalent functionality built-in) to parse the textual expression; it must access the symbol table to look up addresses of variables; it must read debuggee memory to get the current values of these variables; it must use the execution engine to execute function calls in the expression; and it must combine the subexpression results using the specified operators in order to present to the user interface a final result. This is critical functionality for the debugger: It allows the user to apply his or her "theories" against what is really happening in the executing program. For example, the user "believes" a variable should have a certain value or that a function if executed now will produce an expected result, and if this is not the case the user can then alter the course of investigation accordingly.

Operating System Interface

When the debugger kernel needs access to the debuggee, it must use a collection of routines provided by the operating system for this purpose. This debug application program interface (API) portion of the operating system provides the basic functions to create debuggable processes, to read and write this process's memory, and to control the execution of this process. In addition, this API provides a way of notifying the debugger whenever anything "important" happens to the debuggee. Other than responding to this special *debugger API*, the debuggee's operation on and interaction with the OS and underlying hardware are not affected by its being debugged. This is the Heisenberg nonintrusive principle in action. Nonintrusiveness is important because the application the user really wants to debug is the one running natively on the operating system, not the one running specially under the control of the debugger. Therefore, it is an important goal of all operating systems that the debug API be nonintrusive so that it has minimal impact on the debugged application.

Debugger Main Loop

Let's dive one level deeper in our architectural overview to gain a good understanding of how the debugger does its job. A good way to do that is to examine the way the debugger operates its basic "main loop" that is the jumping-off point for all its activities. Again, we are assuming a full-featured graphical user interface debugger for these purposes. One important characteristic of graphical user interface systems like Motif, MS Windows, Mac OS, or OS/2 is that these are "event-based" systems that spend most of their time waiting for an event that requires action. The event may be a user action, such as a mouse movement or button click or a keyboard button press. Or, the event may be one coming from the OS or another application that requires some kind of screen drawing action (for example, an expose event that requires some screen redrawing for windows newly exposed). Because basic windowing-based graphical user interface applications must be set up to respond to all sorts of events in a completely general, asynchronous fashion, this provides a handy mechanism for dealing with the other major type of unpredictable, asynchronous "events" that a debugger will receive: those events caused by significant changes of state in the application being debugged. These events are things like stopping, receiving an exception, terminating, and the like. We find that in widely disparate operating systems like UNIX, Windows-16, Win 32, OS/2, and others that provide very different models for debugging APIs, there are general similarities in how the debugger's main loop should run. The major differentiators are these:

- Single-threaded versus multithreaded
- Debug OS call blocking versus non-blocking
- Direct use of OS message system versus separate notification mechanism

Multithreaded applications are becoming the norm as the mass market operating systems support threads. A **thread** is a single path of execution with its own context that includes program and hardware state. Multiple threads of execution within a single process can easily share data and can be switched back and forth relatively inexpensively. **Processes** are collections of one or more threads; sharing data between processes requires special calls to the operating system. I will go into much more detail on debugging multithreaded applications in Chapter 9.

Older operating systems are typically single-threaded. A single-threaded operating system must have an alternative to a blocking OS debug call. That is, when the call to the basic OS debugger control function is called, it must return control to the caller immediately. This means there is some other means to get notification that a material change of state has occurred in the debuggee that requires action from the debugger or user. It also requires that either the debugger main loop poll for normal windowing events and debugger events or some mechanism exists to get notification of either. The following algorithm presents the model for a debugger's main loop on a single-threaded GUI-based system.

If the OS provides basic support for multithreaded application construction, this can be advantageous to use for the debugger's main loop. This is required if the OS debug call is blocking because the main UI loop of any GUI application cannot block and remain unable to respond to UI events. Multithreaded systems allow the main loop to look just like a normal GUI event-processing thread because the blocking debuggee control is handled by a separate thread. In the secondary thread a loop waits for a material event in the debuggee that will cause a message to be sent to the main GUI loop. It is important to note that this secondary thread has one and only one purpose in life: to intercept a debuggee event and post it (as a message usually) to the normal queue of events processed by the main GUI debugger thread. Then this main loop handles this event (message) from the debuggee thread while the secondary thread goes back to waiting—this time for the main thread to give it a new

Algorithm 2.1 *Single-threaded GUI debugger main loop*

Input	Windows messages as the asynchronous communication mechanism.
Output	UI effects of windows messages or debugger actions due to debugger internal functions.
Method	This algorithm depends on the debug call being non-blocking or else the debugger must be implemented as separate processes. The call to initiate execution returns immediately and a separate call is used to check on the status of the debugee. This latter call is non-blocking and so operates in a polling fashion.

```
cause debuggee to run
loop {
   check for windowing message           // non-blocking call
   if (quit message) then
      break out of loop
   else
      process windowing message
check debuggee for notification          // non-blocking call
if (debuggee notification) {
   handle notification
   re-start debuggee
}
} forever
```

command. This secondary thread is always waiting, either for the debuggee to cause an event to occur or for the main UI thread for a new command.

Operating systems like Windows NT, Windows 95 (Win 32), and OS/2 operate in this fashion because they are multithreaded and have a blocking OS debug API call. UNIX, up until three years ago when threads became part of the UNIX standard, operated in this fashion using separate processes—one for the UI, one for the debugger kernel, and one for the debuggee itself. Mac OS debuggers use a polling approach that explicitly checks for debuggee notifications frequently.

Further discussion of debugger design, features and algorithms requires building up more understanding of the underlying basic mechanisms a debugger requires. So next, in Chapter 3 we present hardware support for debuggers and subsequently, in Chapter 4, we present the operating system debugger support that makes it possible for a debugger to function.

Algorithm 2.2   *Multithreaded GUI debugger main loop*

Input	Windows messages as the asynchronous communication mechanism. Two separate threads of control.
Output	UI effects of windows messages or debugger actions due to debugger internal functions.
Method	The primary thread is the standard GUI windows messages processing thread with the addition of having logic to handle debuggee-related messages coming in from the secondary thread. A secondary thread that is dedicated to waiting for the debuggee communicates with the primary thread via specialized window messages. When the primary thread is processing debuggee messages from the secondary thread, it is responsible for restarting the debuggee when necessary.

secondary thread:

```
loop {
   wait for debug event        // blocking call
   send message about debuggee state to main loop
} forever
```

primary thread:

```
loop {
   wait for message   // blocking call
   if (GUI windows message)
     process GUI windows message
   else if (debuggee message)
     process debuggee message
}
```

3

Hardware Debugger Facilities

Necessary and Sufficient Hardware Debugging Support

The debugger's ability to control the execution of the debuggee depends both on hardware support built into the processor and on sophisticated, specialized debugging mechanisms built into the operating system. In this chapter I will discuss the hardware support typically provided to aid debuggers. Even though the details of the underlying processor are normally accessible only through and via the operating system, debugging services is one area where hardware details show through directly to the debugger. The minimal basic requirements a debugger places on the underlying hardware are quite simple:

1. A way to specify a breakpoint—a specific location in the executing code such that when the processor reaches this location, execution will stop; this can be provided for by simply writing some illegal instruction into the code stream for the debuggee

2. A notification system, also called an interrupt or a trap, that will notify the operating system (and thereby the debugger) that an important event has occurred with respect to the running process

3. The ability to read and write directly out of and into the hardware registers when the interrupt occurs; this includes the program counter register

Other hardware facilities allow additional useful debugger features but this set will allow critical basic debugger functionality to be developed. Note that the processor does not need to support a single-step or instruction trace capability because that can be provided equivalently via breakpoints alone.

Generic Hardware Debugging Mechanisms

First I will describe the basic set of hardware debugging support. In this section I will cover what CPU support for a basic set of debugger capabilities would look like. The set of capabilities I will examine includes the following:

- Breakpointing
- Single-stepping
- Fault detection
- Watchpointing
- Multithread control
- Multiprocessor control

After that, we will describe the specific debug architectures of several important modern CPUs.

Breakpoint Support

Breakpoints are usually implemented as a special instruction that causes a trap to the operating system, which then can notify a special program that has registered itself as a debugger. On architectures with varying length instructions, it is normal for the trap—or breakpoint—instruction to be the length of the shortest possible instruction. This makes it much simpler for the debugger to guarantee breakpoints are placed on instruction boundaries. Table 3.1 shows the format for breakpoint instructions on the various CPU architectures we will be addressing.

TABLE 3.1 *Breakpoint Instructions*

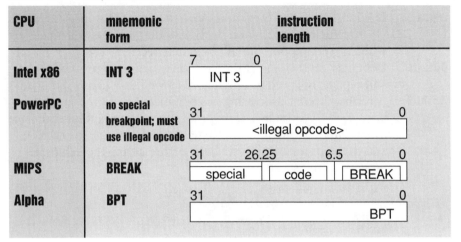

CPU	mnemonic form	instruction length
Intel x86	INT 3	INT 3 (7...0)
PowerPC	no special breakpoint; must use illegal opcode	\<illegal opcode\> (31...0)
MIPS	BREAK	special / code / BREAK (31, 26.25, 6.5, 0)
Alpha	BPT	BPT (31...0)

The debugger, through special interface routines provided by the operating system, has the ability to read and write the text (that is, executable code) space of the debuggee process. Given an address in this text space where a breakpoint needs to be set, the debugger can read the current instruction at that location and save it for later replacement. Then, the debugger writes the special breakpoint instruction at that location. Now, when execution of the debuggee proceeds at full processor speed, if the processor executes one of these breakpoint instructions, a special trap occurs in the operating system without the debuggee executing a single instruction past the breakpoint. The operating system notifies the debugger that the debuggee stopped, why it stopped, and where it stopped, including which thread of execution was running when the stop occurred. It is now up to the debugger to react accordingly. Normally, the debugger will use other OS debug routines to gather up a complete state description of the debuggee that includes copies of all the important registers with their values as of the moment of the execution of the breakpoint instruction. Sometimes, the debugger will want to proceed past this breakpoint. In this case, the debugger must go back to the instruction it saved earlier and replace it, have the debuggee single-step this one instruction, and then replace the breakpoint instruction before allowing the debuggee to again proceed at full processor speed. This procedure is basic to debugger operation and is described in Algorithm 3.1.

Algorithm 3.1 *Breakpoint replace and go*

Input	Previously inserted breakpoint instruction just trapped to the OS. Original instruction at the breakpoint address was saved when the breakpoint initially was inserted.
Output	Debugger must re-insert the saved instruction to proceed and still replace breakpoint instruction as well so it can be hit again.
Method	After breakpoint processing has completed and the debugger is instructed to continue execution of the debuggee, it must replace the original instruction, single-step over that single instruction, and then put the breakpoint back before letting the debuggee proceed at full speed.

```
loc = current_address
address[loc] = saved_instruction
initiate single step in debuggee
when trap occurs {
   if (trap was for single-step completion)
   {
       address[loc] = breakpoint_instruction
       run debuggee full speed
   }
   else
   {
       standard handling for debuggee exceptions
       when re-starting debuggee, re-start same
       thread that stopped
   }
}
```

Single-step Support

Single-step means that the processor is instructed to execute a single machine instruction when it is next processing instructions for the debuggee. Most processors provide a mode bit that controls single-step operation. Typically, this bit is directly manipulated only by the OS on behalf of the debugger through a special debug routine. This bit is part of the processor state so one thread (or process) being single-stepped does not cause other threads (or processes) to also single-step when the OS decides to give control to another thread (or process) not being debugged. When single-stepping, the processor executes one instruction and then causes a trap back to the OS, which in turn notifies the debugger that the requested single-step has completed. With the move toward reduced instruction set computers (RISC), hardware support for single-step has been disappearing because it slows all instruction execution (KANE 1989). That is not an unsolvable problem for debugger design because technically single-step is not needed. A debugger can simulate single-step by decoding the instruction at the current program counter, setting a breakpoint on the very next instruction, and causing the debuggee to run.[1] In this way, "go" has the same effect as single-step. This low-level, single-step functionality is important for several execution control debugger algorithms I will discuss in later sections.

Fault Detection Support

Catching faults in programs being debugged is one of the most critical requirements for a debugger; after all, a debugger is asked to control broken programs most of the time. The major purpose of debuggers is to find program faults. Usually some faults are detected by the processor, such as divide by zero and memory access violations, while the OS detects some others (for example, I/O failure of some sort). In some cases, higher level software systems detect additional faults, such as stack corruption or array bounds check violation. In any case, the OS notifies the debugger that its debuggee has received a fault *before* the debuggee actually is allowed control again. This is critical to the user as the user wants to see what caused the fault before any reactions to that fault can begin. The fault may cause lots of damage to the debuggee environment so that after the fault occurs it may be impossible to detect it any longer. The debugger or its user may decide that some faults are not critical and can be allowed to pass on to the debuggee without causing the program to stop. This is important with faults such as alarm clock that may be necessary for correct operation of the program and should not be considered a fault. In other cases, serious faults also need to be allowed through to the debuggee without intervention by the debugger because the issue being addressed by the programmer in the program is fault handling.

Watchpoint (Data Breakpoint) Support

Watchpoints are notifications presented to the debugger when specified portions of the debuggee's address space are modified. Their purpose is to point out locations in the application where these writes to memory occur, presumably because the results are not as expected; for example, a variable changes value unexpectedly and incorrectly. These are some of the most difficult and

---

[1]But there are times when determining the next instruction is not straightforward, and this mechanism can break down. Such a situation might occur, for example, when the current instruction is a privilege transition instruction.

insidious bugs to detect and fix because their point of detection may not be anywhere near their point of origin. In other words, the place in the code that corrupts some memory is frequently not related to or even near the place that actually faults from using the corrupted memory location.

Hardware support for watchpoints can take on a variety of forms. The most direct is to have special base / limit registers in the processor that specify starting address and run-length.[2] It is then the processor's responsibility to trap on any modifications of data in these addresses and stop the processor before the write occurs. A less common approach—necessary in the absence of data breakpoint registers—is to mark a complete data page as read only, and then, when a page access violation occurs, check to see if the address in that page being accessed is part of the offending data range. In either case the OS notifies the debugger that a watchpoint "fired"; the debugger can then present this information to the user.

Multiprocessor Support

Standard uniprocessors—the ones normally discussed—are architecturally known as single instruction single data (SISD). That is, a single instruction operates on at most a single data store at a time. Two types of parallel architectures are typically employed today. There are multiple instruction multiple data (MIMD) and single instruction multiple data (SIMD) parallel machines. MIMD machines have a small to medium array of processors, each with their own local store. All processors operate on separate instruction streams quasi-independently but in cooperation on a single program. SIMD machines, also known as massively parallel, have a large array of relatively simple identical processors, each with a local store. In SIMD, all processors operate in lockstep executing the same instruction but using different local data stores.

In both types of multiprocessor systems stall detection is very important to debuggers. To provide a controlled debugging environment, debuggers controlling asynchronous multithreaded programs may need to operate only one thread at a time so that no thread can "run away" in an uncontrolled fashion. This works only if there is good notification when the thread being controlled suddenly stalls because it requires some sort of synchronization with

---

[2]Some CPUs have only a single address register (e.g., MIPS) or none (e.g., Alpha) so only one or no out-of-line, non-code-inserted breakpoints can be handled by the hardware.

another thread that is already stopped by the debugger. If this situation is detected, then the debugger can switch control from the thread just stalled to the thread it is now waiting on. If this situation cannot be detected, or if these two threads are actually waiting on each other, deadlock occurs and the debugger then needs to report it as a major program flaw. This same problem exists with thread deadlocks on uniprocessor systems, but the problem is more common and the result more deadly on multiprocessor systems.

A significant issue for debuggers on multiprocessor systems is how or whether other processors stop when a fault occurs in one. On SIMD architectures, by definition, all processors operate in lock step and so this is guaranteed. The problem can occur in MIMD systems because the processors are complex and are more loosely coupled and synchronized. It is a critical issue to address because having a deterministic debugger on MIMD systems is vital to the debugging process.

Contemporary CPU Debug Architectures

All contemporary CPUs provide a similar set of basic support for debugging that gives the operating system and the debugger the tools it needs to provide debugging features to programmers. This basic set includes the following:

- A special instruction that halts execution
- A special mode of the processor to execute a single instruction
- Page protection mechanisms
- Exception or fault detection mechanisms
- In some cases, special debug registers

In this section, I will delve into how a common set of contemporary CPUs implement their debugging support. The CPUs covered include: Intel x86 including Pentium® and Pentium Pro®, the MIPS family of RISC processors, the Motorola / IBM PowerPC® architecture, and Digital Equipment's Alpha® RISC processor.

Intel x86 and Pentium

Most of this description also applies to the x86 family, but the Pentium does introduce some special debugging facilities that the older processors do not have.

First, it should be noted that the x86 family is an extremely complex processor as characterized by the following attributes.

- Variable length instructions: very complex instruction makeup consisting of optional prefixes, one or two primary opcode bytes, possibly an address specifier consisting of the ModR/M byte and the SIB byte, a displacement, if required, and an immediate data field, if required (INTEL 1994).

- Three distinct processing modes: protected mode, virtual-8086 mode, real mode

- Addressing flexibility: addressing of 16- or 32-bit locations

- Breakpoint instruction: INT 3—traps to the debugger interrupt routine

- Debug registers: four registers that contain addresses of code breakpoints allow debugger to not modify the code space for breakpoints; also provide support for data breakpoints (also known as watchpoints)

- Trap flag (TF): single-step mechanism as a mode switch on the CPU status word accessible to the debugger

Code breakpoints are the highest priority processor faults to guarantee they are serviced before any other faults and therefore cannot be preempted. The processor IP (instruction pointer—also known as the PC, for program counter) address will be decremented to the beginning of the breakpoint instruction so that when processing is resumed the instruction that caused the debug fault will be re-executed. In the case of the in-line form of breakpoint (INT 3), the debugger must replace it with the original instruction when processing is resumed.

The processor's TF flag is set directly by the debugger when it needs a hardware-level single-step to occur. This flag in the CPU causes a debug trap to occur as soon as the next instruction completes execution. This will be used whenever the user is in hardware assembly debug mode and wants to advance the processor. It can also happen internally when the debugger is trying to complete a source-level single-step as it executes occasional machine-level single-step operations as it tries to complete a more granular type of step (more details in Chapter 6).

Stack implementation on the x86 processors is very straightforward and similar to older generation minicomputer layouts. Multiple stacks are supported via a stack segment (SS) register. The ESP register points to the top of the stack. Operations that PUSH or POP are relative to and modify the ESP register. The stack-frame base pointer (EBP) usually points to data structures passed on the stack, such as parameters passed to a subroutine. Figure 3.1 shows how the Intel x86 stack is laid out.

MIPS

The dramatic cost/performance advantages offered by RISC CPUs are based on simplifying the instruction set and the ability to process these instructions extremely rapidly. RISC systems demand that sophistication and complexity of design be balanced among CPU, operating system, compiler, and debugger, as opposed to putting an unbalanced emphasis on sophistication in the instruction set. The design philosophy is to maximize instruction pipeline speed, instruction fetch, and register operations on a larger set of fast registers while minimizing the use of slower RAM. This design point results in much higher levels of sophistication in compiler optimizations and some debugger complexity.

The MIPS processor family has specialized calling conventions different from those of other RISC processors (KANE 1989) to meet its paramount objective: speed of execution. Each procedure call tries to optimize performance and

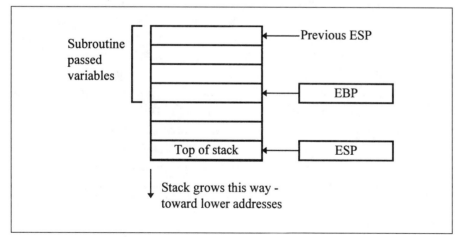

Figure 3.1

The Intel x86 stack. *The stack layout for the x86 architecture shows the relationship between the stack-related registers and the layout of the stack in memory. The stack grows toward lower addresses while heap memory grows from lower to higher addresses.*

uses only the portions of the calling convention absolutely needed. This trade-off favors execution performance over complexity of debugger design. For example, the compilers will avoid using a register as a frame pointer whenever possible. Instead, the debugger must synthesize the frame pointer from ancillary information generated by the compiler (that is, debug information).

On the MIPS architecture, the compiler and debugger follow important implicit rules as opposed to communicating directly through certain dedicated registers. The debugger looks at symbol table information placed there explicitly by the compiler via a ".frame" directive that gives the debugger enough information to synthesize the frame pointer from what it already knows. This way, when there is a leaf routine that does not call any other routines and that does not require any stack local storage, there is no need for frame information and therefore no work need be done to set up a new frame. When a frame pointer is needed it exists only as a *virtual* frame pointer that consists of the stack pointer register value added to the framesize (stored in the symbol table). A symbol table where the debugger can find these synthetic frame pointers must be accessible, or the debugger will not be able to present a stack back-trace. Figure 3.2 shows how frames are synthesized by the debugger.

The other complicating issue with the MIPS processors for debuggers is the *branch delay slot*. Here again, the design trade-off was to speed execution of instructions at the expense of additional compiler and debugger complexity. The rationale is that branch instructions cause the processor to go back to memory and fetch the target address. This causes the instruction pipeline to halt while the address is being fetched. Instead of stalling the instruction pipeline like this, in the MIPS architecture branch instructions are delayed and do not take effect until after one or two more instructions immediately following the branch instruction. It is usually a trivial effort for the compiler designer to handle this because most instructions cause a one-instruction delay. It is easy to move the instruction that would have preceded the branch into the slot afterwards. However, moving an instruction this way causes significant complications for the debugger and its designer. Figure 3.3 shows an example instruction sequence with a typical branch delay slot filled. This branch instruction also happens to be the target of a breakpoint because this instruction is a source code boundary (such as the beginning of an if-statement).

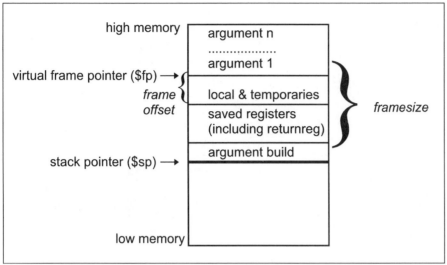

Figure 3.2

MIPS stack layout. *The stack layout and the use of a virtual frame pointer on the MIPS architecture are shown. A leaf function that calls no other functions is simpler. And simpler still is a leaf function that also requires no stack space for local storage.*

Now, if the debugger should stop at this location, if it does not do anything special the instruction

```
move   a0, s0
```

will not have been executed, which almost certainly is wrong (if a variable is inspected it will not have been updated in this example). The debugger must always check to see if the instruction at which it is stopping is a branch instruction; if so, it must check to see if the branch delay slot is filled by other than an NOP.[3] If there is a valid instruction in the branch delay slot it must move the program counter to point to that instruction and execute one single-step to make sure this instruction takes effect before reporting the stop to the user. When execution is about to resume some time later, the debugger must notice that it is about to start with a branch instruction; if the branch delay slot is filled, it realizes that this instruction has already been executed and must replace this with an NOP, do a single-step to execute the branch

---

[3]No-op (NOP) a "do nothing" instruction designed to take up time and space but which causes no side effects.

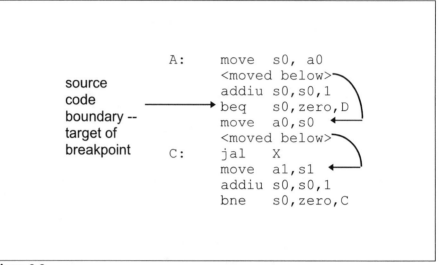

```
                          A:      move    s0, a0
             source               <moved below>
             code                 addiu s0,s0,1
             boundary --          beq     s0,zero,D
             target of            move    a0,s0
             breakpoint           <moved below>
                          C:      jal     X
                                  move    a1,s1
                                  addiu s0,s0,1
                                  bne     s0,zero,C
```

Figure 3.3

MIPS branch delay slot. *Sample code generated for a MIPS processor. Two* move *instructions are shown moved from their logical positions down into the slot after a subsequent branch instruction.*

instruction, and then replace the original instruction so that next time this sequence is executed the correct thing happens. This algorithm is specified in Algorithm 3.2.

Algorithm 3.2   *MIPS branch delay slot breakpoint stop*

Input   Debugger stopping at a breakpoint on a MIPS processor.
Output   Correct behavior such that all instructions that should be executed have been before stop is reported to the user.
Method

on initial stop at breakpoint:

    i. As initial stop is reported by OS to debugger, check to see if current instruction pointed to by the program counter is a branch instruction that has a branch delay slot.

    ii. If the instruction has a branch delay slot, advance the program counter to the slot following the branch.

    iii. Execute a single-step operation.

    iv. When the debuggee returns from the single-step operation, reset the program counter back to its correct position at the branch instruction.

on restart after stop at breakpoint:

   i. If the current instruction is a branch instruction with a branch delay slot, save the instruction in the delay slot and replace it with an NOP.
  ii. With the program counter still pointing to the branch instruction, execute a single-step operation.
 iii. When the debuggee returns from the single-step operation, replace the NOP with the saved instruction.
  iv. Allow the debuggee to proceed at full speed as required by the current execution control operation.

PowerPC

The PowerPC is a RISC processor derived from IBM's POWER workstation architecture (Motorola 1993). Like the other RISC processors, the instructions on the PowerPC are all the same length, 32 bits. There is, however, very little debugger support built into the PowerPC architecture.

The Machine State Register (MSR) has a bit that can be set by the debugger for single-step of individual instructions. When this bit (bit 21) in the MSR is set, as the processor restarts execution, it executes a single instruction and then generates a single-step trace exception that will be processed by the operating system and eventually will get back to the debugger for handling. The PowerPC supports out-of-order instruction dispatch to allow much faster execution by processing some simple instructions while waiting for longer memory-access instructions (like branches) to complete. This is done invisibly by the CPU and is not the responsibility of the debugger. When single-stepping individual instructions, the instructions are processed by the CPU strictly in program order. This does mean that debugging is changing behavior when single-stepping somewhat—this is something for debugger developers and users on PowerPC to watch closely.

There is no special breakpoint instruction on the PowerPC. However, there are special registers that support debugging. HID1 is the Debug Modes Register. This is a supervisor-level register that defines debugging modes—how the registers and exceptions generated during debugging behave. HID2 is the Instruction Address Breakpoint Register. This is the supported way to specify breakpoints in user code. It is advantageous to have breakpoints in a special register, as opposed to inserted into the executable instruction stream, because this avoids issues of instruction caches and interactions between a debugger and page faults. But with only a single register, a debugger cannot provide generalized breakpoint support where multiple breakpoints are set at the same time. To build a standard application debugger that supports multiple breakpoints, some other mechanism will have to be used. One alternative is to use an illegal instruction that when executed will cause an illegal instruction exception, which will halt the processor at the offending instruction. When such an exception occurs during debugging, the debugger must first look at the location of the program counter; if this is the value the debugger uses for special breakpoints and this address matches one the debugger set, then this illegal instruction is actually a breakpoint.

The PowerPC supports address breakpoints through the HID5 Data Address Breakpoint Register. For each instruction that accesses memory, the memory address is compared to the Data Address Breakpoint Register. A match will cause an exception, as determined by how the HID1 register is set. Again, this supports only one data access breakpoint and users will not always be content with just one. At this point, the debugger would need to fall back on the page fault mechanism previously described.

Alpha

The Alpha is also a RISC processor (Sites 1992). Unlike the PowerPC and MIPS RISC processors (prior to the MIPS R4000), the Alpha is a true 64-bit processor. Registers are all 64-bit quantities. There are 32 integer and 32 floating-point registers. All addressing is via 64-bit byte addresses. All instructions are 32-bit quantities. Instructions are always aligned on long word boundaries. The Alpha has a very simple instruction set: All memory operations are load or store. Multiple instructions are issued per clock cycle, but this will be transparent to a debugger. To get the highest possible execution speeds, there is branch prediction support so that the highest probability next instruction is being pre-fetched. Again, this should not be an issue for a debugger.

There is a special breakpoint instruction provided called BPT. Execution of this instruction causes a switch to kernel mode and saves the values in registers R2..R7, the program counter (PC) and the processor status (PS) registers. All are saved to the currently active stack as a stack frame. The PC value saved is the next PC after the BPT instruction so that the debugger, to continue execution after a breakpoint, will have to back up the PC when the original instruction at the breakpoint location is replaced.[4]

There is no instruction-level single-step support. This means that to perform a single-step of a single instruction, the debugger must insert a BPT instruction right after the instruction to be stepped. There are also no specialized instruction or data breakpoint registers so the benefits of out-of-line breakpoints cannot be realized on this processor. Additionally, the only way to implement data access breakpoints will be via the page fault mechanism described previously.

Future CPU Debug Architecture Trends

As CPUs evolve, the need for debugging support will evolve as well. Unfortunately, debugging can often be an afterthought of systems design. And yet, as systems get more and more complex the expectations and requirements placed on debuggers grow substantially.

The general trends for CPUs are toward longer words (64-bits), multiple instruction pipelines, systems built with multiple processors working in cooperation, and special performance features such as branch prediction and speculative execution. Specifically to support debuggers, these architectures will provide more debug registers, special performance monitoring, and profiling registers that enable a debugger to track execution sequencing, timing, and patterns. This allows a "debugger" to actually do profiling of the executing code where the amount of time spent in certain portions of code can be reported back to a user. Further, this kind of information could be used to aid a debugger in reporting on test coverage statistics. Other uses for these registers are planned as well.

---

[4] Note that some processors like the x86 back up the instruction pointer when a breakpoint is hit, and others like the Alpha do not.

4

Operating System Debugger Infrastructure

Necessary and Sufficient OS—Debugger Cooperation

To control a debuggee process, a debugger needs a mechanism to notify the operating system about the executable program it wishes to control. Once this is done, the debugger needs to be able to modify that debuggee's code memory in order to modify the instruction stream with the special break-point instructions. Then the debugger needs to be able to tell the operating system to run the debuggee but notify the debugger if any sort of exceptions (or traps) occur *before* the debuggee itself gets notified or terminated. Once the debuggee does stop for some reason, the debugger needs to be able to gather information from the debuggee's register set and data memory. The debugger needs enough information to know what address in data memory should be read to present stack and variable value information. These are the most basic facilities a debugger must have in order to function. All production operating systems provide this much debugger support and more. There are important distinctions in the way these mechanisms are presented. I will now compare and contrast some of the most prevalent operating system debugging application programming interfaces (APIs).

Generic OS—Debugger Interaction Model

A debugger is a user-level (but highly specialized) application; it is not part of the operating system and it is not even a privileged application. It uses special calls to alert the OS that it is a debugger and that it wants to debug some application or applications. By so doing, the debugger sets itself up to get special notifications of important events in the life of the process it is set up to debug. On contemporary operating systems, for security reasons, interactions between the debugger and the debuggee must go through the operating system. To allow the debugger to run and then give control over to the debuggee requires a context switch that is much more expensive than just a system call. In a context switch, the OS scheduler data structures must be adjusted to reflect which process and thread now has control and the context for that process and thread must be reloaded into memory after the context for the previous one has been saved. On a simple breakpoint, where the debuggee is running and the debugger is waiting for some notification, there are six significant (and expensive) transitions between debugger and debuggee before the debuggee is completely stopped and the debugger is ready to deal with the user's next request.[1]

- Debuggee running hits breakpoint. Transition **#1** to OS to deal with trap.

- Transition **#2** to debugger waiting for event. Debugger now running.

- Debugger requests state info on debuggee. Transition **#3** to OS to deal with request.

---

[1]This is one reason why, as we shall explore in detail later, we try to minimize the usage of machine-level single step which can easily be 1000 times slower than letting the debuggee process run full speed up to the next breakpoint.

- Transition **#4** to debuggee context to get information. Debuggee context now active.
- Transition **#5** to OS to return information.
- Transition **#6** to debugger to handle information. Debugger active.

The picture gets significantly more complex once we factor in graphical user interface (GUI) applications and a GUI debugger dealing with those applications. In operating systems like UNIX, a context switch entailed saving only the processor state (registers and the virtual memory system mappings) and process-specific state information created by the operating system. In the GUI environment a lot more additional state is involved in a context switch. The active window, which window has focus, mouse capture information, and a host of other window-related states must be saved and restored on each context switch.

For a debugger to minimally support debugging of a multithreaded application, the debugger must be notified as soon as the application creates or destroys a thread; it must be able to inquire and set thread-specific program state; and it must be able to detect when the application stops and which thread was executing when it stopped. In Chapter 9 I focus on issues with debuggers and threads.

Like most powerful programming paradigms, threads complicate programmers' lives and are the cause of many complex programming problems requiring special and powerful debugging assistance. In addition to the basic debugging support already mentioned, additional thread-specific debugging support is desirable. The area most likely to need this additional support is interthread communication. Interthread communication may consist of semaphores, queues, pipes, shared memory, or some other mechanism. There is not yet a lot of support for tracking these mechanisms in debuggers, but we may begin to see this as threaded support becomes a mainstream operating system feature.

The following sections describe specific operating systems and the APIs and other facilities they provide for debuggers. I will work in roughly chronological order starting with "legacy" systems and how they supported debuggers.

Legacy OS Debugging Support

Three major systems constitute our examination of legacy systems debugger support. We cover Windows 3.1 augmented by TOOLHELP, the UNIX ptrace () approach and finally the Mac OS debugging support.

Windows 3.1 and TOOLHELP

Microsoft provided TOOLHELP.DLL long after Windows 3.x was shipping after it realized that people needed a way to get at "internal" OS functionality to build debugging aids and when books were published that were essentially documenting "undocumented" features (SCHULMAN 1992). TOOLHELP.DLL allows an application to obtain state information about Windows internals as well as all applications running on Windows. This information was not available previously except to Microsoft-built applications. Additionally, TOOLHELP provides critical functions necessary to build a debugger. Unfortunately, this interface is completely different from the Win32 debug API (or the 16-bit debugging interfaces within the newer Win32-based operating systems).

It is especially critical for a GUI debugger that uses the same basic Window messaging system as GUI applications to have excellent control over the tasks in the system as well as the message flow for itself and its child processes. Table 4.1 describes the important debugger TOOLHELP facilities. The TOOLHELP call is listed on the left with the resulting behavior next to it on the right.

TABLE 4.1   *TOOLHELP Calls and Behaviors*

TOOLHELP Call	Behavior
InterruptRegister	The heart of a TOOLHELP debugger.
InterruptUnRegister	Needed for handling interrupts and exceptions to the debuggee; enables debugger to "hook" and chain interrupts. Exceptions the debugger typically cares about:
	Divide by 0 (and other math errors)
	Single-step instruction
	Breakpoint

	Stack fault	
	General protection fault	
	User attention	
MemoryRead **MemoryWrite**	Enables the debugger to read and write to any address in the form of selector:offset. This pair of calls is not technically necessary because the debugger and debuggee are in the same memory space, and they are unprotected from each other. But using these calls leads to better discipline—unfortunately, at the cost of noticeably poorer performance.	
NotifyRegister **NotifyUnRegister**	This pair of calls is for debug notifications; the debugger registers what events it wants a callback on:	
	NFY_LOADSEG	need to save breakpoints in the code segment just being reloaded
	NFY_STARTDLL	need to get debug information for the module (DLL) just being loaded
	NFY_STARTTASK	a new task has been loaded, but its first instruction has not yet been executed
	NFY_EXITTASK	a task is exiting, and this is a chance to clean up
	NFY_DELMODULE	a DLL or EXE is being removed so can clean up
	NFY_RIP	called when FatalExit is called and when the system is terminating the application
	NFY_OUTSTR	output strings captured by debugger
	NFY_INCHAR	indicates whether to continue after a system-detected API usage error (e.g., invalid Window handle argument)
StackTraceFirst **StackTraceCSIPFirst** **StackTraceNext**	The debuggee's first stack frame, the debugger's own stack, and the way to get successive debuggee stack frames, respectively.	

TABLE 4.1   *(Continued)*

TaskGetCSIP **TaskSetCSIP**	Calls to obtain and modify the CSIP (program counter) of a task necessary for a debugger each time debuggee stops for any reason other than termination.
TaskSwitch	Allows debugger to execute code in the debuggee directly, which is needed by a debugger to evaluate expressions within the environment of the debuggee. Also necessary to do I/O in the context of the debuggee.
TerminateApp	Kill the debuggee without calling normal exit procedures.
LockInput	**Not in TOOLHELP but required by GUI debuggers.** Keeps control of the input queue so that the debugger has complete control over all messages going to debuggee. LockInput prevents a context switch away from the debugger, and this is critical for all production GUI debuggers designed to handle GUI applications. Without this call, GUI debuggers will frequently become hung or at best unstable when debugging GUI applications even if these applications are "well-behaved."

UNIX ptrace()

UNIX `ptrace()` is an example of a true debugger application program interfaces (API). It was one of the first dedicated APIs designed to support production-quality debuggers. A call to `ptrace()` is considered non-blocking. This means that calls to `ptrace()` made by the debugger return immediately—the OS has all the information and resources it needs to satisfy this request; the debugger may continue whatever processing it needs to do. This usually means the debugger goes back into some UI processing loop looking for events caused by the user pressing keyboard or mouse buttons. The debugger finds out when the debuggee stops or in some important way changes state through the `wait()` system call. The `wait()` call can be either blocking or non-blocking, giving the debugger designer a lot of flexibility in how the debugger should be set up. An important point about `ptrace()` is that the debugger must instantiate a process to be debugged using `ptrace()` so that the OS can set the "tracing" flag on the process to know how to behave when the process gets exceptions. More recent flavors of UNIX have offered a `ptrace()`

"attach" capability that substantially relaxes this restriction. UNIX `ptrace()` and `wait()` are described next.

The function prototypes for ptrace and wait are as follows:

```
int
ptrace(PTRACEREQ request, int pid, char* addr, int data, char *addr2);
int wait(&wstatus);
```

Table 4.2 lists the possible values of PTRACEREQ on the left and the resulting behavior on the right.

Algorithm 4.1. describes how a debugger based on UNIX `ptrace()` would function.

MacOS Debug API

Mac OS employs debugger technology based on a series of callbacks. This is an old code base that, like Windows 3.1, seems not to have built-in debugger support from the beginning.[2] Additionally, the rather simple—and not very robust—debugging model is that the debugger runs in the same process context as the OS services it requires. This is why the debugger API is largely made up of callbacks—the debugger uses certain APIs to "register" itself as a special agent—that the OS service routines will call as certain events of interest to the debugger occur. Those exceptions and their meanings in MacOS are listed in Table 4.3.

A debugger for System 7.5 or Mac OS will share a similar internal architecture to one built for Windows 3.1 using TOOLHELP. In both cases, the support is minimal and not very clean. The interfaces are based on "hooking" existing OS routines for the debugger's purposes or on callbacks. Both systems are not capable of very robust operation because the debugger and the debuggee as well as the OS are in the same process context. Table 4.4 lists the main functions used to set up debugging using the MacOS callback approach.

Contemporary OS Debugging Support

In this section we will delve into the contemporary operating systems support for debuggers. Things have changed dramatically and debug APIs are now robust and full-featured. I will cover UNIX's more modern `/proc` debugging

---

[2]This will change when Copeland, a complete rewrite of the Mac operating system, comes out in 1997.

TABLE 4.2   *Possible PTRACEREQ Values in Calls to* `ptrace()` *and Their Behaviors*

PTRACEREQ Values	Behavior
`PTRACE_TRACEME`	The debugger `forks()` itself into two processes, one of which makes this call on behalf of the debuggee. It registers the debuggee as wanting to be traced. Immediately after making this call for the debuggee, that version of the debugger process overlays itself (using `exec()`) with the debuggee process.
`PTRACE_PEEKTEXT` `PTRACE_PEEKDATA`	This is the way to inspect a single word in the debuggee's code or data address space. The TEXT form is the way to get at instructions and is part of the breakpointing mechanism.
`PTRACE_POKETEXT` `PTRACE_POKEDATA`	A single word is written to the debuggee's code or data space.
`PTRACE_CONT`	The debuggee's execution is continued from wherever it stopped previously. The program counter can be reset at the same time optionally.
`PTRACE_KILL`	This forces the debuggee to terminate.
`PTRACE_SINGLESTEP`	Similar to PTRACE_CONT, this continues execution of the debuggee but if possible only a single machine instruction is executed before it stops and notifies the parent process (debugger).
`PTRACE_SYSENTER` `PTRACE_SYSEXIT`	This is a very useful capability for monitoring or hooking system calls. The debugger can be instructed to stop on certain system calls, all calls, or none and can be further directed to stop on entry, exit, or both. And the debugger can "hook" a call and change parameters to it or return values from it.
`PTRACE_ATTACH` `PTRACE_DETACH`	If a process is already running it can become the debuggee via ATTACH. DETACH will release a debuggee to be an untraced process.
`PTRACE_GETREGS` `PTRACE_SETREGS`	Whenever the debuggee stops, the debugger may want to examine or modify its registers.

interface, OS/2's debugging API called DosDebug(), and finally the Win32 debug API used for both Windows NT and Windows 95.

Algorithm 4.1 *UNIX ptrace debugging algorithm*

Input	Debugger process and the full path name of debuggee process desired.
Output	Debuggee under full control of debugger process via ptrace.
Method	From initial debugger (parent), create new (child) process

When the child exists but is still just a copy of parent, establish that it wants to be a traced process.

Child portion of this pair now execs the debuggee process overlaying that process on itself.

Meanwhile, parent process waits until new child debuggee process is ready.

Parent debugger can now control child debuggee via `ptrace()` calls waiting (or polling) whenever child debuggee is running. Parent's wait call returns whenever the child debuggee process stops or terminates.

```
fork();                         // create second process
if (pid == 0 )                  // new process has special pid
{                               // this is the child
    ptrace( PTRACE_TRACEME );
    exec( new process that will be debuggee );
}
else
{                               // this is the parent
    wait( pid, &status );
}
while (!TERMINATED(status))
{                               // the main debugger loop
    ......                      // do things to debuggee
    ptrace(PTRACE_CONT);   // start the debuggee running
    wait( pid, &status );
}
```

UNIX /proc

Newer UNIX systems support `/proc` instead of (or in addition to) `ptrace()` (FAULKNER 1991). `/proc` is a device driver interface to all system processes. It presents all processes as files in a directory called `/proc` within the standard UNIX file system. With `/proc`, the debugger can just use standard accesses to a device driver to control any process in the system according to standard UNIX file protection mechanisms. Typical sys-

TABLE 4.3 *Mac OS Exceptions and Their Meanings*

MAC OS Exceptions	Meanings
unknownException	An unknown exception occurred.
illegalInstructionException	An illegal instruction opcode was executed.
trapException	The processor trapped. This may be for special OS functions, or it may be an application fault.
accessException	Memory access violation ocurred.
unmappedMemoryException	A violation of memory mapping occurred.
excludedMemoryException	An attempt to access excluded memory occurred.
readOnlyMemoryException	An attempt to write to read-only memory occurred.
unresolvablePageFaultException	An unresolvable page fault occurred, probably a system-level problem.
privilegeViolationException	An attempt was made by the application to violate established privileges—a privileged instruction was executed.
traceException	A single-step operation completed.
instructionBreakpointException	A breakpoint was hit.
dataBreakpointException	A data breakpoint fired (watchpoint).
integerException	Some type of integer math exception occurred (e.g., divide by zero, overflow).
floatingPointException	Some type of floating point math exception occurred.
stackOverflowException	The applications stack overflowed, that is, it exceeded its allotted space or ran into memory allocated for some other program structure (e.g., heap).
terminationException	Exception occurred at termination to allow the debugger to catch exiting processes.

TABLE 4.4 *Mac OS Debugging Functions and Their Purpose*

MAC OS DEBUG	
Function	**Purpose**

`KillProcess`
`StopCurrentProcess`
`ResumeProcess`
	These are process control APIs. Debuggers can use these functions to control the debuggee process.

`FragAddNotifyProc` `FragRemoveNotifyProc`	The debugger installs callbacks here to get notifications from the Code Fragment Manager that notify the debugger when code gets loaded and unloaded on behalf of the debuggee.
`SetDebuggerNotificationProcs`	The debugger installs callbacks via this function into the Thread Manager. These callbacks will notify the debugger when a new thread is created or if one is terminated.
`InstallExceptionHandler`	This is a critical function whereby the debugger is notified when an exception occurs and all the information the debugger needs about the exception is passed in via an exception structure at this time.

tem calls used to access /proc are open(), close(), lseek(), read(), write(), and ioctl(). This is a much more general interface than ptrace(), and one of its benefits is that the debugger need not have set up a process for debugging ahead of time as with most ptrace()s. This is a big advantage because now a debugger can "attach" to any process, even one that was not initiated by the debugger.

Most of the debugger execution control mechanisms are implemented in /proc via special ioctl() operations listed in Table 4.5.

A process being traced through /proc will stop due to events of interest as specified by one of the above ioctl() calls, when it is specifically directed to stop via PIOCSTOP, or due to reasons external to /proc such as ptrace() or job-control stop. Unique to UNIX via this /proc interface, and some variants of ptrace(), is the system calling control afforded a debugger. As you can see above in PIOCSENTRY, the debugger can control stop on entry and/or stop on exit from system calls. This allows the debugger to modify arguments on entry to a specific system call and to modify return values on return from system calls and thus gives a powerful "hook" mechanism to debuggers or similar tools potentially completely changing system call behavior invisibly to the debuggee. It also provides a way for user-level code to simulate obsolete system calls without making the system support a feature forever. Perhaps an even more powerful use of this capability to trace entry and/or exit from system calls is the ability of the debugger to have the debuggee execute any system call on its behalf with any arguments the debugger requires. This means that anything not provided explicitly via /proc but needed by the debugger in the debuggee's address space, is still accessible if it is available via system call at all. Of course, not perturbing the debuggee here is difficult and becomes a big intrusiveness issue.

UNIX's /proc does not explicitly provide a breakpoint mechanism. Instead, it provides very general non-specific read and write system calls to

TABLE 4.5 *UNIX ioctl() Commands and Their Behavior*

ioctl() commands	Behavior
PIOCSTATUS	Get general process status.
PIOCSTOP	Direct a process to stop.
PIOCWSTOP	Wait for a process to stop.
PIOCRUN	Make stopped process run again.
PIOCSTRACE	Define a set of traced signals (software exceptions).
PIOCSFAULT	Define a set of traced machine faults (hardware exceptions).
PIOCSENTRY	Define a set of traced syscall entries (OS calls being traced).
PIOCSEXIT	Define a set of traced syscall exits (OS call tracing).
PIOCGREG	Get values of process registers (hardware state when stopped).
PIOCSREG	Set values of process registers.
PIOCMAP	Get virtual memory address mappings (for debuggee's memory).

the user application's code address space. The debugger must determine the address in code space to place the breakpoint, and it then reads that location to save the existing instruction and writes the breakpoint instruction into that location. Usually, the hardware dictates what breakpoint instruction is used, but sometimes it is defined by the operating system as a special form of illegal opcode. Execution of this instruction causes a trap to the OS kernel. If the debugger using `/proc` has specified this type of fault (exception) to be of interest, then the process will stop and the debugger will become active because it was waiting (blocked) in a PIOCWSTOP `ioctl()` call.[3]

UNIX's `/proc` provides the debugger with the capability to control multiple processes. When a process being controlled **forks** a child process, the debugger can arrange to be notified so that it can also control the new child process. As UNIX adopts a multithreaded programming model, `/proc` needs some work to keep up and provide the necessary level of control over all threads in all controlled processes. Fortunately, the `/proc` model is sufficiently general and sufficiently flexible to allow this.[4]

OS/2 DosDebug()

OS/2 provides a very different debug API, one that is blocking. The **DosDebug()** call to make a debuggee start executing does not return control to the caller (that is, debugger) until the debuggee process has stopped or terminated. This means that an OS/2-based debugger that needs to continue to process user input—such as respond to mouse events—must be implemented using separate threads of execution. This way one thread can block after calling **DosDebug()** while a second thread continues to process standard windowing events. An OS/2-based debugger must deal with separate address spaces for each debuggee and must deal with multithreaded applications. The **DosDebug()** interface provides support for these aspects of debugging and is the only way for a debugger to interact with its debuggee (PIETREK 1993). The two most basic APIs needed to initiate a debugging session are listed in Table 4.6.

---

[3]Alternatively, the /proc file descriptors can be considered in the same way other file descriptors are used in the `select()` system call, which allow a debugger to wait for multiple events (such as keyboard and mouse) at the same time as waiting for the debuggee to stop.

[4]/proc could present process files as hierarchical with "subfiles" representing threads. This model has been implemented in some UNIX kernels recently.

TABLE 4.6 *The Two OS/2 APIs Used to Set up and Then Control Debuggee Processes along with Descriptions of Their Behavior*

OS/2 debug APIs	Behavior
`DosStartSession()`	This is used to initiate the child process establishing the debugger as its controlling parent.
`DosDebug()`	This is the synchronous OS API for debugging interactions. It takes a pointer to a debugger buffer that contains information about the process and thread to be queried or controlled. On successful return, information in the structure is filled in by the operating system to give feedback to the debugger on the results of the last command or query

```
PVOID pDbgbuf;
APIRET rc;
rc = DosDebug()(pDbgBuf);
struct DbgBuf {
    ULONG   Pid;
    ULONG   Tid;
    ULONG   Cmd;
    ULONG   Value;
    ULONG   Addr;
    ...
};
```

Table 4.7 lists possible values of the DbgBuf.Cmd parameter passed to `Dos-Debug()` on the left with the behavior resulting from `DosDebug()` when called in this fashion.

Weaknesses in the OS/2 Debug Support

There are several problems in the debug support on OS/2 that make building a robust debugger all but impossible. We briefly outline them here. Several of these problems are not unique to OS/2 but plague the other curent OSs as well. In particular, lack of adequate thread debugging support and lack of adequate debugger/debuggee context switching() support in the GUI manager is pervasive.

1. OS/2 has only a single input queue that all threads and processes share. This includes a GUI debugger. This makes a debugger on OS/2 as primitive and unreliable as GUI debuggers on TOOLHELP Windows 3.x systems. This brings in all sorts of problems and deadlocks

TABLE 4.7   *Possible Values of the Dbg Buf. Cmd Command Parameter to DosDebug with the Resulting Behavior of DosDebug()*

DbgBuf.Cmd Value	DOS Debug behavior
`DBG_C_ReadMem` `DBG_C_WriteMem`	The word specified by the Addr field in DbgBuf is returned in the Value field (for read) or is written into debuggee memory (for write).
`DBG_C_ReadReg` `DBG_C_WriteReg`	This reads or writes the register set of the specified thread in the debuggee. The DbgBuf contains the fields corresponding to the register set that gets filled in.
`DBG_C_Connect`	This is the connect to debuggee command. This is the first `DosDebug()` command issued by the debugger and allows it to establish communication with the debuggee child process.
`DBG_C_Go`	This initiates execution of the debuggee. All non-frozen threads are allowed to execute user code immediately.
`DBG_C_Continue`	This is the way to continue debuggee execution after the debuggee has caused some notification to the debugger that stopped the process's execution.
`DBG_C_Term`	This terminates the debuggee prematurely.
`DBG_C_SStep`	This causes the specified thread to execute only one machine instruction and then cause a notification.
`DBG_C_Freeze` `DBG_C_Resume`	This prevents specified threads from executing (freeze) or reverse this action (resume). This, if exposed to the user, allows users to specify which threads shall be allowed to execute next time the debuggee is run.
`DBG_C_ThrdStat`	This gets thread status information on the specified thread with respect to its frozen/thawed state as well as its runnable/blocked state.
`DBG_C_SetWatch` `DBG_C_ClearWatch`	These are watchpoint control commands that allow the setting and clearing of data access breakpoints.

that make debugging flaky programs (the ones that need debugging the most) almost impossible.

2. There is no notification given by this or any multithreaded OS to the debugger when one or more of the independent threads con-

trolled by the debugger blocks. This is serious because it makes the debugger freeze and gives no feedback to the user about why or where there is a problem. This is exacerbated by the fact that the API gives (and encourages) debuggers to allow users to zero in on and control individual threads by freezing all other threads—a handy thing to be able to do.

3. The GUI system on OS/2 is called Presentation Manager. It runs very much like a user application as opposed to being integrated into the operating system. However, to applications like a GUI debugger, PM is very much a systems service. When a GUI application and the debugger are both using PM simultaneously and one of them gets into trouble and grabs a critical drawing semaphore, other applications that need to draw on the screen to function are frozen out. Until PM and its critical system resources are integrated into the OS, OS/2 will continue to be a non-robust environment on which to build debuggers.

Win32 Debug API

With the advent of Microsoft Windows NT and its common Win32 API, and with the more recent incarnation of Win32 through Windows 95, a new debug API has come into prevalent use. Like `DosDebug()` this is a blocking debug API meaning that the system call does not return to the caller until the request is satisfied. So, in a similar fashion to `DosDebug()` systems, a call to `WaitForDebugEvent()` is used to block and wait for an event. Unlike both UNIX `ptrace()` and OS/2 `DosDebug()`, the debuggee does nothing special to allow itself to be debugged. Instead, the debugger (parent) calls `CreateProcess()` with a special flag or uses `DebugActiveProcess()` on an existing process. Win32 assumes a multithreaded process model so individual thread contexts of a debuggee—the register values—can be examined using `GetThreadContext()` and their state altered using `SetThreadContext()`.

Breakpoints or code patching uses `ReadProcessMemory()` and `WriteProcessMemory()`. The debugger must explicitly wait for a state change in the debuggee by blocking or polling in `WaitForDebugEvent()`. A pointer to a DEBUG_EVENT structure is passed to and filled in by `WaitForDebugEvent()` that indicates why the state of the debuggee changed. Because NT and its newer Windows cousins are multithreaded operating systems, this will typically be done by having one thread in the debugger dedicated to waiting for the executing debuggee to change state, while all other debugger threads go off and process user interface events or perform some other actions. This is vastly preferable to any sort of polling approach that is also supported by the API and that has been necessary in UNIX `ptrace()` models to date.

The types of events that cause a debuggee's state change are listed on the left in Table 4.8 with their meanings described to the right.

Weaknesses in the Win32 Debug Support

There are several weaknesses or omissions in the debug support on Win32 that make building a robust debugger difficult.

1. Windows 95 fails to save the debug registers of the Intel x86 processor on context switches. This means that they are effectively unusable by the debugger because their state will not be saved on context switches and whatever information the debugger placed in them will disappear the next time the OS switches to a different process.

2. The OS gives the debugger no notification when one or more of the independent threads controlled by the debugger blocks. This is a shared omission with the OS/2 operating system, as described earlier. This reflects the early state of support by all vendors for effective debugging of multithreaded applications.

3. No abstraction is provided for single-step and data breakpoints or watchpoints so the debugger must dive down into hardware register details to provide these capabilities. And in so doing, the debugger loses its ability to remain nicely modular and thereby makes portability more difficult.

4. There is no support for a 32-bit debugger on Windows 95 to debug a 16-bit application. On NT, there is a special API called VDMDBG for doing this. On Windows 95, you must only use a 16-bit hosted debugger to debug 16-bit applications.

5. Another Win 95 bug, which makes development on that platform difficult is the inability to terminate a multi-threaded application when a thread has a pending but unreported debug event.

6. While Win32 provides on *attach* capability, there is no detach which is limiting. It is very useful when you suspect an application is hung

TABLE 4.8   *Possible Win32 Debug Events and Their Meanings*

WIN32 DEBUG Events	Meaning
CREATE_PROCESS_DEBUG_EVENT	Generated whenever a new process is created, the debuggee spawns a new process or the debugger attaches to a running process.
CREATE_THREAD_DEBUG_EVENT	Generated whenever a new thread is created in a process already being debugged and once for each existing thread when the debugger attaches to a running process.
EXCEPTION_DEBUG_EVENT	Generated whenever an exception occurs in the process being debugged. These exceptions include programming errors such as access to inaccessible memory and divide by zero. They also include special debugging exceptions such as breakpoint, single-step, and watchpoints.
EXIT_PROCESS_DEBUG_EVENT	Generated whenever the last thread in the debuggee process has exited.
EXIT_THREAD_DEBUG_EVENT	Generated whenever a thread that is part of the debuggee process exits.
LOAD_DLL_DEBUG_EVENT	Generated whenever a new DLL is loaded by the debuggee process.
OUTPUT_DEBUG_STRING_EVENT	Generated whenever the debuggee executes the special API OutputDebug String; the debugger can capture the string and print it out as directed
UNLOAD_DLL_DEBUG_EVENT	Generated whenever the debuggee unloads a DLL.

to attach to it, monitor its state, and detach without disturbing its operation. UNIX supports this while Win32 does not.

The Win32 debug API is sketched out in Table 4.9. This is not a complete description of the API.

The basic algorithm for a debugger's main loop on Win32 is described next in Algorithm 4.2.

This basic algorithm is also shown in Figure 4.1.

Hybrid OS Debugging Support

In this third section describing various OS support for debugging we will look at what I call "hybrid" debugging support. By this I mean 16-bit debugging on a natively 32-bit operating system. This is a temporal phenomenon, as we are in the middle of a massive transformation of 16-bit systems becoming 32-bit systems and thousands of 16-bit applications will continue to be built and debugged to run on both the older 16-bit as well as the newer 32-bit operating systems. I examine two very different such hybrid systems: 16-bit debugging on NT and on Windows 95.

16-bit Debugging under Windows NT

The Windows-on-Windows (WOW) subsystem on NT[5] creates a self-contained 16-bit environment within the 32-bit operating system. This 16-bit DOS/Win16 subsystem is a complete simulated x86 environment. There is a special debug API specifically designed to allow 32-bit debuggers to debug 16-bit applications running within this WOW subsystem. A 16-bit debugger running within the WOW subsystem can debug another 16-bit application within the same WOW subsystem via TOOLHELP as if it were Window 3.1 (at least theoretically). The special debug API for 32-bit debuggers acting on 16-bit NT applications is called VDMDBG. At issue is the fact that the 16-bit environment is a *simulated* protected-mode DOS environment and the 32-bit debugger is in another process's context. As such, this debugging mechanism needs to provide some code within this simulated environment for protected-mode interrupt handling. Back in the 32-bit NT environment specialized APIs are needed to field information from the simulated environment and send it to the debugger as well as code for handling it within the debugger and for special service routines to help assist the debugger in its tasks.

---

[5]WOW is now more frequently referred to as the VDM—Virtual DOS Machine interface.

TABLE 4.9 *Win32 Debug API Functions and Their Behaviors*

Win32 debug functions	Behavior
`ContinueDebugEvent`	Continues the thread in the debuggee that previously reported a debugging event.
`DebugActiveProcess`	Allows attaching to an active process and from there continue normal debugging. Win32, however, does not provide a detach facility. The debugger now has control until process termination.
`DebugBreak`	Can be placed in the source code of a program to be debugged. If called when being debugged it forces an exception that stops the process and gives control to the debugger.
`FatalExit`	When called from the debuggee, transfers control to the debugger. This function terminates the application and has no return back to the calling thread.
`GetThreadContext` `SetThreadContext` `GetThreadSelectorEntry`	The thread context is the set of information saved on behalf of a thread whenever it is stopped. This information includes all the processor register values. On x86 architectures, it is possible to get the thread's selector entry as well.
`SuspendThread` `ResumeThread`	Same as freeze and suspend thread in OS/2; allows explicit suspension of a thread so that it will not run. Can be reversed using resume.
`ReadProcessMemory` `WriteProcessMemory`	Reads and writes debuggee process memory.
`OutputDebugString`	Can be placed in the debuggee that when executed will cause the process to stop and give control over to the debugger. It passes a string as a side effect.
`WaitForDebugEvent`	The blocking call that the debugger executes while the debuggee is running that will return only when the debuggee stops and causes a debug notification to be passed to the debugger.

Our standard two-thread Win32 debugging main loop is used. When the debug event is being processed after a return from `WaitForDebugEvent()`, if it is the special value STATUS_VDM_EVENT, then the debugger knows

Algorithm 4.2 *Win32 debugging algorithm*

Input   Debugger process and the full path name of debuggee process desired.

Output   Debuggee under full control of debugger process.

Method   Use two threads; one for tracking the debuggee and one for tracking the user. Messages pass between the two threads using special codes.

Primary thread (thread1):

```
// Send message to Thread2 to create new debuggee
// Set up debuggee as needed (breakpoints, etc.)
// Send message to Thread2 to start debuggee
    PostMessage();          // to Thread 2
                            // to create debuggee
for (;;)
{
    WaitForSingleObject();
    if (special debug message)
        <process debug message>
    else
        <process normal windows message>
    PostMessage();          // to Thread2
                            // to continue debuggee

}
```

Secondary thread (thread2):

```
CreateProcess( <path name of .EXE> , debug_flag );
WaitForDebugEvent( );
// can now set breakpoints, inspect, modify memory
// and initiate execution control
for(;;)
{
    WaitForMessage( );      // from Thread1
    ContinueDebugEvent();
    WaitForDebugEvent();

    // process exception that stopped debuggee
    PostMessage();          // to Tread1 on why debuggee
                            stopped

}
```

this is an event from the 16-bit environment. From here on, the debugger needs to operate on this debuggee using the special API from the

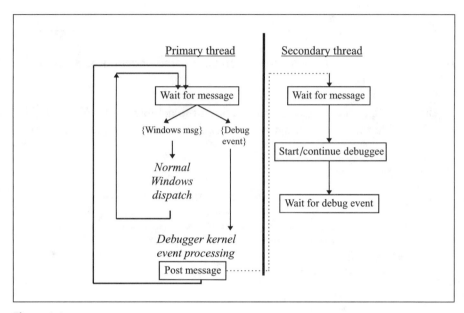

Figure 4.1

Win32 debugging loop. *Diagram showing basic two-threaded algorithm for inner debugger processing loop.*

VDMDBG.DLL that specializes in dealing with a debuggee running in the 16-bit DOS/Win16 simulated environment.

Because the debugger and the debuggee are in completely different environments, the method of communicating between has to be via exceptions. NTVDM is the name of the simulated environment. If NTVDM detects it is being debugged, it will raise exceptions on behalf of the debuggee and the Win32 debugger should receive them. The exception returns to the debugger a 4 DWORD value. Word 1 contains the type of event that has occurred out of the list of possibilities shown in Table 4.10.

The set of functions unique to NTVDM that are used either in addition to the standard Win32 debugging APIs or in some cases instead of those in Win32 are described in Table 4.11.

VDMDBG allows a 32-bit NT-based debugger to extend its capabilities and continue to debug 16-bit DOS and Windows applications. But the cost in design and special-case code is high because once the event comes back as STA-TUS_VDM_EVENT the debugging logic is quite specialized to the NTVDM subsystem. And, unfortunately, as we are about to revisit, this same subsystem is not provided on the other major platform for Win32: Windows 95.

16-bit Debugging under Windows 95

On Windows 95, there is absolutely no support for a 32-bit debugger to control a 16-bit process. No VDMDBG support is provided (and, I am told, there never will be). Microsoft's position is that 16-bit debuggers can control 16-bit applications by using TOOLHELP and 32-bit debuggers can control 32-bit processes using the standard Win32 debug API. But, Microsoft cautions, do not try to mix the two: Do not write a 32-bit debugger that will try to control a 16-bit process. This leaves Win32 debugger developers with a complex development matrix, shown in Table 4.12.

Java Debugging Support

Because Java is so new to the programming landscape, I need to begin with a brief overview of Java [SUN 1995].[6] Java is a programming language that has naturally evolved from C++ to address some specific needs of programmers and application users. Those needs include a higher degree of simplicity, platform independence, network awareness, and security, among others. Java is an interpreted environment currently, and Java applications run unmodified on a host of platforms including UNIX, Mac, and Windows variants. Applications written in Java can either be stand-alone or can occur as applets that operate typically within an Internet browser. A Java "compiler" currently transforms Java-written text into a well-defined standard byte stream. On each platform, a virtual machine receives this byte stream and executes native code on that specific CPU on behalf of the byte stream in interpreted fashion (like Smalltalk). The byte stream is compact and efficient so that applets streaming down off the Internet execute as rapidly as the interface to the Net allows, and even stand-alone Java applications read from local disk run reasonably efficiently. There are just-in-time compilers, and there will be direct-to-hardware implementations of Java compilers over time to get higher degrees of efficiency. The distinction is that a just-in-time compiler takes a stream of byte-codes (either from disk or coming down off the Net) and on-

---

[6]For the latest, up-to-date, publically accessible information about Java including debugging support, visit http://java.sun.com.

TABLE 4.10 *The List of All Possible Exceptions Raised in the 16-bit Simulated NTVDM Environment and the Meanings of Those Exceptions*

Word 1 of NTVDM exceptions	Meaning
`DBG_SEGLOAD`	*Segment Load Notification* A Win16 selector has just been created, and it maps to a module's segment.
`DBG_MOVE`	*Segment Move Notification* A segment has changed from one selector number to another (or it has been discarded).
`DBG_SEGFREE`	*Segment Free Notification* A segment is being released.
`DBG_MODLOAD`	*Module Load Notification* An event signifies that a module is going to take up a range of memory.
`DBG_MODFREE`	*Module Free Notification* A module is being freed.
`DBG_SINGLESTEP`	*Int 01h break* This special debugger-specific event needs to be tied back into the debugger's breakpointing and single-step logic.
`DBG_BREAKPOINT`	*Int 03h break* Typically, the special event signifying a breakpoint was hit. Typically this will be a breakpoint set by the debugger and as such will be part of the debugger's breakpointing and single-step logic.
`DBG_GPFAULT`	*General Protection Fault* This is probably a fatal error in the application (or some other serious error). The debugger will want to intercept these and give the standard application fault handling such as showing the location and stack where the fault occurred.
`DBG_DIVOVERFLOW`	*Divide Overflow* This needs to be tied into the standard debugger logic for serious application fault presentation.

`DBG_INSTRFAULT`	*Invalid Opcode Fault* An application error has ocurred that needs to be reported to the user in the standard ways.
`DBG_TASKSTART`	*Task starting* All of an application's image has been loaded but it has not yet executed the first instruction so that the debugger can insert any breakpoints or do other housekeeping functions before debuggee execution begins.
`DBG_TASKSTOP`	*Task stop* This is provided so the debugger can clean up and do necessary housekeeping after an applications image has been unloaded.
`DBG_DLLSTART`	*DLL starting* A DLL has been loaded, but none of its code has been executed yet. This allows the loading of new symbols into the debugger's symbol maps and allows any necessary setting of breakpoints destined for code in this DLL.
`DBG_DLLSTOP`	*DLL stop* A DLL has been unloaded so the debugger can and should clean up its symbols, breakpoints, etc.

the-fly, a class at a time, generates native machine code for the byte codes. A native Java compiler would treat Java as a language like C, C++, or Pascal and would translate the textual representation directly into a specific hardware instruction set.

A debugger for Java applications (or Java applets running within a browser) runs as part of the Java run-time system local to the user. The Java application being debugged may be running locally, running remotely, or a combination of both. The client and server (or local and remote) portions of the application may be running on completely different platforms. Java is a multithreaded application system so each portion of a complex client-server application may execute in multiple threads.

TABLE 4.11   *The NTVDM Functions Used by a Debugger and the Descriptions*
of Those Functions

NTVDM debug functions	Description
VDMProcessException	Every exception is passed to this function. If it's extraneous and not important to the debugger it will return FALSE and the debugger can continue execution. If it returns TRUE then analysis of the exception arguments tells the debugger how to act.
VDMGetThreadSelectorEntry	This is used to get the descriptor table entry for the specified VDM thread corresponding to the specified selector. This is just like the TOOLHELP function GetThreadSelectorEntry() except that this works in the simulated DOS/Win16 environment.
VDMGetPointer	This function is used to convert 16-bit addresses into flat 32-bit addresses.
VDMGetThreadContext	The context (all register values and related state) of the specified thread in the simulated DOS/Win16 environment is retrieved. No matter what system NT is running on, the simulated environment is always x86.
VDMSetThreadContext	This is the API to modify the thread context (that is, change the value of a register or change the state of the processor) in the simulated environment.
VDMGetSelectorModule	This is a helper function for a debugger in this environment to enable the debugger to map a code or data address to the module it belongs to.
VDMGetModuleSelector	This is the opposite of VDMGetSelectorModule—the selector is returned for the given module.
VDMModuleFirst	This begins enumerating all the modules currently loaded in the 16-bit Windows environment. It's basically the same function as the TOOLHELP ModuleFirst.

`VDMModuleNext`	This continues enumerating all the modules loaded. It is the same as TOOLHELPs ModuleNext.
`VDMGlobalFirst`	This begins enumerating all the global blocks of memory currently allocated in the 16-bit Windows environment. Same as TOOLHELPs GlobalFirst.
`VDMGlobalNext`	This continues enumerating all the global memory blocks. It is the same as TOOLHELPs GlobalNext.

Four key requirements for a debugger for the Java programming language are as follows:

1. The interface should be object-oriented in the same manner as the language.

2. Java language runtime features such as threads should be fully supported.

3. Remote debugging should be possible.

4. Security should not be compromised under normal operation.

To fulfill these requirements, the Java debugger API is included as part of the standard system packages.[7] This API is a set of Java Objects (written in Java and fully integrated into the Java system) that assumes all Java applications run remotely (local is just a special loop-back case). The debugger API uses the notion of a proxy for objects under observation so that, for example, there are classes in this API for `RemoteObject`, `RemoteStackFrame`, etc. This means that the remote debugger that our client user interface is talking to will, on our behalf, create references to objects we wish to examine. Because Java is a "garbage collection" environment, this is necessary to make sure these objects are not destroyed by the remote run-time's garbage collector if all other references to an object disappear.

The basic class used by a Java debugger is the `RemoteDebugger` class, which is a "viewer" for the Java Runtime being debugged. The methods in the `RemoteDebugger` class perform general operations, such as returning

---

[7]One debug API for Java is provided by SUN and is supported by the virtual maching shipped by SUN. However, other vendors such as Microsoft Symantec and even Netscape are shipping VMs with very different debug APIs. This area is developing rapidly and will remain confused until one vendor dominates.

TABLE 4.12 *Win32 debugger Development Matrix*

Platform	Application	Solution
Win32 / NT	32-bit	Use x86 debug registers
	16-bit	Use VDMDBG API
Win32 / Win95	32-bit	Use INT 3 breakpoints
	16-bit	Use thunking or DDE to a 16-bit debug engine using TOOLHELP; or give up

instances of `RemoteClass` or `RemoteThread`. Then, more specific data inquiry operations are supported through the methods of these returned classes. To get a class's methods, for example, the `RemoteClass` method `getMethod()` would be used. To print one of those method's names, its `getName()` method would be used. The `RemoteDebugger` class and its methods are described in Table 4.13.

The debugger communicates with the Java interpreter being debugged via a socket-based, proprietary protocol that is not extensible by debugging clients, for security reasons. The Java interpreter doing the debugging needs notification of debugging events that occur in the remote Java interpreter, and this is set up via the `DebuggerCallback` interface. Through this interface's methods, the local Java debugger is notified of breakpoints and exceptions in the debuggee. The class `DebuggerCallback` is described in Table 4.14.

The other classes in package java.tools.debug with brief descriptions of their methods are listed in Table 4.15. First, class `RemoteValue`, which is the basic class for dealing with (that is, inspecting) remote variables is described. The `RemoteValue` class gives the debugger access to a copy of a value in the remote Java interpreter. This value may be a primitive type, such as a Boolean or float, or an object, class, array, and so on.

Next, we show the set of classes that extend `RemoteValue` for dealing with basic types. Clearly, because these classes extend `RemoveValue`, any methods of `RemoteValue` are available and three additional methods (get, toString and typeName) are provided. See Table 4.16.

```
public class extends RemoteValue
public class extends RemoteValue
```

```
public class extends RemoteValue
public class extends RemoteValue
public class RemoteFloat extends RemoteValue
public class extends RemoteValue
public class extends RemoteValue
public class extends RemoteValue
```

The RemoteObject class allows access to an object in a remote Java interpreter. Remote objects, like remote values, are not created by the local debugger—the remote agent creates a reference to the requested object and returns to the local debugger this RemoteObject class for querying. Each remote object has a reference cached by the remote Java interpreter, to protect against being garbage-collected during examination. The Remote Debugger's gc() operation is used to free references to objects that are no longer being examined. See Table 4.17.

For the aggregate types, a set of classes extends RemoteObject. These classes include RemoteArray, RemoteClass, and RemoteString. See Table 4.18.

The class RemoteClass includes methods to manipulate breakpoints within a class. In Java, breakpoints are much easier to deal with for a debugger than in C, C++, Pascal, or similar languages. All code resides in one class or another—there are no header files—so breakpoints are always specified with respect to a class and a line number within that class. See Tables 4.19 and 4.20.

The way in which execution control, variable access, and context information are all so seamlessly accessible as part of the built-in system makes Java an ideal environment in which to build a debugger. For example, each variable and method—generically referred to as fields—within a RemoteClass are accessible as RemoteField. The description of class RemoteField follows in Table 4.21.

The stack in Java, in principle, is like a stack in any procedural language. However, more like Smalltalk than the *compiled to native code* languages, the stack is maintained exclusively in the Java run-time machine. Classes that provide all the necessary infrastructure to completely present stack information to the Java debugger user are provided through classes StackFrame, RemoteStackFrame, and RemoteStackVariable. See Table 4.22 through 4.24.

TABLE 4.13   *Class RemoteDebugger with All of Its Methods Described*

```
class RemoteDebugger extends Object
class RemoteDebugger (String host, String password,
DebuggerCallback client, PrintStream console, boolean verbose)
throws Exception
```

RemoteDebugger Methods	Method description
`void` `close(boolean)`	Closes the connection to the remote debugging agent.
`RemoteClass` `freeClass(String)`	Finds a specified class by its string name. First the remote debugger will try to find the class in its known set and if not successful, the request will be passed to the remote interpreter.
`int` `freeMemory()`	Reports the free memory available to the Java interpreter being debugged.
`void` `gc()`	Frees all unreferenced objects. While the remote debugger is examining objects, it keeps a reference so that no objects can be garbage-collected during examination. This method allows those objects to now be freed.
`RemoteObject` `get(int)`	Gets an object from the remote object cache identified by ID.
`String[]` `getExceptionCatchList()`	Returns the list of the exceptions the debugger will stop on.
`String` `getSourcePatch()`	Returns the source file path the Agent is currently using.
`void` `itrace(boolean)`	Turns on/off instruction tracing. This is a printout control for each instruction executed by the remote interpreter. This is not information accessible to the remote debugger.
`RemoteClass[]` `listClasses()`	Lists the currently known classes.

`RemoteThreadGroup[]`
`listTreadGroups`
`(RemoteThreadGroup)`
	Lists threadgroups given a RemoteThreadGroup tag.

`RemoteThreadGroup` `run(int, String[])`	Loads and runs a runnable Java class, with any optional parameters. The class is started inside a new threadgroup in the Java interpreter being debugged. Although it is possible to run multiple runnable classes from the same Java interpreter, there is no guarantee that all applets will work cleanly with each other. For example, two applets may want exclusive access to the same shared resource, such as a specific port.
`void` `setSourcePath(String)`	Specifies the list of paths to use when searching for a source file.
`int` `()`	Reports the total memory usage of the Java interpreter being debugged.
`void` `trace(boolean)`	Turns on/off method call tracing. This is just a printout control. If on, each method call of the remote interpreter is printed out.

The class `RemoteStackFrame` provides access to the stack frame of a suspended thread.

A `RemoteStackVariable` represents a method argument or local variable. It is similar to a `RemoteField`, but it is much more transient in nature.

Lastly, the final two classes that make up the Java debug API complete the picture by bringing in the concept of threads as a fundamental aspect of the Java language. These final two classes are `RemoteThread` and `RemoteThreadGroup`; see tables 4.25 and 4.26. Because the fundamental unit of execution in Java is the thread, it is here that we finally see the execution control methods such as step and continue. First we will take a look at class `RemoteThread`.

A Thread group can contain a set of Threads as well as a set of other Thread groups. A Thread can access its Thread group, but it can't access the parent of its Thread group. This makes it possible to encapsulate a Thread in a Thread group and stop it from manipulating Threads in the parent group.

TABLE 4.14   *Class Debugger Callback with All of Its Methods Described*

PUBLIC CLASS DEBUGGERCALLBACK EXTENDS OBJECT	
Debugger Callback methods	**Method description**
`void breakpointEvent (RemoteThread)`	A breakpoint has been hit in the specified thread.
`void (RemoteThread, String)`	An exception has occurred in the specified thread; the error text is specified in the given String.

TABLE 4.15   *Class RemoteValue with All Fits Methods Described*

PUBLIC CLASS REMOTEVALUE EXTENDS OBJECT	
Remote Value methods	**Method description**
`String description ()`	Returns a description of the `RemoteValue`.
`int fromHex (String)`	Converts hexadecimal strings to ints.
`int getType()`	Returns the `RemoteValue`'s type.
`boolean isObject()`	Returns whether the `RemoteValue` is an Object (as opposed to a primitive type, such as int).
`String toHex(int)`	Converts an int to a hexadecimal string.
`String ()`	Returns the `RemoteValue`'s type as a string.

TABLE 4.16   *Class Remote* and All the Shared Methods Described*

SHARED METHODS OF REMOTE*	METHOD DESCRIPTIONS
`char get()`	Returns the appropriate type's value.
`String toString()`	Returns the appropriate type's value as a string.
`String typeName()`	Returns this RemoteValue's type as a string

TABLE 4.17 *Class RemoteObject and All of Its Methods Described*

PUBLIC CLASS REMOTEOBJECT EXTENDS REMOTEVALUE	
Remote Object methods	**Method descriptions**
`String description ()`	Returns a description of the object.
`RemoteClass getClazz ()`	Returns the object's class.
`RemoteField getField (int)`	Returns an instance variable, specified by slot number.
`RemoteField getField (String)`	Returns an instance variable, specified by name.
`RemoteValue getFieldValue (int)`	Returns the value of an object's instance variable.
`RemoteValue getFieldValue (String)`	Returns the value of an object's instance variable.
`RemoteFields[] getFields ()`	Returns the instance (non-static) fields of an object.
`int getId ()`	Returns the ID of the object.
`String toString ()`	Returns object as a string.
`String typeName ()`	Returns the `RemoteValue`'s type name ("Object").

A full-featured debugger can be built in Java that deals with local and remote Java applications. A screen-shot for such an early Java debugger is shown in Figure 4.2.

TABLE 4.18 *Class RemoteArray and All of Its Methods Described*

PUBLIC CLASS EXTENDS REMOTEOBJECT

RemoteArray methods	Method descriptions
`String arrayTypeName (int)`	Returns the element type as a string.
`String description ()`	Returns a description of the array.
`RemoteValue getElement (int)`	Returns the array element whose index in the array is specified as an argument.
`int getElementType ()`	Returns the element type as a "TC_" constant, such as "TC_CHAR".
`RemoteValue[] getElements ()`	Returns a copy of the array as instances of RemoteValue.
`RemoteValue[] getElements (int, int)`	Returns a copy of a portion of the array specified by the arguments representing the range of elements as instances of RemoteValue.
`int getSize ()`	Returns the number of elements in the array.
`String toString ()`	Returns a string version of the array.
`String typeName ()`	Returns this RemoteValue's type ("array").

Table 4.19 *Class RemoteObject and All of Its Methods Described*

PUBLIC CLASS REMOTECLASS EXTENDS REMOTEOBJECT

RemoteClass methods	Method descriptions
`void catchExceptions ()`	Enters the debugger when an instance of this class is thrown.
`String clearBreakpoing (int)`	Clears a breakpoint at a specific address in a class. Return an error string if any.
`String clearBreakpoingLine (int)`	Clears a breakpoint at a specified line. Returns an error string if any.
`String`	Clears a breakpoint at the start of a

`clearBreakpoingMethod` `(RemoteField)`	specified method. Return error string if any.
`String description ()`	Returns a String description of the class.
`RemoteObject` `getClassLoader ()`	Returns the classloader for this class. ClassLoader is an abstract Class that can be used to define a policy for loading Java classes into the runtime environment. By default, the runtime system loads classes that originate as files by reading them from the directory defined by the CLASSPATH environment variable.
`RemoteField` `getField (int)`	Returns the static field, specified by index.
`RemoteField` `getField (String)`	Returns the static field, specified by name.
`RemoteField` `getFieldValue (int)`	Returns the value of a static field, specified by its index.
`RemoteField` `getFieldValue (String)`	Returns the value of a static field, specified by name.
`RemoteField []` `getFields ()`	Returns all the static fields for this class.
`RemoteField` `getInstanceField (int)`	Returns the instance field, specified by its index.
`RemoteField[]` `getInstanceFileds ()`	Returns all the instance fields for this class.
`RemoteClass[]` `getInterfaces ()`	Returns the interfaces for this class.
`RemoteField` `getMethod (String)`	Returns the `RemoteField` for the method specified by name.
`String[]` `getMethodNames ()`	Returns the names of all methods supported by this class.
`RemoteField[]` `getMethods ()`	Returns the class's methods as a vector of `RemoteFields`.
`String getName ()`	Returns the name of the class.

Table 4.19 *(Continued)*

`RemoteField[]` `getStaticFields ()`	Returns all the static fields for this class.
`RemoteClass` `getSuperclass ()`	Returns the superclass for this class, that is, the class that this class extends.
`void ignoreExceptions ()`	Don't enter the debugger when an instance of this class is thrown. This is how the debugger user can be selective about which exceptions will cause execution of the remote interpreter to stop and return control to the debugger.
`boolean isInterface ()`	Returns true if this `RemoteClass` is an interface.
`String` `setBreakpointLine (int)`	Sets a breakpoint at the source line number in a class passed as an argument. Return string, if present, is an error description.

`String`
`setBreakpointMethod`
`(RemoteField)`
	Sets a breakpoint at the first line of a the class method specified as an argument. String return, if present, is an error description.

`String toString ()`	Returns `RemoteClass` as a string.
`String typeName ()`	Returns the name of the type of this class as a string.

TABLE 4.20 *Class RemoteString and All of Its Methods Described*

PUBLIC CLASS REMOTESTRING EXTENDS REMOTEOBJECT	
RemoteString methods	**Method descriptions**
`String description ()`	Returns the string value, or "null."
`String toString ()`	Returns the string value, or "null."
`String typeName ()`	Prints this `RemoteValue`'s type ("String").

TABLE 4.21 *Class RemoteField and All of Its Methods Described*

PUBLIC CLASS REMOTEFIELD EXTENDS FIELD	
RemoteField methods	**Method description**
`String getModifiers ()`	Returns a string with the field's modifiers, such as "public," "static," "final," etc.
`String getName ()`	Returns the name of the field.
`String getType ()`	Returns a type string describing the field.
`RemoteValue getValue (int)`	Returns the value of the field as identified by the index given as an argument.
`boolean inStatic ()`	Returns whether the field is static (a class variable or method).
`String toString ()`	Returns a String that represents the value of this Object.

TABLE 4.22 *Class StackFrame and All of Its Methods Described*

PUBLIC CLASS STACKFRAME EXTENDS OBJECT	
StackFrame method	**Method descriptions**
`String toString ()`	Returns a String representation of the value of this Object.

TABLE 4.23   *Class RemoteStackFrame and All of Its Methods Described*

PUBLIC CLASS REMOTESTACKFRAME EXTENDS STACKFRAME

Remote StackFrame methods	Method description
`int getLineNumber ()`	Returns the source file line number.
`RemoteStackVariable getLocalVariable (String)`	Returns a specific (named) stack variable. Facilities are provided in `RemoteStackVariable` to indicate if the variable is out of scope currently.
`RemoteStackVariables[] getLocalVariables ()`	Returns an array of all valid local variables and method arguments for this stack frame.
`RemoteClass getRemoteClass ()`	Gets the class this stack frame references.
`InputStream getSourceFile ()`	Gets the source file referenced by this stackframe.
`String getSourceFileName ()`	Gets the name of the source file referenced by this stackframe

TABLE 4.24   *Class RemoteStackVariable and All of Its Methods Described*

PUBLIC CLASS REMOTESTACKVARIABLE EXTENDS LOCALVARIABLE

RemoteStackVariable methods	Method description
`String getName ()`	Returns the name of a stack variable or argument.
`RemoteValue getValue ()`	Returns the value of a stack variable or argument.
`boolean inScope ()`	Returns whether variable is in scope.

TABLE 4.25   *Class RemoteThread and All of Its Methods Described*

PUBLIC CLASS REMOTETHREAD EXTENDS REMOTEOBJECT

RemoteThread methods	Methods description
`void cont ()`	Resumes this thread from a breakpoint, unless it previously suspended.

`void down (int)`	Changes the current stack frame to be one or more frames lower (as in, toward the current program counter).
`RemoteStackFrame[]` `dumpStack ()`	Dumps the stack in the form of a vector of `RemoteStackFrame` classes.
`RemoteStackFrame` `getCurrentFrame ()`	Gets the current stack frame.
`int` `getCurrentFrameIndex ()`	Returns the current stack frame index.
`String getName ()`	Returns the name of the thread.
`RemoteStackVariable` `getStackVariable (String)`	Returns a stack variable from the current stack frame as named by the String argument.
`RemoteStackVariable[]` `getStackVariables ()`	Returns the arguments and local variable from the current stack frame.
`String getStatus ()`	Returns the thread status description.
`boolean isSuspended ()`	Returns whether this thread is suspended.
`void` `resetCurrentFrameIndex ()`	Resets the current stack frame index.
`void resume ()`	Resumes execution of this thread (that is, "un-suspends" it).
`void` `setCurrentFrameIndex (int)`	Sets the current stack frame index.
`void step (boolean)`	Continues execution of this thread to the next function (if arg is true) or line.
`void stop ()`	Stops the remote thread.
`void suspend ()`	Suspends execution of this thread—it will stay suspended until resume is called on it.
`void up (int)`	Changes the current stack frame to be one or more frames higher (as in, away from the current program counter).

TABLE 4.26 *Class RemoteThreadGroup and All of Its Methods Described*

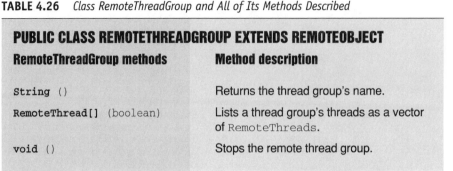

PUBLIC CLASS REMOTETHREADGROUP EXTENDS REMOTEOBJECT	
RemoteThreadGroup methods	**Method description**
`String ()`	Returns the thread group's name.
`RemoteThread[] (boolean)`	Lists a thread group's threads as a vector of `RemoteThreads`.
`void ()`	Stops the remote thread group.

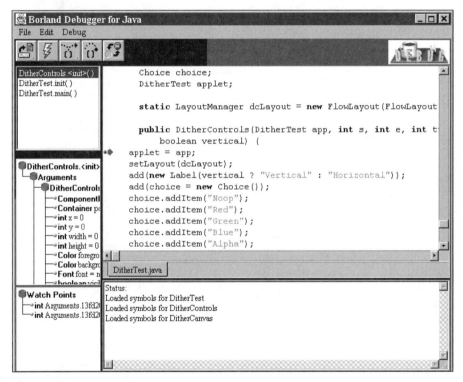

Figure 4.2

Java debugger. *The main context window in a Java debugger. Here a single window, which is thread-specific, shows the annotated source code, the stack trace, and the current variables.*

Controlling Execution

The heart of a debugger is its process control or execution control "kernel." This is the portion of the debugger responsible for controlling the process or processes being debugged. To do this the debugger must gain control of the debuggee, be able to determine its state, set breakpoints, run the process, and terminate it. This section examines in depth the key algorithms associated with these debugger activities.

Initiating Program Execution

The first job of a debugger with respect to controlling execution is the creation of the debuggee from scratch or via attachment to an existing process. Next up is to get that debuggee ready to run under the debugger's control. In this section we will explore how these steps are taken.

Creating the Debuggee

The first thing the debugger must do, once the user has specified what executable is to be debugged, is to initiate the calls to the OS that create the debuggee. The OS needs either to create the debuggee process for the debugger explicitly through a special call or to attach the debugger to an existing process. In either case, the OS must be able to control the debuggee completely as directed by the debugger. Typically, the new process is loaded such that it has all but executed its first instruction but is in every other way ready for execution. The debugger gets notifications from the OS whenever a material event occurs with the debuggee; all notifications result in the debuggee being stopped for examination. The debugger gets its first notification about a new debuggee once all the setup is done and the debuggee is ready for debugger control.

For execution control purposes, putting the debuggee under control of the debugger in this fashion has one important goal: to change the behavior of exceptions or signals generated in or by this debuggee process. Instead of the normal handling of exceptions—where the application gets a chance to handle an exception and then the OS does what it needs to with it—the debugger is notified first. Exceptions cover a wide variety of events including "illegal instruction," "user interrupt," "floating point overflow," and so on. Most importantly, special events like "breakpoint hit" and "single-step completed" are exceptions that notify the debugger that something of interest has happened.

This "event-driven" concept of debugging has been extended to include a variety of non-exception events, but ones critical to effective debugging. A list of typical events is shown in Table 5.1.

Attaching to Running Program

Attaching to a running program is a very important facility for multiprocess, post-mortem, or just-in-time debugging (initiating a debugging session only after a fault has occurred but before the OS has flushed the just-faulted process). For some operating systems, it is also the way to control a process spawned by the current debuggee.[1]

For multiprocess debugging, the debugger, needs to be able to debug any and all processes that interact with the debuggee. To fully understand what is going wrong, it may be necessary to have all interacting processes under the control of the same debugger.

Post-mortem debugging is the process of examining the memory image of a process that has faulted and was terminated. Its state at the time it faulted was saved to disk for examination. Just-in-time debugging is related, but instead of

---

[1]Win32 does not require an attach in this case since it provides explicit events as child processes spawn and die.

TABLE 5.1   *A List of Generic Debugger Events with the Causes of These Events*

Debugging	Causes of this event
process created	This event occurs whenever a debuggee is initially created explicitly by the debugger or implicitly when an attach to a running process occurs. On some systems this event also occurs if the debuggee spawns a new process. The debugger will probably have some internal process data structures that must be created at this time.
thread created	Whenever the debuggee causes a new thread to begin execution this event occurs. If an attach to a running process occurs, one of these events arises for each active thread in the new process. A debugger that handles multiple threads must have an internal structure that tracks the state of each thread. This structure must be created as a result of this event.
process exited	This event occurs when the debuggee process terminates. No other events from the debuggee can occur after this. This event is a chance for the debugger to clean up its internal record keeping and to release any resources it maintained on behalf of the debuggee process.
thread exited	As the debuggee terminates threads this event occurs. It also occurs in conjunction with the **process exited** event as an entire process shuts down. On some systems as spawned processes exit this event is passed on. Again, this is the opportunity for the debugger to release any resources and clean up as a thread terminates.
module loaded	Modules, either DLLs or EXEs, are the compiler-generated units that, combined, make up a working program. When the initial process is getting started there is a module-loaded event for the initial EXE. Subsequently there is a module-loaded event for each DLL as it is loaded. The main activity within the debugger on module loaded events is symbol table loading from the new module. New symbols, breakpoint locations, files, etc. must be added to the already loaded ones coming from the new module.
module unloaded	As this event occurs, some module is being unloaded from the running process. This may occur during normal execution or as the entire process itself is shutting down. In either case, the debugger must deal with the fact that some symbols are no longer mapped to any existing module, and some breakpoints also may no longer exit.

TABLE 5.1 *(Continued)*

output string	A special event exists in some OS debug APIs to allow users to programmatically force debug events to occur. It takes the form of a special 'printf' that is passed to the debugger instead of printed out on any output device. Usually the debugger is just expected to stop and show the string that was just passed from the debuggee.
exception	This is probably the most important event the debugger ever receives from the debuggee. This event is used to capture breakpoints, single-step completion, watch point firings, and real faults in the running program. In all of these cases, the debugger determines if the stop should be made visible to the user, and if so, the state of the debuggee at the time of the stop must be captured for presentation to the user. The type of exception will determine further how the debugger behaves.

an image written to disk, when the OS issues a fatal exception but before the process is flushed from memory, the OS allows a debugger to attach to the process to examine its memory image. At this point, the user cannot continue execution of the process but its registers, current stack trace, location of fault, and its variables can all be examined by the user. Frequently this is enough for the user to be able to tell what happened and go fix the problem.

When the debugger attaches to an existing process, it is able to "catch up" with the state of the debuggee via a series of notifications. There will be a notification at attach time for each module loaded and each thread created that is currently active in the debuggee process.

Setting a Breakpoint

Breakpoints are special instructions inserted into the executable text image by the debugger that, when executed by the debuggee, cause it to halt execution immediately and to "trap" to the operating system. These special instructions are defined by the CPU architecture. Sometimes they are just a special value of a general "interrupt" instruction (Intel 1990). Or it may be a special dedicated breakpoint instruction (Kane 1989). In either case, it is an instruction designed to trap immediately to a special OS breakpoint exception handler.

A lot of debugger issues revolve around breakpoints that may not be immediately obvious. Breakpoints are *the* basic mechanism used by a debugger to control the debuggee process. Breakpoints can be used to aid single-step, provide special user convenience features such as "run-to-here," allow function evaluation, provide selective or conditional program control that stops the debuggee only under user-defined conditions, and a whole host of other possible features. Table 5.2 is a quick synopsis of some of the uses for breakpoints.

Causing the Debuggee to Run

Once the programmer has set the necessary breakpoints and wishes to execute the program to the first breakpoint, the debugger will begin execution of the debuggee. Execution may be either "run full speed until some debug event occurs" or it may be "execute a single machine instruction" and then generate a debug event. The latter is—as I have discussed—a convenience to the debugger technically not needed and not even available on some architectures. In either case, the operating system has been directed to context switch from the debugger to the debuggee. What actually occurs is as follows: The debugger is the active process and it makes a call into the operating system to initiate the debuggee; control switches over to the operating system to complete this system call; the operating system gets the debuggee process ready to run and context switches to it; the debuggee now is the active process and runs according to the scheduling algorithms in the operating system. The debugger will still get its time-slice and become the active process so that it can process user events, but a critical thread (or process) within the debugger is idle until the debuggee stops. Usually the debuggee, once executing, is able to achieve full processor speed with very little overhead due to debugging. But once a debugging event occurs, the debuggee is stopped, the operating system saves its stopped context (the values of all hardware registers), and control transfers to the waiting debugger.[2] At this point the debugger must discover why the debuggee stopped, where it stopped, and what is its context. The *why* is usually indicated by a special flag or value set in a return code either from the blocking debug execution function or in the blocking wait function. The *where* is usually available in

---

[2]Actually, whenever any process is stopped or preempted by the operating system, its context must be completely saved so that it can be started up at a later time; for a debugger, the operating system just gives easy access to that saved context.

TABLE 5.2   *Generic Breakpoints and How They Are Used by a Debugger*

BREAKPOINT TYPE	WHAT IT DOES
user breakpoint	This is the most frequently used kind of breakpoint. The user specifies a place in the code where he or she wishes execution to stop, usually by pointing in the source or edit view to the line where the breakpoint should be set. Certain conditions can be attached to this breakpoint that control when it actually activates and really stops the process.
single-step	Continuous instruction-level single-step is unacceptably slow just because of the sheer number of instructions that would need to be stepped in many cases. Some processors do not even support single-step mode. Breakpoints are used to advance the execution short amounts to get the effect of statement single-step. Even instruction step can be accomplished using only breakpoints by decoding the current instruction and placing a breakpoint on the very next instruction.
run-to-here	This is a form of user breakpoint, but one that is frequently referred to as a "once only" breakpoint. That is, once the debuggee stops for any reason all these "once only" breakpoints are permanently removed.
finish function	Frequently, this feature is offered to users as a convenient way to complete whatever function the current execution point is in. The way this is implemented usually requires finding the return address of the current function and placing a temporary internal breakpoint there.
function evaluation	When a function within the debuggee must be executed in isolation from the normal path of execution (as for breakpoint conditional expression evaluation), the debugger must set up a very controlled environment. The stack must be manipulated prior to calling the function, and a breakpoint must catch execution as the function exits so that only the desired function is executed.
messagepoints	Message points, also known as windows message breakpoints, are normal breakpoints placed in a special place in the code that will capture Window message events. In addition, these breakpoints know

	something about window messages so that the arguments can be evaluated for adherence to some required pattern for stopping.
profiling	Even profiling may in some cases use breakpoints if the profiling strategy requires examining each function and recording some information as each one is entered and/or exited. Profiling integrated into a debugger might use this sort of strategy.

the saved context that contains the values of all the processor registers at the time debuggee execution halted, including the program or instruction counter, which points to where in memory the debuggee was executing when it stopped. And the context just requires reading an OS-maintained buffer of all the registers saved when the debuggee halted. This typically includes all hardware, general-purpose, floating-point, and status registers. A critical piece of context information needed by the debugger and its user is the debuggee program stack that shows the function call stack that traces the history of execution up to the moment it stopped. One or more hardware registers gives the debugger enough information to reconstruct the stack, which itself resides in debuggee data memory.

Debuggee-generated Events during Execution

From a design standpoint, the most challenging aspect of a debugger's execution control is the event-driven nature of debug notifications. A characteristic of debugging control APIs is that because they are notification based, the debugger sets the debuggee running and must wait for a notification some time later. Whenever the debuggee is executing, the debugger is waiting for one of these notifications. As soon as the debuggee stops for any reason, a notification is passed by the operating system to the debugger to break it out of its wait state and alert it to take some sort of action. The debuggee will not continue execution until the debugger directs it to do so. The types of action taken for each type of notification are discussed in the following sections.

Breakpoint, Single-step Events

When the notification is **breakpoint,** the debugger needs to check its stored list of breakpoints to find out which breakpoint has been hit. It does this by getting the saved state for the debuggee and querying the stop location (that is, the program counter). The list of breakpoints, typically not very large, is scanned to look for this address. More than one may match. Some of the breakpoints in this list may be internal breakpoints for use by the debugger as helpers in its execution algorithms. For example, statement stepping at the source code level uses internal (not visible to the user) breakpoints so that statement step operates faster (see Chapter 6 for more details). In some cases the debugger may find no breakpoint in its list that matches this stop address. This is possible because the breakpoint instruction may have been inserted into the running program by an agent other than the debugger. The user, for one, may have explicitly coded the special breakpoint instruction into the debuggee. In this case the debugger should act still as if it hit an explicitly set breakpoint but it will have to resort to a CPU view to show where execution stopped instead of a source view.

Thread Creation/Deletion Events

When the debuggee process creates or deletes a thread of execution the user interface must be notified so that user-visible changes can occur. Additionally, thread-specific data structures maintained by the debugger will need to be affected by thread creation and deletion. It is critical that the debugger is aware of each thread and maintains context information about each one because one of the more important functions the debugger provides is its ability to control these separate threads and to detect problems in multi-threaded applications. Typically, the low-level *wait* in the debugger kernel will return when the thread creation or deletion notification occurs, once the appropriate data structure cleanup and user interface notification occur, the kernel just restarts the debuggee with no other changes to debuggee or debugger state. If the thread getting "deleted" is the main thread of execution, this is not just a matter of data structure cleanup; the process itself is about to exit. A lot more work needs to be done here as all data structures maintained on behalf of the debuggee need to reflect the fact that the process will soon no longer exist.

Process Creation/Deletion Events

Some debuggers are designed to handle debugging multiple processes. In this case, notification from the initially started process that it has spawned a new process is important for the debugger to be able to track the new process. For this to work the debugger must be provided with the "attach" capability. This allows a debugger to request an attachment to an already running process, after which this new process is controlled in the same fashion as the process that was initially created by the debugger. Normally, the attach facility causes several notifications immediately after the attach succeeds, including process created, thread created (for each active thread), and module loaded (for each dynamic load library loaded). As processes exit, the process-deleted notifications come in to the debugger, allowing it to clean up all internal data structures related to the process just exiting. And if it is the initially debugged process that is exiting, this is the last notification the debugger will get about the debuggee, and no further control over this process is possible.

Data Access (Watchpoint) Events

The watchpoint feature (also known as data access breakpoints) is not one that has been widely adopted and standardized. However, it is one of the more important features a debugger can provide because data corruption is a common and very difficult type of bug to isolate. Watchpoints are supported in more recent CPUs; that support is, in some cases, exposed through the debug APIs in some operating systems. For example, some versions of UNIX/ptrace() have a "data access breakpoint" interface. In other operating systems, while not explicitly exposed, there are usually mechanisms to bypass the operating system and work directly with the hardware if it supports watchpoints. In this case, the notification may be very similar to breakpoint. To detect the difference, the debugger must get the entire state of the stopped debuggee and examine certain hardware status registers that will specify the precise cause of the exception. Watchpoint notification, whether direct or indirect through hardware register examination, indicates that a location or region in memory was accessed. The program counter will point to the offending instruction or one instruction past the offending instruction. This will probably cause a hard stop of the debugger and get reported to the user as an attempt to modify the variable he or she wanted to watch. Presumably, the programmer discovered a corrupted memory location or variable and now wants to determine where and when this corruption took place.

Module Load/Unload Events

Module load and unload notifications occur whenever a dynamic load library (DLL)[3] is loaded or unloaded by the debuggee. This is important information to a debugger because code the user may want to debug may exist in these DLLs. This means that symbol table information that contains important debugging information may need to be examined and processed on module loads. Furthermore, the user may have set breakpoints in source code for which the executable, residing in a DLL, has not yet been loaded. In this case, at the moment the DLL load notification occurs, the debugger must resolve these breakpoints—compute the correct location in the text space— and immediately get them inserted into the newly loaded DLL text. Similarly, when a DLL is unloaded, the corresponding symbol table information must be noted by the debugger, and any breakpoints in this DLL must be re-marked as unresolved in case this DLL gets reloaded at a later time. Once this symbol table and breakpoint processing is completed, the debugger must continue execution of the debuggee until the next notification.

Exception Events

True exception events—as opposed to breakpoint, watchpoint, or single-step events disguised as exceptions—are program faults such as floating point divide by zero or illegal memory access. These are the kinds of bugs the debugger must help the user find and eliminate. These exceptions almost always cause a hard stop that gets reported to the user but frequently indicate such a serious problem that execution cannot proceed in any meaningful way even if the user so desired. There are several classes of exceptions; some are so severe that meaningful execution cannot proceed while others do not prevent continued execution. Some of these may be automatically ignored by the debugger with execution proceeding immediately, such as software timer interrupts. But others point to severe programming errors like executing code outside of the program's text space (for example, following a bad pointer to a function and executing this pointer indirectly), or attempting to access a memory location that is not a legal address (which probably means a pointer is bad or a memory location has been corrupted), or attempting to extend the

---

[3]The term DLL is a Win32 term for what is generically a shared library. The UNIX equivalent term is shared object (SO). I will use the term DLL throughout but it can be thought of in the more generic sense.

stack beyond the limit set by the operating system (which probably means infinite recursion). The various operating systems allow differing degrees of selectivity on a debug exception. Win32 is one extreme with no degree of selectivity—the debugger hears about everything. UNIX/proc and even TOOLHELP allows some control ones which exceptions are passed along to the debugger. OS/2 has an extremely high degree of selectivity in this regard.

Other Events

Many new operating systems present a special type of exception that allows users to programmatically control when the debuggee generates an exception through special system calls the user can insert in the source code of the program being debugged. Usually this call accepts a string as an argument that is then emitted to a special debug string monitoring tool; it also causes an exception when run under the debugger. Under Windows and Win32 this OS call is called OutputDebugString().

Another type of debug exception provided by some operating systems allows one to stop the debuggee whenever it is about to execute an operating system call. This is a very useful type of event because frequently at issue is the interface between the user's program and the operating system. This "system call exception" notification is available on some UNIX variants and may begin to appear in PC systems as true protected operating systems begin to take over the PC platforms.

Continuing Execution

Continuing execution after the debuggee has stopped is fairly straightforward. All of the debug APIs have a function to continue execution. However, several options for the debugger do exist. First is the issue of changing the program counter location. If the stop is at a breakpoint, the PC and breakpoint must be dealt with, as I shall describe in detail in the next chapter. If the restart is to execute a function to be evaluated in the debuggee context, the PC must be adjusted first and reset later. I will discuss function evaluation in detail in Chapter 8.

Besides determining if the PC or current breakpoint must be manipulated, there is the issue of whether to pass into the debuggee any idea of why it was stopped. If the stop was caused exclusively by what the debugger did (on behalf of the user) you probably do not pass this information into the debuggee as it is about to continue execution. But if the stop was due to an exception caused within the debuggee's executing environment, then a real choice exists as to whether the debuggee should "see" the exception. For example, a user may decide a divide-by-zero is not critical and more can be learned by allowing execution to continue, fooling the debuggee into thinking the fault never occurred.

Terminating Execution

Contrary to intuition, terminating a debuggee can be quite tricky and problematic. This may be simply because the logic in the operating system associated with process termination in conjunction with the debug APIs can be fragile. Termination of the debuggee can occur in many ways. The process itself can exit normally. A fatal exception may occur. Some other process can cause it to terminate. The debugger can try to force early termination. Forcing termination explicitly occurs under a couple of circumstances. The user may request "termination" or "reset" of the process being debugged as offered in some debugger UI menu. This would occur when the user wants to start the process again from the start or switch to a different process to debug. It also is necessary if the same executable is to be rebuilt because if the debugger has the file open, the linker will not be able to modify it.

Breakpoints and Single Stepping

Breakpoints

Breakpoints are key to all debugger execution control—almost all execution control algorithms, at some point, involve breakpoints. These algorithms frequently require a special breakpoint be set, perhaps completely invisible to the user. This section describes a set of requirements for breakpoint algorithms, data structures for breakpoints, and various scenarios and algorithms that may be used by debuggers to fulfill the requirements stated.

Requirements for Breakpoint Algorithms

Following is a list of requirements for a debugger's basic breakpoint mechanisms. Breakpoints must adequately support execution control functionality and provide the rich set of functionality nedeed for a modern debugger:

- User may insert source-level or instruction level breakpoints.

- Some high-level breakpoints may map onto many text addresses such as breakpoints in C++ templates.

- Each user-created breakpoint must be represented and maintained uniquely.

- There can be many user-created breakpoints at the same source code or text address location.

- Some user-created breakpoints will be temporary ("once only") and must be removed at the next stop.

- Breakpoints may have associated conditions that must be evaluated by the debugger to determine if the stop really should occur.

- Breakpoints may have side effects that must be acted on by the debugger when activated but that may or may not actually be represented to the user as a debuggee stop.

- Breakpoints set in not-yet-loaded modules must be resolved when these modules get loaded.

- Internal breakpoints created by the debugger must be maintained so that they are invisible to the user.

- On multiprocessor architectures, high-level breakpoints may require interprocessor synchronization.

Breakpoint Data Structures

Typically there need to be at least two "levels" of breakpoint representation: the logical and the physical. The **logical breakpoints**—usually corresponding to those set by the user—are those associated with a point in the source code. The **physical breakpoints**—those that relate directly to executable machine instructions—are the points in the text space where actual hardware breakpoint instructions get written. It is the physical level that must store the original instruction (or part thereof) that must be replaced if the breakpoint is to be removed. The logical level is responsible for representing a breakpoint as fully resolved (that is, it has a mapping to a physical address) or as not yet resolved as when a breakpoint is set in a module that will not be loaded until some time later during debuggee execution. Special kinds of breakpoints called "conditional breakpoints" may or may not actually stop when the breakpoint "fires" depending on the value of an associated condition.

These conditions associated with a breakpoint are maintained at the logical level. This is true even for logical breakpoints set in disassembled instructions presented to the user in a machine or CPU view. Conditions are Boolean expressions that are evaluated by the debugger upon breakpoint activation. If the Boolean expression evaluates to false, the breakpoint activation is ignored and execution automatically resumes without the user ever being notified of the stop. If the Boolean expression evaluates to true, the breakpoint activates and the user is notified the process has stopped. Such conditions as *pass counts*, *window message received*, and *expressions* that must evaluate to true for valid stop are also maintained at the logical level.

A many-to-one relationship may exist between logical and physical breakpoints, as shown in Figure 6.1. We do not restrict the user from setting two distinct breakpoints (perhaps with different conditions) at a point in the source code that maps to the same physical location. In fact, as we shall explore later, C++ templates cause the logical to physical mapping to be many-to-many. Because we expect the number of breakpoints to remain relatively small, the most effective approach usually employed is to have two separate structures for logical and physical breakpoints where the node in each list maintains an address that is the link between the two. The downward mapping from logical to physical occurs when setting, deleting, or modifying a breakpoint. This downward mapping results in a physical address to be used as a lookup or search token in the physical breakpoint list. The upward mapping occurs when a breakpoint triggers due to the debuggee executing a breakpoint instruction. This upward mapping results in a physical address from the OS that maps uniquely to one node in the physical breakpoint list. This same address is then used to search the logical breakpoint list to find all logical breakpoints that mapped into the given physical address. At this point, any associated conditions can be evaluated to determine if this stop of the debuggee should be reported to the user because some user-created breakpoint met all its conditions for stopping the debuggee. Because of the inherent many-to-one mapping between logical and physical, it is necessary for the physical level to know when all logical breakpoints referring to a single physical address are deleted or disabled. This is easily accomplished with reference counts on the nodes in the physical breakpoint list. A node is actually deleted, removed from the list, and its original instruction restored only when its reference count drops to zero.

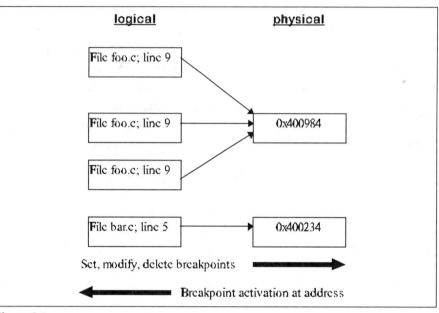

Figure 6.1

Breakpoint two-way mappings. *This figure shows that in some cases, several logical breakpoints map onto a single physical breakpoint location. The mappings are used in both directions. Logical-to-physical on set, modify or deletion of breakpoints. Physical-to-logical whenever a hardware breakpoint event occurs.*

Breakpoint Setting and Activation

The basic breakpoint setting algorithm, based on the data structures described above, is shown in Algorithm 6.1. The user specifies that a source line in the editor or source view should have a breakpoint set on it. This algorithm is then run to map that to a physical breakpoint location in the code space.

Algorithm 6.1 *Breakpoint setting (source level)*

Input	File name and line number or file offset in source file.
Output	Physical location of breakpoint or error indication.
Method	Map from file name plus line number to physical address using symbol table, logical breakpoint, and physical breakpoint.

    i. Request symbol table agent map given file name and line number information into physical address (notify if given module not yet loaded);

    ii. Create logical breakpoint object with this information contained;

   iii. Create (or increment reference count if already exists) physical breakpoint object;

   iv. Physical breakpoint agent must now insert breakpoint instruction and save original instruction at that location;

The physical breakpoint object is very simple and looks like Figure 6.2. These structures are probably kept in a linked list because there are never so many of them that the linked list overhead becomes an issue.

There are two sides to this coin: setting the breakpoint and then hitting it once the process starts executing. Algorithm 6.2 shows the steps necessary once a breakpoint fires.

Breakpoint Validation

When a breakpoint is set by a user there may not be an address at which to physically place the breakpoint instruction yet. This can occur because there may not yet be a valid mapping from the source code the user can see and manipulate and the executable code, which executes on the processor. The breakpoint may be in code in a dynamically loaded library (DLL) that has not yet been loaded. Or, perhaps no process is loaded at all because the user is modifying the source code and the compiler has not yet translated the source code into executable text. In either case, the breakpoint set by the user, a logical breakpoint, will exist without any associated physical breakpoint until some later time—it remains invalidated. In fact, it may never be a valid breakpoint because it may have been set on a non-executable statement. Unless the editor parses the text being edited, it cannot know, until a statement table is built by the compiler, which places in the source text represent breakpointable locations. Once the process finally gets loaded or the appropriate DLL is loaded, a validation algorithm must complete the mapping of invalidated logical breakpoint to physical.

Validation of breakpoints must get triggered at the earliest possible moment. This is easy in the case of invalidated breakpoints in a process not yet loaded as a debuggee. When the process is first created no instructions are executed before the debugger has a chance to process all the invalidated breakpoints and get physical breakpoints inserted. It is slightly more problematic for DLLs loaded at run-time. More recent operating systems have provided a debugging *event* or notification when a module load or unload occurs. This

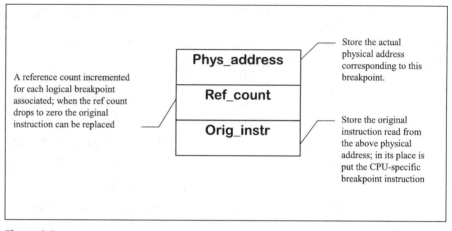

Figure 6.2

Simple physical breakpoint structure. *This structure holds the physical address in instruction memory where the breakpoint instruction will be placed. The original instruction is saved so that when the breakpoint must be removed the correct original instruction can be replaced. There is also a reference count due to the fact that multiple logical breakpoints may map to the same physical location. This allows the debugger to easily maintain the breakpoint and this corresponding data structure until the ref_count drops to zero.*

notification causes the debuggee to stop execution whenever a DLL is loaded but before any instruction in that DLL actually executes. This gives the debugger a chance to validate these DLL breakpoints in time to catch any breakpoints that might get hit as the DLL executes. Provision needs to be made within the debugger's execution control algorithm to process this kind of notification and validate all breakpoints in the source code associated with a DLL. The same procedure will have to run on initial startup for statically loaded libraries and on attach, where all previously loaded libraries will generate a series of module load events.

Older operating systems (like Windows 3.1 or before) required extensive trickery to accomplish this—although they support DLLs there was no debugger notification of these modules being loaded. Catching the call to the run-time routine (LoadLibrary()) that causes these loads was necessary. Debuggers would have to find this routine in the operating system's list of external entry points at debuggee startup time, set a special breakpoint in this routine that would trigger whenever a load module was requested, and handle this breakpoint being hit as if it were a module load notification. Algo-

Algorithm 6.2   *Breakpoint activation*

Input	OS notification that debuggee stopped at certain address due to breakpoint.
Output	Stop or continue debuggee according to below method.
Method	Map from physical location back to source file and line number using physical and logical breakpoint structures.

    i.   Scan logical list of breakpoints for this address (there may be more than one);

   ii.   Apply any conditions associated with this breakpoint (this may even involve more execution if the condition involves expression evaluation);

  iii.   If a condition does not evaluate to true move on to the next item in the list, ignoring this one any further;

   iv.   When no more breakpoints at this address are found, determine if any had either no conditions or had conditions that evaluated to true;

    v.   If so we report stop;

   vi.   Else we continue the debuggee as if no stop occurred at all.

rithm 6.3, to perform breakpoint validation, should be used whenever a debuggee process is created and at each subsequent module load event during debugging. The unverified list may indeed not be empty at the end of this process. This is because a file containing

1: #ifdef _IN_EXE

2: I=Ø;

3: #else //_IN_DLL

4: I=1;

5: #endif

is compiled into both an .EXE and DLL, a breakpoint on line 4 will show up as invalid in the EXE but can later be verified when the DLL is loaded.

Temporary Breakpoints

Breakpoints can have numerous attributes associated with them. They can be valid or invalid, as we have seen. They can be temporary or permanent. Temporary breakpoints—sometimes thought of as firing "once only"—are used to implement features such as "run-to-main" or "run-to-here." Run-to-main

Algorithm 6.3   *Breakpoint validation*

Input	OS notification that a module load has occurred.
Output	Processing of breakpoint list validating as many as possible.
Method	As processes are created and when modules are loaded, find all unverified breakpoints and remap them from logical to physical.

    i. Get module name being loaded either executable or DLL;

    ii. Determine list of source files used to build this module from the compiler-generated symbol table modules section;

    iii. Find all not-yet-validated breakpoints that match a file name from this list;

    iv. For any matches, use the line number in the breakpoint object to lookup in statement tables a breakpoint address;

    v. Report failure on those breakpoints on line numbers not in the list;

    vi. Set physical breakpoints in executable code and mark breakpoint as validated;

    vii. Continue with step iv above until all list entries have been examined.

is used at debuggee startup to quickly execute past all startup code and to stop on a program's main routine—logically considered by the programmer to be where the program starts.[1] Run-to-here allows the user to point to source code where he or she desires the program counter to be and quickly have the debuggee execute up to that point. These and other examples of temporary breakpoints are a convenient way to move execution to a certain point but do not require explicit setting and unsetting of breakpoints by the user. The debugger handles this invisibly. A temporary breakpoint is set, the debuggee is started running, and once it stops the temporary breakpoint removed. Typically, the temporary nature of the breakpoint is one of its attributes. In other respects it is just like all other breakpoints. Thus, the algorithm for cleanup of temporary breakpoints just requires a scan of all breakpoints whenever the debuggee stops, wherein the normal algorithm for breakpoints is applied to each one.

Internal Breakpoints

Like temporary breakpoints, internal breakpoints can be just an attribute associated with a breakpoint object. Internal breakpoints are invisible to the

---

[1]Erroneously, however, because C++ static constructors are executed before main and can be a problematical and error-prone area. Even in C, if # pragma startup is used the exact same problem occurs.

user but are key to the debugger's correct handling of many of its algorithms. These are breakpoints set by the debugger itself for its own purposes. I will discus several situations where internal breakpoints are used.

The basic source-level single-step algorithm uses a combination of internal breakpoints and full-speed run to key internal breakpoints placed for optimal stepping speed, as compared to machine-stepping instruction-by-instruction through hundreds or thousands of instructions. This is especially critical on source statement *step over*. Step over is a statement step in the context of the current function scope running any descendent functions full speed to completion. For statement step over, we typically use an internal breakpoint on a function's return address to allow that function and all its descendents to run at full speed. *Step into* is a statement step that goes into any descendent functions found during the current operation. Even step into uses internal breakpoints to quickly run over stretches of code as long as possible up to some branch instruction, again for performance reasons. Both of these algorithms will be described in much more detail later in this chapter.

Some processors, especially the newer generations of very high-performance RISC processors, do not provide any hardware single-step support because it can complicate a processor that is focused on simplicity and performance. In this case, the debugger has no choice but to set internal breakpoints and run to the next breakpoint to simulate the single-step functionality. To do this correctly, the debugger must decode the current, about-to-be-executed instruction. If the next instruction is non-branching, the debugger may set the breakpoint just past that instruction and run. If the debugger detects the next instruction as a branch instruction it must decode the target of the branch and set a breakpoint there to correctly "single-step" over the branch instruction. Or the debugger could trace to both possible targets of the branch instruction and set breakpoints at both addresses to avoid the prediction of the branch target.

During expression evaluation, when the debugger must use the debuggee to evaluate a function in an expression entered by the user, internal breakpoints are used to carefully control execution so that just the desired function is executed. An internal breakpoint must be placed at the return address of the function being called so that once evaluation completes, the debuggee stops to allow complete cleanup so that normal debuggee execution can proceed later. More details on the expression evaluation algorithm appear in Chapter 8.

If a very different model of stepping is required, internal breakpoints may be employed to accomplish this different approach. For example, where a program consists entirely of a collection of disjoint user-written, event-driven small functions, stepping off the end of one of these functions may mean the debugger must run the program to the beginning of the next user-written function. This would require a special internal breakpoint to catch the run from the end of one function to the beginning of the next function.

One additional consideration about internal breakpoints is critical in debugger design. This is the question of when (if ever) these breakpoints are visible to the user. In a disassembly view, where machine instructions are disassembled into their mnemonic equivalents, we may want to ignore the existence of internal breakpoints and show the underlying instruction instead. But a hex memory dump may want to show the exact contents of memory even if this includes the debugger-inserted internal breakpoints.

Side Effects

Breakpoints can be used for much more than just a way to stop the debuggee program and give control to the user. Side effects on breakpoints allow a lot of interesting debugging approaches. It is perhaps best to think of breakpoints as probe points where test data can be extracted as the program runs and does not necessarily stop. We can program the debugger to do anything we deem useful when a breakpoint activates by associating *actions* to be performed when a breakpoint evaluates its condition (if any) to be true.

Logging is a simple action that can be performed at a breakpoint. Frequently all that is desired is a record of the activation of a breakpoint in some sort of historical readout. All the debugger is directed to do is to emit some characteristic information about the breakpoint that can be collected for the user to review. The debugger may or may not be directed to stop at this particular breakpoint. This is very similar to a debugging technique familiar to all programmers: inserting print statements directly in the source code that record some sort of history of execution when the program runs. However, the breakpoint history record approach via a debugger has the advantage of not requiring the program to be recompiled.

Pass counts are another frequently used side effect. **Pass counts** are simple expressions to be evaluated by the debugger upon breakpoint activation. The debugger must record the number of times this particular breakpoint has activated. This information is compared against a *threshold*—the pass count —specified by the debugger user. This is a common way to control a certain number of passes through a programmed loop before execution of the debuggee stops. This is for bugs that follow the pattern "it happens after N times through the loop."

A more general form of expression evaluation than pass counts is possible and common as well. Everything from specialized expression languages using debugger-created variables, to the full expression syntax of the debuggee's programming language using debuggee-based variables, is possible. This can be an extremely complex and involved portion of the debugger, and it is covered in detail in Chapter 8. Here it suffices to say that as with other breakpoint side effects, on breakpoint activation the expression may be evaluated. If this is a conditional breakpoint, then the expression is evaluated for its Boolean value. If true, the breakpoint will cause a stop; otherwise, execution will continue. Or, the expression may be tied to the logging feature and the value of the expression recorded in the viewable log. These uses of expression evaluation are a way to have the debugger "patch" the debuggee program without modifying the program or even compiling it at all. In the first case, an expression evaluated at breakpoint activation may itself have side effects that "fix" some problem or deficiency in the program being debugged. For example, the expression may set a variable to zero that was previously uninitialized in the program that seems to fix a problem. This "fix" can now be tested and verified before modifying the program itself. The logging expression case is like having added a print statement to the program and recompiled it except not as fast or in as flexible a manner as having the debugger do it.

Other side effects are possible as well. For instance, it is useful in message-based GUI program debugging to carefully track the GUI messages received at a specific function. Specialized breakpoint side effects can be created that track the GUI messages being processed when the breakpoint activates. Then either evaluating this in a conditional sense to determine if a stop should occur or simply logging the receipt of that message and proceeding is possible.

Finally, arbitrary "actions" may be associated with a breakpoint as a further side effect. These actions can consist of any of the capabilities of the debugger that can be expressed in some type of macro language as a single or linked set of functions. For example, setting another breakpoint may be the desired action when a special breakpoint activates. The trend is toward more and more configurable tools that can be driven from a macro or embedded programming language. Once a debugger can be driven in this fashion any of its capabilities can then be associated as an action.

C++ Templates and One-to-Many Problems

Breakpoints set in source code that is then replicated by the compiler pose special problems. This scenario creates a one-to-many mapping from source code to executable. Breakpoints in inlined code, some breakpoints on function returns (depending on the compiler), and some breakpoints on for-loops (again, depending on the compiler) all share this characteristic. However, the problem is extreme in C++ templates, and the debugger design must handle this extreme case smoothly as C++ templates are becoming very prevalent.

As the breakpoint setting algorithm looks up a file name / line number pair it may find that many executable modules have this mapping and that many physical addresses correspond for locating the physical breakpoint instruction. At this point the debugger may opt to give the user a chance to filter this down to select just the ones intended to receive the breakpoint. This may work well for C++ templates because each of the C++ templates represents an instantiation for a distinct type and the user may be thinking of only one of these types as he or she sets the breakpoint.

Code Patching by the Debugger

Breakpoints are also the basis for more extreme code modifications attempted by some debuggers. Instead of inserting a special breakpoint instruction at a given location and saving the original instruction away in debugger memory, any instruction could be inserted into the executable code stream by the debugger. Specifically, a branch or jump instruction could be inserted. What this means is that very general code patching is possible. Suppose, for example, a special monitor routine needs to be called upon entry to every function. The debugger could place this monitor routine in code memory and then insert special stack manipulation and jump instructions to cause in-line redirection to this monitor routine. This allows us to make these significant changes to the debuggee program without a recompile. There are lots of uses for code patching in debuggers and other tools related to debuggers such as profilers.

Using standard debugging techniques the user may have a theory about what will fix the bug, but rebuilding the entire program may take so long that some faster way to verify if the proposed fix works is frequently required. One way to offer this capability is to allow users to modify the debuggee program with new and/or different code without re-compilation. The most common way to do this is through the function evaluation capability described in Chapter 8. Used in conjunction with a breakpoint that allows an associated expression evaluation, this kind of code patching support is straightforward. As long as breakpoints have an option that allows the user to specify that execution does not actually stop but some expression will get evaluated instead, and as long as general expression evaluation includes debuggee function invocation, the desired code patching capability is provided as desired. Further refinement that provides one more level of support for incremental code modification is to allow these function invocations to support breakpoints. This extra level of generality allows a rich set of features to be offered to the debugger user, which may lead to powerful debugging support for difficult debugging problems even in large, complex programs.

Single-step

Single-step is important because users need to be able to "watch" execution proceed. Frequently the failure mechanism, to be understood, must be "eased into." It is also important to understand the side effects occurring close to the failure point, which stepping allows. To fully support breakpoints and single-step in its various forms, the debugger needs to have a very sophisticated execution control mechanism. The main reason for this is the asynchronous nature of debug event notifications that occur whenever the debuggee stops. It is not correct to start a single-step assuming the next stop must be the completion of the just initiated single-step—it could stop instead for a breakpoint or exception. This requires a fairly involved set of states maintained by the debugger that correctly describes the state of the debuggee with respect to its current execution algorithm. Motivation for this statement comes easily with a simple example. During statement step, which requires many internal breakpoints and instruction-level steps, a divide-by-zero occurs, but the sin-

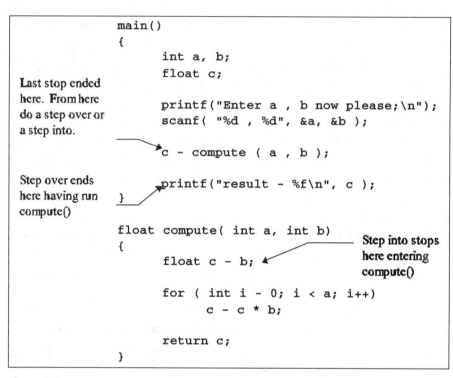

```
                        main()
                        {
                                int  a,  b;
                                float  c;
Last stop ended
here. From here         printf("Enter a , b now please;\n");
do a step over or       scanf( "%d , %d", &a, &b );
a step into.
                        c - compute ( a , b );

Step over ends          printf("result - %f\n", c );
here having run
compute()               }


                        float  compute( int a,  int b)                    Step into stops
                        {                                                 here entering
                                float  c - b;                             compute()

                                for ( int i - 0; i < a; i++)
                                        c - c * b;

                                return c;
                        }
```

Figure 6.3

Sample code showing step over versus step into.   *This figure shows sample code to explain the difference between step over and step into. When the program is stopped on a statement containing a call to a function, step into visits the function while step over stops on the line after the function returns.*

gle-step initiation is forgotten as less important than the divide-by-zero. The debugger must report the exception if this type of exception is supposed to be reported and then stop after cleaning up all the state being maintained for the statement step. Typically this is best handled by a finite state machine that gets its initial state from the user-requested command. Each notification from the OS about the debuggee stopping is a transition in this finite state machine, possibly to a new state. Breakpoint notifications occur at several points in the state diagram for this finite state machine. If the debugger was executing a statement step and this was an internal breakpoint, then the debugger must determine if the current location corresponds to a valid source statement boundary that represents the completion of one source step. If not, execution proceeds either to another internal breakpoint or via instruction level single-step.

Step Into versus Step Over

We define "step into" to mean execution proceeds *into* any function in the current source statement and stops at the first executable source line in that function. "Step over," sometimes referred to as "skip" instead of step,[2] treats a call to a function as an atomic operation and proceeds past any function calls to the textually succeeding source line in the current scope. Figure 6.3 shows the distinction on a simple code fragment.

Step into could be implemented by using machine step repeatedly checking at each instruction step to see if the current address matches a source statement's starting address. In practice it is a serious performance problem to do this. This fact, plus the existence of processors that do not support machine-level step, leads us to an algorithm that decodes instructions and advances the processor via breakpoint plus full-speed run. More on this later in this chapter, where we discuss smart, fast stepping algorithms. First, here is Algorithm 6.4, the basic algorithm for stepping.

Algorithm 6.4 *Source step into*

Input	Current statement and instruction pointer address.
Output	A new statement and instruction pointer address for the next statement to be executed.
Method	

    i. Note current statement location;
set moved_flag := false;

    ii. On each debug stop notification (and after initial setup):

    iii. Set simulated_pc := real_pc;

    iv. If (moved_flag == true and simulated_pc points to beginning of a statement) then
step into is completed so report new location to the user and exit this algorithm;
else if (no source avail) we can either run or "run to first source" (see page 128)

---

[2]Step over, aka skip, is called "next" in some older debuggers such as some variants of UNIX's dbx.

    v. Get and decode the instruction pointed to by the simulated_pc in debuggee text address space;

    vi. If (this instruction is not any sort of branching instruction and it is not an exact match for the beginning of a source statement) then
advance our simulated_pc to the next instruction;
go back to step iii;

    vii. If (simulated_pc does match beginning of a new source statement and real_pc != simulated_pc) then
set a temporary breakpoint here;
set the moved_flag := true;
set the debuggee running;
wait for the next debug notification;
clean up internal breakpoint just hit;
go to step iii;

    viii. If (this is a branching instruction) then
        either
            machine single-step one instruction;
        or
            decode the branch target;
            set a temporary breakpoint at that address;
set the moved_flag := true;
start the debuggee running;
wait for the next debug notification;
clean up internal breakpoint just hit (if any);
go to step iii;

The algorithm for step over begins just like step into but it notes a "call" instruction during instruction decode as special, and once the called function has been entered, a breakpoint is inserted at the return address of this function by looking at the current stack frame. A full-speed run then gets the debuggee rapidly through this function and any functions it calls (assuming no breakpoints or exceptions are encountered along the way). Once this return address breakpoint is reached, after breakpoint cleanup, the basic source step algorithm is continued. The result will be to skip over a function and to step to the textually next source statement within the current function scope. Algorithm 6.5 for step over is shown next.

Algorithm 6.5 *Source step over*

Input	Current statement and instruction pointer address.
Output	A new statement and instruction pointer address for the textually 'next' statement.
Method	

    i. Note current statement location;
set moved_flag := false;
set in_function flag := false;

   ii. On each debug stop notification (and after initial setup):

  iii. Set simulated_pc := real_pc;

  iv. If (moved_flag == true and in_function flag == false and simulated_pc points to beginning of a statement) then
        step over is completed so report new location to the user and exit this algorithm;

   v. If (in_function == true) then
        use current stack frame to find return address for the new current function;
        set internal breakpoint at this return address;
        set in_function := false;
        set debuggee running;
        wait for debug notification;
        go to step iii;

   vi. Get and decode the instruction pointed to by the simulated_pc in debuggee text address space;

  vii. If (this instruction is not any sort of branching instruction and it is not an exact match for the beginning of a source statement) then
        advance our simulated_pc to the next instruction;
        go back to step iv;

 viii. If (this instruction is a function call instruction) then
        set in_function := true;
        machine single-step into this function;
        wait for debug notification;
        go to step iii;

   ix. If (simulated_pc does match beginning of a new source statement and real_pc != simulated_pc) then
        set a temporary breakpoint here;
        set the moved_flag := true;

```
                    set the debuggee running;
                    wait for the next debug notification;
                    clean up internal breakpoint just hit;
                    go to step iii;
        x.  If (this is a branching instruction) then
                    either
                                machine single-step one instruction;
                    or
                                decode the branch target;
                                set a temporary breakpoint at that address;
                    set the moved_flag to true;
                    start the debuggee running;
                    wait for the next debug notification;
                    clean up internal breakpoint just hit (if any);
                    go to step i;
```

Smart, Fast Source-Step

If a debugger implements source-step by using a series of machine single-steps, checking the text address reached each time against the statement address table, single-step will be painfully slow at times and users will not tolerate it. Typically, machine single-step is roughly 1000 times slower than full-speed run to a breakpoint. There is a tremendous cost to a call to the OS debug API due to several context switches (debugger to OS, OS to debuggee, debuggee to OS, OS back to debugger) and OS scheduling delays as well as CPU overhead. Second, the number of instructions to execute may be large. If there is a call to a library routine such as `printf` that does not have associated source code to stop in and show the user, thousands of individual calls to machine single-step would be required

This is why Algorithms 6.4 and 6.5 used instruction decoding as a fundamental part of the algorithm, as opposed to multitudes of instruction steps. Skipping over entire functions by setting a breakpoint at the return address and running full speed to this breakpoint dramatically decreases the number of single steps attempted, which in turn dramatically speeds up source step.

Instruction decoding involves reading a debuggee text address (at the current program counter usually) and applying a CPU-specific lookup to determine the type of instruction at this location. If the instruction is a procedure call instruction, the debugger knows one machine step will execute that instruction and end up at the first instruction inside that function. Now, typically obtaining the value in a special register gives the debugger the return address where a breakpoint can be set to enable skipping over the entire function rapidly.

More extensive instruction decoding can be used to decrease usage of machine single stepping even more. Sequences of in-line, that is, non-branching, instructions can be grouped together and executed all at once by setting a breakpoint at the end of such a block of instructions. If these sequences tend to be long, this approach can save a large percentage of calls to the OS debug API. This level of instruction decoding just requires detecting branching instructions versus non-branching instructions.

This can be taken a step further by decoding targets of branches and setting a breakpoint only when an instruction decode requires dynamic data or a statement boundary has been reached. In fact, this approach is required if the processor does not support machine single-step. And even on processors that do support it, it may be faster not to use it and to fully decode instructions always running full speed to the next breakpoint.

It is possible to go even further and completely emulate each instruction (for those instructions where this is even possible) so that even data dependent branches can be decoded correctly. In most cases this would allow a source statement to be "executed" without ever running the CPU. It is not clear whether this is important enough to justify the significant extra logic in a debugger. One last important point about instruction decoding in debuggers is that this area is one of only three in a typical debugger that are processor-specific and non-portable. The three areas that are processor-specific and non-portable are the following:

1. Instruction decoding as used in stepping algorithms
2. Stack back-trace unwinding or "walking"
3. Disassembly and CPU view register presentation

It is worth keeping these aresa isolated from all other debugger functions to enable easier porting to new processors.

Pathologic Stepping Problems
Nothing is as simple as being able to uniformly apply the above simple algorithms and get the correct behavior out of single-step in all cases. Many

contemporary debuggers have anomalous stepping behavior under some circumstances. Two examples of commonly found anomalous behavior are single-*line for loops* and attempting to step into "missing" routines. Because the debugger's basic approach to stepping is so simple, it can be argued that these stepping problems stem from incomplete or inconsistent information provided by the compiler. We will examine these issues in more detail in the following sections.

Single-line For Loops

Many C/C++ compilers given the source

```
for ( i = 0; i < 1000; i++ )
    a += i;
```

generate this code (x86 variant shown):

```
        xor     eax, eax
@2:
        add     edx, eax
        inc     eax
        cmp     eax, 1000
        jl      short @2
```

and will generate only one breakpointable address for this single syntactic language statement (even though it resides on two textually distinct lines). This means that a user single-stepping from the beginning of the for-loop will see the debuggee advance all the way through the for-loop, stopping on the next line textually after the for-loop. The user might be surprised by this result because if he or she had written

```
for ( i = 0; i < 1000; i++ ) {
    a += i;
    b *= i;
}
```

stepping will naturally step to each line inside the {} 1000 times.

Debugger stepping algorithms need to be prepared to deal with this single-line for-loop situation. If the compiler does not help the debugger, the debugger can still behave correctly. A simple-minded approach would be to notice if the CPU branch instruction within a single-source statement branches backward to an address still within the same statement. Now the debugger considers this branch instruction as a stoppable location (even though it does not match the beginning of a source statement, as expected by our source-stepping algorithm). This solution is not foolproof because compilers are not prevented from generating backward branches within a statement.

Similar to the single-statement for-loop is multiple return instructions from within a single function. In this case there is no one-to-one mapping between source and statement line number tables. This situation has many breakpointable locations for a single source line (the function's closing }), whereas the for-loop example had several source lines and only one break-pointable location. The debugger must be able to deal with both types of scenarios.

Step into "Missing" User Routines

Source-level single step should present the "illusion" that the high-level language *is* being executed directly, one statement at a time. But sometimes, the reality of how a debugger implements single-step comes in direct conflict with this illusion. Then, something has to give. Either the user will be suprised—usually not in a positive way—or the debugger will have to do something extraordinary to satisfy this conflict.

One example of this is the classic dilemma of source stepping through a mixture of functions with debug information (the ones supplied by the user) with functions without debug information (as supplied by a run-time library, for example). If a user routine calls a library function that in turn calls a user routine (a "callback"), the standard step algorithm will not give the desired results. The "hidden" user routine—the one called by the immediately con-tained library (no debug) routine—will never be seen by source step. This is not a contrived example. It is now extremely common, especially in event-driven systems like Microsoft Windows and UNIX X-Windows, because a user supplies user routine pointers to the basic event-processing loop. Top-level user code calls the library event-processing routine, which on some events calls these user-supplied dispatch routines. Because single-step *into* promised to take you to the next executed source statement that has debug information, it has broken its promise. Instead, as step into detects it has entered a routine—the one in the library—it sets an internal breakpoint at this function's return address and runs full speed over this function and all the functions it calls. It also just ran over the user function called from inside the library routine. This is a serious flaw in single-step and one not easily solved.[3] Previously, debuggers that tried to solve this were unacceptably slow as they machine-stepped (slowly) through the non-debug routines until they detected a new routine that had debug information. The performance penalty of this approach is so extreme as to make any debugger employing it laughable.

There are two workable solutions to this problem. One is to build into the stepping algorithms a "run to first source" feature. To implement this, a breakpoint is placed on all procedure entry points. This way, stepping off the end of a function or into code with no source will stop the next time a user-written function is entered. This solution requires very fast lookup, setting and unsetting of a large number of function entry point breakpoints. The alternative is to use page protection set for all user-written code pages that will cause a page protection violation as soon as user code is about to execute again.

If the OS provides APIs to control the memory access permissions on a page-by-page (in the OS sense) basis, these can be used to set the code pages of the debuggee corresponding to the portion having debug information as not executable and not readable. When step into lets the debuggee run full speed to the internal breakpoint set at the non-debuggable function's return address, if user code gets called before that internal breakpoint is hit, a page protection violation exception will cause the debuggee to stop. The debugger will then be able to use this exception that stopped the debuggee to reset the page protection and to continue stepping as before into the user's "hidden" routine as desired. This is a major advancement for debuggers because this stepping problem has plagued all debuggers to date. Algorithm 6.6 shows this modification to the standard step into algorithm.

C++ Global Constructors and Destructors

A similar flaw in source step occurs at initial startup and on final shutdown of a C++ application. As a C++ program starts up, after initial loading into memory and execution of the run-time startup code, all C++ global constructors must be executed *before* the function 'main' begins execution. However, most debuggers run to main and stop there, presenting the illusion to the user that program execution actually begins at 'main.' The goal was to run to the first user code, which was most easily accomplished by running to 'main.'

---

[3]Currently, I know of only Borland's Delphi and C++ debuggers as ones that specifically address this issue.

Algorithm 6.6   *Step into "hidden" debuggable routines*

Method   This is a modification to Algorithm 6.4.
 i. Perform all steps of the step into algorithm up to and including setting the breakpoint on the return address of the first non-debug routine found;
 ii. Before letting the debuggee run full speed do the following:
 iii. Set all code pages of debuggee as non-executable and/or non-readable using the memory access API of the operating system;
 iv. Run the debuggee full speed;
 v. If (internal function return address breakpoint hit) then
     continue normal processing of step into algorithm;
    else
     set all debuggee code pages back to executable
     go back to step i of algorithm 6.4

This was reasonable for C-language debuggers, but in C++ the critical bug may be in one of the constructors that execute before main. Therefore, running to main does not yield the expected or desired result. On the other hand, machine-level stepping will be too slow to be usable to avoid this problem. Here at least, unlike the previous scenario, it is possible to get help from the run-time library as to where the constructor chain begins. The global destructors executed after main returns present the same situation. (In fact, bugs here are quite common as a user begins to track down memory leak bugs.) The same technique used for hidden routines works here but it critically depends on a page protection API provided by the OS.

Step-related Algorithms

There are a series of features a debugger may provide that superficially do not appear directly related to stepping algorithms. But, in fact, a wide range of these features do directly utilize the stepping algorithm. The list we will briefly consider includes the following:

- Animation
- Software watchpoints
- Finish function
- Reverse execution

- 'Slime' trail mode
- C++ exceptions

Animation

Animation is used to dynamically show the progress of execution through the program. It is sort of a "watch the bouncing ball" for a computer program. It is implemented by continuously executing the step-into algorithm pausing at the end of each statement step to refresh the views but then immediately resuming stepping. This is a marginally useful feature, usually used for demonstrations, program learning, or testing. A debugger supporting a scripting or macro capability—a very useful feature—can easily overlay animation on the standard step-into feature without engineering in animation.

Software Watchpoints

Software watchpoints are data access breakpoints that are not implemented via hardware assist. A watchpoint "watches" a range of data addresses in debuggee memory and activates—stopping the debuggee—if any modification is attempted. For memory corruption bugs this is a critical feature. There may be no hardware assist or the limit on the number of locations watchable has been exceeded which causes the need for software implementation. One approach to implementation in software is to invisibly, even on a "run" request, use the single step algorithm checking the specified address ranges for change on each step completion. Totally accurate results actually require using machine-step granularity, but in practice this is much too slow. Even using source step granularity is so slow that clear warning about slow stepping to the user is prudent.

Alternative implementation strategies may be more effective, depending on the OS facilities provided. For example, if the debugger can mark a page of debuggee data memory as read-only, then an attempt to write into that page would cause an exception that the debugger would catch. On this type of exception the debugger would check the exact address of the access attempt, and if it intersects a watchpoint, activate that watchpoint. Otherwise, the page must be made writable, the process stepped a bit, and then re-marked read-only before a full-speed run can be resumed.

Finish Function

A feature that can be thought of as "finish the current function" is very useful at times. Once a user finds that he or she has stepped into a function inadvertently he or she might like to run quickly to a point just after the call to this function. There are two ways to offer this kind of functionality. One is to require users to use the call stack to select one stack frame prior to the current function. This will show the place from where the current function was called. Here a breakpoint or "run-to-here" could be performed. Shorthand for this—and more convenient to the user—would be an explicit "finish function." The implementation of this is just the latter half of the step-over algorithm. The result is to very quickly take the user to the source line immediately succeeding the call to the current function.

Reverse Execution

Truly effective reverse execution would be a very valuable feature for a debugger. Some interpretive language systems can perform true reverse execution because they have complete control over all program states. Debuggers in compiled language systems must settle for a very limited form at best. When a bug is observed it would be very valuable to "back up" a little to examine program state thoroughly just before the fault occurs. This would allow the user to zero in very quickly on the cause of a fault. In a compiled language system this would require noting all memory accesses and saving memory state prior to any changes so these can be reversed. This requires instruction single-stepping and decoding all instructions for their reversible state. Even so, many instructions are simply not reversible, such as I/O instruction or any calls to OS or library routines. Because it requires special processing during single-step, reverse execution requires a mode set by the user. Only when this mode is set does the debugger single-step and save the state of each memory location about to be modified. These limitations make reverse execution a practically useless feature. The goal of backing up from where the fault occurred can almost never be met. In spite of its limitations, users still request the feature in debuggers, and some commercial debuggers (for example, Turbo Debugger) have attempted to implement it.

Slime Trail

Because "where am I" and "how did I get here" are perhaps the most frequent debugging questions, a debugger should be prepared to answer them. "Where am I" is covered by source views, disassembly views, and a stack back-trace. But "how did I get here" is not completely answered by a stack trace. Functions entered but already left do not appear on a stack back-trace. For this reason, some debuggers have a "slime trail" mode that shows all statements and functions executed up to the current execution point. This is usually done just like animation using single-step—instead of showing the user each step, a record is emitted for each statement that is viewable at a later time by the user.

C++ Exceptions

C++ exceptions consist of a "throw" at the point of detection and a "catch" of the prescribed type at some point programmed to handle the fault more cleanly. The most important benefit of C++ exceptions is that the compiler guarantees all destructors for all automatic objects will get called on the way up the stack from the throw to the catch. Defects can occur anywhere including in the throw logic, catch logic, or any destructors in between. Thus, the debugger must aid in tracing through this code. An implementation strategy for C++ exceptions is to have the debugger aware of a single, well-specified run-time library special dispatch routine where all C++ throws are initiated. From here, users can be given the option of running immediately to the catch point or stepping through each destructor in succession. In this latter case, the step algorithm is used once again to trace through the destructors as if they were a series of nested routines.

Event-driven Stepping Models

The standard stepping model presented so far assumes a user builds programs by building up a series of routines, one directly calling another. Another model occurs frequently in strictly event-driven systems such as that provided by Visual Basic and Delphi. Each user function represents an action taken on some system-specified event. The user associates one function with each event. But these user functions are only directly called from system dispatch routines (which will not have debugging information and will thus be "invisible" to debuggers). Our standard stepping algorithm will fail completely on this model. Even if a stop at a breakpoint occurred in one of the user's routines, stepping off the end of this function will end up back in system code that was responsible for calling the user function. The simplest algorithm for handling this type of programming model, and the one employed in Visual Basic and Delphi, is to have the debugger detect when it is about to step off the end of a user function and at that moment set breakpoints at the beginning of every user routine in the entire system. Once the user routine returns, the debugger must cause the debuggee to run at full speed. Eventually, the debuggee will hit one of the special breakpoints and stop at the start of another user routine. We specify this in Algorithm 6.7.

Algorithm 6.7 *Event-driven stepping model*

Input	Current statement and instruction pointer address.
Output	A new statement and instruction pointer address for the 'logical' next statement.
Method	The key is detecting stepping off the end of a user routine and then catching the next time execution moves back into user code.

    i. Detect step off end of user routine;
   ii. Get list of all user routine entry points from symbol tables;
  iii. Set internal breakpoint at each entry point (or, if memory protection is available, mark all debug information code pages as inaccessible);
  iv. Run debuggee full speed;
   v. Stop at special breakpoint will occur some time later;
  vi. Remove all special breakpoints;
 vii. Revert to standard stepping algorithm.

I should note that one of the unsolved stepping problems mentioned earlier is closely related to this stepping model issue. The problem of stepping from user routine to system routine that calls another user routine is identical to this VB model. However, in standard programming models, setting breakpoints on each and every user routine whenever single-step needs to run full speed to a breakpoint is impractical. Unfortunately, some other solution must be employed to address this problem.

7

Discovering Program Context

Where am I? The most important thing a debugger can do to help the user track down problems in the program being debugged is to provide easy-to-understand context information.

Source-level View

The most important component of answering "Where am I?" is the source view. Users think in terms of their source code. They have a fairly detailed map of their program or at least their subsystem in their minds. So, directory location, file name, routine, and actual source line are all critical to answering the key context questions. Older UNIX command-line debuggers based on dbx exemplified this problem by showing only one to three lines of source context on a stop. It was intensely frustrating to use dbx because there was never enough context—and context is critical in debugging.

The Program Stack

The second most important part of the context story is the function call stack back-trace. It tells you "How did I get here?" The program stack is a data structure supported by the hardware, the operating system, and the compiler. The register set of the CPU provides a *stack and/or frame pointer,*[1] and its instruction set includes special instructions for calling sub-routines that utilize and manipulate this stack pointer. The stack pointer points to a location in memory that stores the currently executing address just before the CPU jumps to the first instruction of a new routine; this then becomes the *return* address. As each routine is called via these special instructions, more and more return addresses are stored there in successive memory locations, creating a stack. As a routine executes its final instruction, the return, it resets its instruction pointer to the return address stored on the stack and "pops" that frame off the stack and discards it.

More than the return addresses are stored on the stack. Also stored there are local variables used just within the associated function. This makes a convenient way to keep track of variables local to a routine and allows that memory to be freed when the routine returns. Stack space is also used for other similar, per-routine types of local storage such as thread-local storage, destructor-chains for exception handling, and more. The operating system usually sets up stack space for each process (thread) as it is created, and it manages stack space limits so that when a process (thread) runs out of stack space the operating system causes a system error to occur.

A **stack trace** is a list of the procedure activation records or *frames* currently on the call stack. The algorithm for finding the frames on the stack is called **stack unwinding**. Like disassembly, unwinding is useful to both the user and the debugger itself. When a fault or breakpoint occurs, the user needs a stack trace to answer the question, "How did the program get here?" When the debugger implements a command like "run the program until the current function returns," it needs to unwind the stack to find the parent procedure's frame pointer and return address.

---

[1] Some CPUs provide both a stack and a frame pointer; some RISC CPUs provide only a stack pointer, and the frame pointer must be synthesized from symbol table information generated during compilation. See Chapter 3.

Each frame on the stack is delimited by a pair of addresses: a frame pointer on the side nearest the base of the stack and a stack pointer nearest the top. Rules called the **procedure calling conventions** dictate where various pieces of data, such as the return address, lie within each frame. Once the debugger knows the boundaries of a frame, using the procedure-calling conventions, it can retrieve the return address saved within that frame and map it to the name of the procedure containing that address. At its simplest, a printed stack trace might show only the procedure name, but a symbolic debugger can also show the names of its formal arguments and the statement that it was executing.

Once it has unwound the stack, the debugger can also retrieve the values of local variables belonging to frames below the topmost. These variables have values placed on the stack so with adequate symbol table information the debugger can completely decode all necessary local variables information.

The algorithm for unwinding a stack varies depending on the calling conventions for the machine and compiler in question. I will describe a traditional set of conventions, but for almost every statement I make there is a counterexample in some environment. Stacks may grow upward or downward; registers may be saved by the parent or the child; arguments may be pushed on the stack or passed in registers; and so on. To cope with this, the author of a debugger has three recourses: first, teach the debugger to deal with the general case; second, if possible, get the compiler to indicate via the debugging tables whenever it diverges from the general case; third, teach the debugger to disassemble the code and figure out for itself how the stack was built.

For a traditional stack, registers hold the frame pointer address and stack pointer address for the current frame. Each procedure call pushes the return address onto the stack, and the child procedure then pushes the parent's frame pointer address onto the stack before it alters the frame pointer and stack pointer to build its own frame. This creates a stack that (omitting details and assuming the stack grows downward) looks like the one shown in Figure 7.1.

The debugger needs to "unwind" the stack, that is, follow the chain of stack frames back to the initial program entry point, each time the debuggee stops. Even if the stack view is not being displayed, this information is still needed for variable inspection. Algorithm 7.1 describes the process of unwinding a stack.

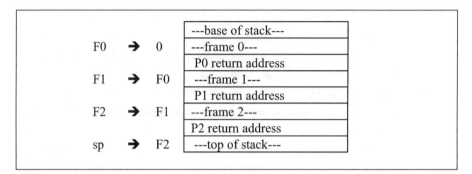

Figure 7.1

Traditional, downward-growing stack. *A standard downward-growing stack is shown. The most recent or current frame is at the bottom (lower address) while the origin is at the top. Each frame includes the calling procedure's return address.*

Some systems store a sentinel value such as zero at the base of the stack. The algorithm could test for this to decide when to stop, but because an errant program can change the stack in unpredictable ways, the algorithm is more robust if the debugger records the base address before the program starts executing and uses the termination test in step iii.

If the debugger wants to show the values of local variables in frames prior to the topmost one, the unwinding algorithm must also restore saved registers.

Algorithm 7.1 *Unwinding a (traditional, downward-growing) stack*

Input	Current registers and stack
Output	List of frames on stack
Method	Follow the chain of frame pointers saved on the stack

    i. Let S and F be the values of the stack pointer and frame pointer for the current frame. Let P be the current program counter.

    ii. Print a description of the frame based on S, F, and P.

    iii. If F >= base_of_stack, stop.

    iv. Let S = F + (size_of_pointer). Replace P with the value stored at S.

    v. Let S = S + (size_of_pointer). //now contains next function address

    vi. Replace F with the pointer stored at F.

    vii. Go back to step ii.

This need arises because a parent procedure may have allocated a variable to a register, and its child or grandchild may have saved that register in its own stack frame and then changed the value of the register.

The procedure-calling convention gives rules about which registers need to be saved, which procedures must save them, and where within the stack frame the saved copies lie. Typically, the child must save the values of certain registers before changing them and must restore the saved values before returning to the parent. (Sometimes the rules put the burden on the parent, and sometimes they partition the register set so that parent and child share responsibility.) Sometimes the calling convention pushes a bit mask onto the stack to indicate which registers were saved; otherwise, you must hope that the debugging tables contain this information, or you must (as mentioned earlier) teach the debugger to disassemble the code and decide for itself.

Dealing with saved registers makes the example and the algorithm a bit more complicated. Figure 7.2 shows the same downward-growing stack, but this time fills in more details including where saved registers are placed as the stack grows.

We now expand our stack-unwinding algorithm to include dealing with saved registers. The saved registers gives the debuggee context at the point when that stack frame was created. For variable inspection, that saved information is crucial to correct scope resolution. Algorithm 7.2 adds these details.

It's important to understand that R is not an accurate version of the value that the registers had when the corresponding procedure was active because it only recovers the value of a register if it was saved; values of unsaved registers are lost if the registers are overwritten.

Special Problems in Unwinding the Stack

A robust debugger must handle some special cases not covered by the algorithm above. For example, stopping during the procedure **prologue**, the code that constructs the stack frame, requires special handling. If a program stops at the first instruction of the procedure, the frame pointer still points to the parent's frame even though the program counter lies within the child; if it stops part way through the prologue, the debugger may find that the stack

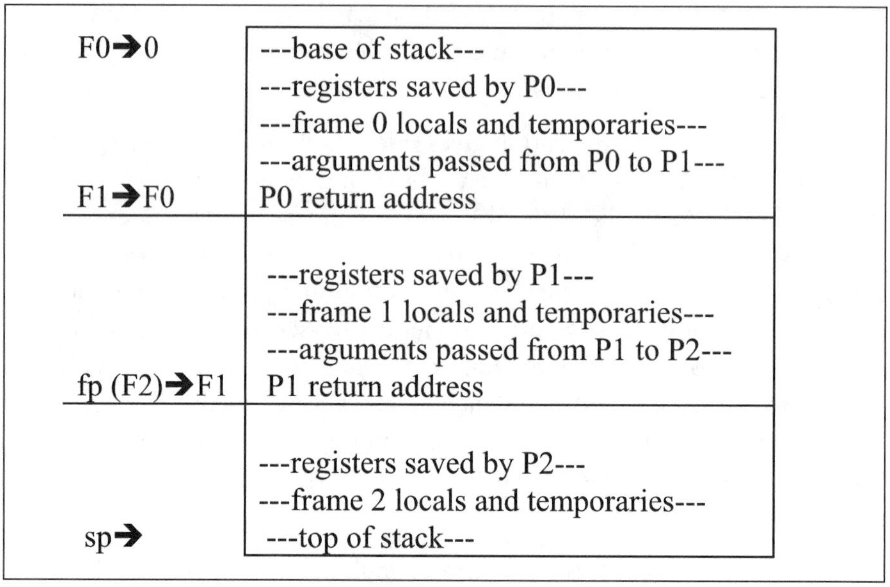

Figure 7.2

Downward-growing stack with details.   *Further expansion of Figure 7.1, this figure shows more details about what is contained within each frame.*

pointer has not advanced to make room for local variables or that some registers remain unsaved. Similar problems occur during the **epilogue**, when the procedure is in the process of removing its frame and restoring registers. The solution is heuristic and implementation-dependent: As usual, it may involve reading the debugging tables or disassembling code.

Also, a robust debugger must not fail or run unreasonably slowly when the number of frames is large. If, for example, the stack overflows due to an unlimited-recursion bug, the user will want to see the topmost few frames on the stack while ignoring the thousands lying below. As I will remind you frequently, the debugger is designed to work on buggy programs, not just ones that work totally as expected.

Tracing a Corrupted Stack

Bugs sometimes destroy part of the current stack frame. For example, if the stack grows downward, writing past the end of a local array (stored on the stack) can wipe out the return address and the saved copy of the caller's frame pointer. Because the normal stack-tracing algorithm starts with the

Algorithm 7.2   *Unwinding and restoring registers*

Method	Build on unwinding the stack the incorporation of the saved registers and the evaluation of local variables using those saved registers.

     i.   Let S and F be the values of the stack pointer and frame pointer for the current frame. Let P be the current program counter.

    ii.   Let R be a copy of the current registers.

   iii.   Print a description of the frame based on S, F, and P.

   iv.   Evaluate local variables using R.

    v.   If F >= base_of_stack, stop.

   vi.   For each data register saved in this frame, copy the saved value into R.

  vii.   Let S = F + (size_of_pointer). Replace P with the pointer stored at S.

 viii.   Let S = S + (size_of_pointer).

   ix.   R is loaded from saved registers on the stack as specified by the calling convention!

    x.   Replace F with the pointer stored at F.

   xi.   Go back to step iii.

---

current frame, damage to this frame can prevent it from showing any of the earlier frames, even if they are undamaged. A similar problem occurs if the operating system pushes a non-standard frame onto the stack. For example, many UNIX implementations push a non-standard frame before invoking a user-written exception handler. And both OS/2 and Windows 95 perform special "thunking" steps when passing from 32-bit code into 16-bit code that obliterate the stack for the debugger.

When the normal algorithm fails, the debugger can often find the undamaged earlier frames by starting at the base and working "backward" toward the top of the stack. Then at the point where the normal and "backward" algorithms both fail, it can print out a message indicating that the stack is corrupted. Almost no debuggers do this, yet it is extremely useful because when debugging, context is everything: The user needs as much information as possible as to where the program is and how it got there.

The backward Algorithm 7.3 is heuristic. It works by searching for saved frame pointers and assumes a stack-construction convention that saves each return address at a fixed offset relative to each saved frame pointer.

Figure 7.3 shows a typical corrupted stack.

The normal algorithm would use the current frame pointer and program counter to print:

<information for F4, procedure P4>

Then it would discover that the saved frame pointer and return address are nonsensical due to corruption and would print:

<corrupt or nonstandard stack frame at F4>

Then the backward algorithm would decipher these frames:

<information for F0, procedure P0>

<information for F1, procedure P1>

<information for F2, procedure P2>

At this point, the backward algorithm would fail because it reaches the top of the stack without finding a saved copy of F3. If possible, the debugger should reverse the order of the frames deciphered by the backward algorithm and print the entire stack in consistent order:

<information for frame F4, procedure P4>

<corrupt stack at memory location F4>

F0 ➔ 0	--base of stack--- ---frame 0--- P0 return address
F1➔ F0	---frame 1--- P1 return address
F2 ➔ F1	---frame 2--- P2 return address
F3 ➔ F2	---frame 3--- ---corrupted (formerly P3 return address)
F4 ➔	---corrupted (formerly F3)
	---frame 4---
sp➔	---top of stack---

Figure 7.3

A corrupted stack. *Using the same type of stack as shown in figures 7.1 and 7.2, shown here is one where at frame 3 the information necessary for unwinding the stack has been corrupted. A normal stack unwind would show frame 4 and stop.*

Algorithm 7.3   *Backward stack trace*

Input	Current registers and stack
Output	List of frames on stack
Method	Linear search for frame pointers saved on the stack

i. Let F be the frame pointer for the initial frame at the base of the stack and let P be the procedure corresponding to that frame. (Typically the stack starts with a run-time procedure or the main program, so that the debugger knows this information a priori.) Set the search position S to match F.

ii. Starting at S and working toward the top of the stack, look for a copy of F within the stack. If the stack conventions require that a saved frame pointer be aligned, use that knowledge to speed the search.

iii. If S reaches the top of the stack, the algorithm has failed.

iv. If the search finds what appears to be a saved copy of F at position S, then examine the saved return address, which should occur at a fixed offset from the saved copy of F (the offset depends on the conventions for the stack frame; often the two are adjacent). If this does not appear to be a plausible return address (for example, if it is improperly aligned or does not lie within the executable section of the program) then the search has not yet succeeded; advance S toward the top of stack and go back to step ii.

v. If the search has succeeded, then print the appropriate information for the frame whose frame pointer is F and whose procedure is P. Set F to match S, set P to be the procedure containing the newly discovered return address, advance S toward the top of stack, and go back to step ii.

<information for frame F2, procedure P2>

<information for frame F1, procedure P1>

<information for frame F0, procedure P0>

Unwinding Nontraditional Stacks

In the past decade, some RISC architectures have diverged from the traditional stack mechanism. Architectures such as MIPS avoid using an explicit frame pointer register. In the traditional scheme, the stack pointer address changes during the execution of a procedure, providing extra storage for temporaries or for the construction of argument lists. The procedure must address its local variables at offsets relative to the frame pointer, which remains fixed. If the compiler can compute the maximum amount of storage that the procedure requires, however, it can push that amount onto the stack at the outset of the procedure and leave the stack pointer fixed. Then the procedure can use offsets from the stack pointer, eliminating the need for a frame pointer.

Without a frame pointer, however, the debugger can no longer find the boundary between a frame and its predecessor. Originally the MIPS compilers provided the frame size within the debugging tables. Today they emit prologue and epilogue code according to a set of rules that makes it easy for the debugger to discover the frame size by disassembling code.

The SPARC architecture actually provides two separate stacks, one implemented in memory and the other superimposed on a circular list of registers. Each procedure sees only a small "window" of registers within the circular list. A procedure call uses the memory stack to hold return addresses and data that the compiler does not allocate to registers. The call also pushes the window forward toward the top of the register stack, exposing a new group of registers. (The old and new windows overlap partially so that the compiler can pass arguments using the registers in the overlapped region.) When the register stack fills the circular list, this causes the operating system to copy registers to the memory stack, freeing them for reuse.

Thus, a SPARC debugger needs to unwind both stacks in parallel, and it needs to recognize that the series of frames on the memory stack may be interrupted by a copy of registers caused by the register overflow trap.

Assembly-level Debugging

No matter how robust or how feature-rich the source-level symbolic GUI debugger is, there will be critical times when it is necessary to dive down into the details of how the actual instructions execute on the hardware. Several types of information typically are provided relative to assembly-level debugging. Disassembly is where the machine code generated by the compiler is decoded back into mnemonic assembly code. The hardware registers and flags are usually shown. Usually their values can be changed (carefully).

Sometimes there are integer as well as floating-point registers, and both must be shown. The stack as actually laid out in memory is shown. And several sorts of memory views can be provided to allow raw memory to be viewed and formatted in special ways.

Disassembly

Disassembling machine instructions is useful in several key algorithms in a debugger. Obviously, certain difficult bugs require the user to examine the instructions that implement the source program. And even if the user never chooses to look at an instruction, the debugger itself will probably rely on disassembly in implementing other operations. (For example, tracing the stack may require the debugger to examine each function prolog to decide which registers have been saved or which of several possible calling sequences was used.) To implement fast statement stepping, the debugger must allow the program to run at full speed, after first placing a temporary breakpoint instruction at each place where the program may leave the confines of the current statement—whether by call, branch, or fall through. And if the hardware provides no support for instruction-stepping, the debugger must operate as it would for fast statement-stepping, placing temporary breakpoints at each instruction that would otherwise follow the current instruction. All of these operations involve decoding instruction opcodes, decoding register fields, and computing branch targets. See Figure 7.4.

Because disassembly underlies so many other operations, instruction decode performance matters. Fortunately, instruction formats are designed to let the CPU hardware decode them rapidly without excessive complexity, and that means that table lookup using multiple tables (which is the closest software analog to hardware decoders) usually works well.

It is wise to provide separate disassembler queries for use on behalf of the user and by the debugger itself because the user's needs and the debugger's needs are very different, and the disassembler can thereby satisfy the debugger's needs more rapidly.

For example, the user may not know where instruction boundaries lie, may want to disassemble backward through memory, and may need to see a string representation of the entire instruction. The debugger usually knows

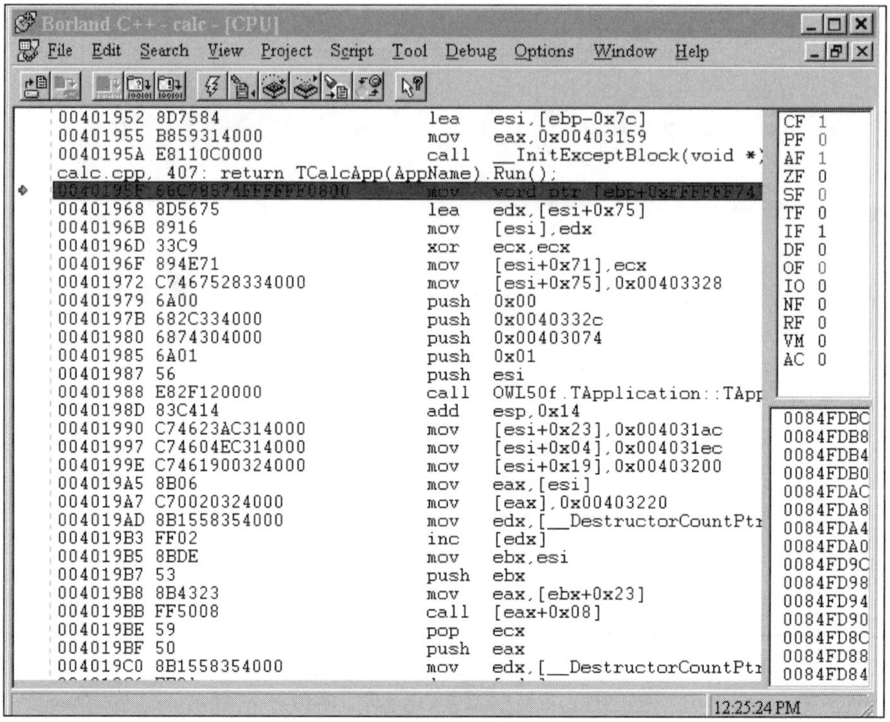

Figure 7.4

Disassembly view. *The typical disassembly view shows what looks like symbolic assembler code listings. However, this assembler code is synthesized by the debugger reading actual instructions directly out of memory.*

exactly where each instruction starts and only disassembles forward. Even more important, the debugger often does not need to decode an instruction completely. Instead, it needs answers to questions like "Does this instruction alter the program counter?" or "Does this instruction alter memory?" When the answer is negative, the debugger may proceed to the next instruction without asking further about the current one.

Disassembling backward generally is not possible on many machines, either because instructions vary in length or because the compiler and assembler insert data between instructions; thus, the debugger must rely on external clues or on heuristics. To understand why, consider that the CPU itself decodes instructions only in the forward direction. Given an address that is known to be the start of a legal instruction sequence, the instruction formats are designed to allow one unique interpretation. But given an address that is known to be the end of a legal instruction, there may be a large variety of legal sequences having different starting addresses but the same ending address. Even worse, the debugger often cannot assume that the beginning of one legal sequence is the end of the previous legal sequence because the compiler or assembler may insert data (such as case statement dispatch tables or constants) between a pair of instruction sequences when the earlier sequence ends with an unconditional branch or return instruction. The best solution is to use clues provided by the debug information: Each statement boundary and each function entry point define the start of a legal sequence.

In the absence of any clues, a "windowing" heuristic is sometimes effective, as described in Algorithm 7.4. The basic premise of this algorithm is to establish "windows" over the instruction sequence and keep moving the window until the forward disassembly at the top of the window ends up with the observed ending sequence at the bottom of the window.

This heuristic relies on the existence of invalid instruction formats and the assumption that data bytes within the instruction stream are unlikely. An incorrect guess is likely to be interrupted by an invalid opcode, which will cause the algorithm to shift by one byte and attempt a different sequence. Each shift increases the probability of "synchronizing" with the correct sequence, but each pass takes time and risks making the presentation of the disassembly view appear sluggish.

Viewing Registers

The registers view is simple and straightforward. The CPU defines the number, names, and lengths of its registers. The debugger must accurately represent that. In addition, it needs to provide a means to change the value of a register. Direct manipulation is best. This means allowing the user to edit the printed value of the register directly within the view and not in a separate edit dialog. It is good to show changed register values in a different color. These changes will not actually be recorded in the hardware until the next time execution of the debuggee begins, so no effect of these changes can be observed until then. A debugger may want to allow different formatting options such as octal, decimal, hex, or binary, on register values to help the user correlate back to his or her expectations. It is worth noting that no CPU

Algorithm 7.4 *"Windowing" reverse disassembly heuristic*

Input	Given current address is A.
Output	ASCII readable assembly language text for a series of instructions preceding A. Also output is the new starting address.
Method	Keep moving a window backward until forward disassembly correctly gets back to a known good place.

    i. Choose the number of instructions you wish to disassemble backward and multiply by the maximum instruction length L to get a window size W;

    ii. Guess that there is an instruction boundary at address A-2*W, and disassemble forward;

    iii. If (we encounter an invalid instruction) then
treat its first byte as data and continue disassembling at the next byte of memory;

    iv. If (resulting sequence ends at A) then
return the set of instructions which fit within the window between A-W and A
else
guess a new starting point A-2*W+1

    v. Repeat the guessing process up to A-2*W+L until success;

    vi. Or, if we do not succeed, return the sequence that has the fewest data bytes between its last legal instruction and address A.

view known to me displays the saved registers as one moves up the stack. This would be extremely valuable.

Memory Dumps

Several sorts of memory dumps are useful. A specialized form of memory dump is the stack view. It is very helpful to annotate the stack view with current stack pointer, frame pointer, and, if possible, any symbolic routine names known. Another memory view that is useful is the raw memory dump, which shows address range and memory contents within that range. Both scroll bars and explicit entry of hex address should be possible. When memory is displayed corresponding to what is viewed in the disassembly view, this should be noted. Formatting choices for memory values shown should be provided including as bytes, words, long words, and then as strings, floats, octal, hex, decimal, and binary. Frequently, hexadecimal math is needed during debugging so a simple hex calculator integrated into the memory view is a nice feature. Finally, again it should be possible to modify memory values through direct manipulation.

8

Inspecting Data and Variables

The execution control algorithms we have just described perform half of the task of debugging: letting the user run and stop the program at will and inspect debuggee context via source, stack, and CPU information. Once the program has stopped, data inspection algorithms perform the other half of the task, letting the user examine and alter the program's data structures. Execution control lets the user understand the "where" of a bug; data inspection lets the user understand the "how."

Evaluating Expressions

Ideally, a symbolic debugger can display data by evaluating an expression that uses the same identifiers and syntax that appear in the source program. This requires the debugger to implement an interpreter for the expression syntax and semantics of one (or, in the case of a multilanguage debugger, more than one) source language.

Many issues for the debugger's interpreter are no different from those covered by the literature on conventional interpreters. The primary difference is that the debugger's interpreter does not allocate its own storage for variables, but instead accesses them within the debugger's child process at the addresses specified by the debugging tables emitted by the compiler. This is critical because what the user is after is the use of the actual values being used by the running program.

One obvious implementation is to adapt the parsing and semantics phases of the compiler that emits the programs on which the debugger must operate. The adapted compiler front-end reads the text typed by the user of the debugger and builds its parse tree as usual. It consults the debugging tables to obtain the identifier and data type information, which in the original compiler would have been placed in the compiler's own symbol table by declaration statements. Then it performs its usual semantic checking and annotation. Next, a new piece of debugger-specific code walks the tree, replacing variables with values obtained from the child process. Finally, the usual constant-folding code within the compiler combines the values and delivers a result.

This approach saves some duplication of work, and it encourages the compiler and the debugger to behave alike; in particular, the debugger can even deliver the same error messages that the programmer is accustomed to receiving from the compiler. The most important advantage to this approach is that *the debugger evaluator is now guaranteed to use the same language syntax and semantics as used in the construction of the underlying program.* The alternative is to build an expression evaluator and language parser as a special dedicated piece of code in the debugger.

There are significant differences between the compiler's needs and the debugger's. If possible, anticipating the debugger's needs when designing the compiler will minimize difficulties.

For example, whereas a compiler always evaluates an expression in the context of the current scope, a debugger may let the user point to any frame on the stack and evaluate an expression as if that were the topmost frame. At best this simply requires passing an extra parameter to the existing compiler code, which maps identifiers onto symbolic information; at worst it requires considerable new work. For example, one simple compiler symbol table organization allocates a block of symbol table entries on a stack at the beginning of each new scope and deallocates the block at the end of the scope. The algorithm for searching the scoping hierarchy is implicit because relevant scopes appear on the stack in the proper order and irrelevant ones have been discarded. This scheme is not sufficient for a debugger, however, because all scopes are present in the debugging tables all the time; the debugger must therefore explicitly choose which scopes to search.

Even within a particular scope, the debugging tables are unlikely to use the same data structures as the normal compiler symbol table. One good solution to this problem is to provide pairs of symbol-table access methods, one for the compiler and the other to translate the object file debugging tables into the data structures the compiler expects to see.

Such translation may need to operate in a "lazy" or "as-needed" fashion. Consider an expression that refers to a single data member of a C++ class. A complete translation of the class would need to process its base classes and then each of those classes' base classes in turn. If the class hierarchy is highly intertwined, this could ultimately require translating every user-defined type in the entire program.

If the debugger supports more than one language, additional problems arise because the user can attempt to evaluate an expression that combines operators from one language with operands generated by different languages, leading to undefined results. An easy solution is to tag each symbol with its source language and to refuse to mix languages within a single expression, but the user may consider this draconian: such a debugger would, for example, refuse to copy a value from a Pascal global integer to a C global int. A better solution is to build checks into the code that translates data structures from the debugging tables into data structures within the compiler symbol table. Gross mismatches are easy to exclude: for example, one cannot map a C pointer onto any FORTRAN 77 data type. Subtle matches still require care: for example, although it might seem that a Pascal tagged variant record maps easily onto a C union embedded within a structure, that might not be true if the C semantics phase assumes that such a union will have a name (because the C parser would not permit its omission), and the absence of a name causes a bug. Or consider the problems that might result if a C++ compiler, which assumes that any symbol named "this" will have a structured data type, encounters a Pascal scalar global named "this."

Adapting the compiler for use within the debugger may also require extra work in constant folding; whereas a compiler-writer can decide that it isn't profitable to fold a difficult and rare combination of operator and operand types, the user will complain if this causes the debugger to reject a legal expression.

Scope Resolution

If a debugger is meant to work with more than one language, it must avoid the temptation to build into its symbol-access methods any assumptions about identifier scoping because these differ among languages. Instead, each language-specific evaluator must bind identifiers onto data items using the rules for the language. For example, a Pascal evaluator that fails to find an identifier in the scope of the current function will next search the statically enclosing function; a C evaluator will next search the scope of the file; and a C++ evaluator will next search for a data member belonging to the same class as the function.

It is useful to extend the syntax of each language while in the debugger's evaluator subsystem to let the user specify variables that exist but that are not currently in scope. For example, the special inspector syntax "#gcd#i" might specify the variable "i" in function "gcd", letting the user examine this variable whenever a frame for "gcd" exists on the stack. Or "##i" might permit the user to examine a global variable named "i" even though the current function redeclares the name "i" as a local variable.

If you allow the user to set a watchpoint (a data breakpoint) on a local variable in procedure X, which is stack allocated, you must somehow ensure that the watchpoint does not fire on some other variable that happens to use the same memory when procedure X is not active. Either the debugger must automatically disable the watchpoint when procedure X returns and reenable it on the next call to procedure X, or it must ignore spurious firing of the watchpoint when procedure X is inactive. It must also deal with the possibility that procedure X may be recursive.

A home table is a list of program-counter ranges where each range specifies a variable's location when the program is executing within that range. If the debugger uses home tables to track when the compiler moves variables into and out of registers, it may need to deal with the fact that the variable spends part of its time in a register instead of memory. There is no hardware or operating system support for an exception if a register's value is modified so the watchpoint will not fire and the debugger will not have been truthful.

Automatic Redisplay of Expressions

Some debuggers will automatically reevaluate an expression each time the child process stops. This feature (sometimes called an "inspector") can require extra work to achieve both correctness and good performance.

First, the evaluator must separate the mapping of identifiers onto symbols from the rest of the evaluation work. This ensures that each identifier has the same meaning each time the debugger reevaluates the expression; it also reduces the cost of reevaluation because only the first evaluation must search scopes to resolve identifiers. Second, it must provide a list of the scopes required, so that the debugger avoids reevaluating an expression unless the stack contains a frame for each of those scopes.

Invoking Functions during Evaluation

The ability to invoke a function during expression evaluation is important in languages like C++ because the user may inadvertently use an operator in an expression that has been overloaded with a function. Following is a sample fragment of C++ code showing function overloading that makes a simple operator actually turn into a function call.

```
operator+ cadd(int,int);
c = a + b; // this '+' calls function cadd()
```

Although the debugger can interpret most expressions, as opposed to gener-ating native code, an expression that invokes a function poses a problem. It is generally not practical to parse the entire function, process it semantically, and then use the resulting tree to drive an interpreter. Even if all this was done, the debugger's expression "language" must remain completely "bug compatible" with the compiler, and this is virtually and practically impossible.

Thus, most debuggers that permit expressions containing function calls employ a trick. Instead of interpreting the function invocation, the debugger builds an argument list using the stack within the child process, sets a break-point at the function return address, and starts the child process running at the beginning of the function. When the child process reaches the breakpoint,

Algorithm 8.1 *Invoking a function during expression evaluation*

Input	Function and actual argument list
Output	Function return value, plus side effects
Method	Use the child process to execute the desired function

  i. Evaluate each of the actual argument expressions and save the resulting value in the debugger address space. (Remember that any of these expressions may itself invoke a function.)

  ii. Save the child process registers and program counter.

  iii. According to the calling conventions of the target machine and compiler, push onto the stack (or copy into a register) each of the actual argument values. (For example, the rules for a non-scalar return value may require you to allocate space on the stack prior to pushing the arguments.) If the language allows user-written exceptions, set up the necessary machinery so that if the function throws an exception, the run-time system will not unwind past this point without giving control back to the debugger.

  iv. Choose a "distinctive" return address. Set a breakpoint at that address. As dictated by the calling conventions, push the address onto the stack or copy it into a register.

  v. Copy the starting address of the function into the program counter register.

  vi. Run the child process.

  vii. When the child encounters the breakpoint, retrieve the return value according to the calling conventions (a non-scalar return value may lie within the space mentioned in step iii.)

  viii. Remove the breakpoint set in step iv.

  ix. Restore the registers and program counter saved in step ii.

the debugger retrieves its return value and restores the child process stack and registers to their original state.

The trick assumes that it is safe to invoke a function at a point where no function invocation appeared in the original program. Fortunately, the assumption is valid for most code generators today. (Given a sophisticated optimizer, this can be invalid because it is equivalent to inserting the function invocation at the current point in the program; even the techniques for debugging optimized code fail to address this because they merely describe the original program graph to the debugger.) As a concrete example, consider a function that makes up-level references to a variable that is dead or enregistered at the current point in the program.

The return address used in this algorithm should be "distinctive" enough so that neither recursive nor non-recursive calls to additional functions will erroneously trigger the breakpoint. The debugger must also anticipate that the function may not return: It may encounter a breakpoint set by the user, or may fault, or may terminate execution of the child process, or may stop executing via a non-local goto or C language "longjmp" that bypasses the normal return address.

An easy solution is to disable user-set breakpoints temporarily and to treat a fault as an error that reports failure to the user and restores the child process state. Process termination or non-local goto constitutes a more serious error because it may be impossible to restore the state. I should emphasize that encountering breakpoints during function evaluation, while it might add on interesting set of capabilities to the user, is quite dangerous if not handled very carefully in the debugger. The most significant issue is reentrancy. The debugger itself has recorded a stop and recorded critical debuggee state information. Now a disjointed path of execution is being followed where another stop is encountered. What is shown on the stack? What are the other threads of execution doing? If they are not frozen they just got to run and create unforeseen side effects. In general, I'd suggest the return on investment for this capability is very low: don't allow breakpoints during function evaluation.

Compiler-generated Debugging Information

A symbolic debugger depends on the compiler and linker to emit debugging tables (often called a "symbol table," but not to be confused with the symbol table used within the compiler itself) that describe the mapping from names and statements within the source program onto the object program (MICROSOFT 1993).[1] But a compiler usually emits the object program and the debugging symbol table separately, so an error in the symbol table appears to the user to be a "bug" in the debugger.[2]

---

[1] Nearly all symbol table encodings are proprietary, an issue which makes it difficult for vendor X to handle vendor Y's encoding and for the encoding to improve through open review.

[2] In fact, as a user of a debugger, many of the bugs you have encountered have almost certainly been due to compiler-debug information problems, operating system bugs, or other issues not directly controlled by the debugger developer.

Ideally (as explained later in connection with the question of debugging optimized code) the debugger might do better to access the same intermediate data structures that the compiler uses to represent the program, but that approach is not common practice due to problems with bulk and information hiding. Instead, the debugging symbol table provides only the information the debugger is thought to need. Often the author of the debugger has no voice in the design of the symbol table, and some debuggers must cope with a variety of formats, typically by translating them into an internal form.

A debugging symbol table must deal with a number of issues:

- Does the symbol table cater to the compiler or to the debugger?
- How does it divide the work among compiler, linker, and debugger?
- Does it permit incremental processing and caching of information?
- Can it support a variety of target machines?
- Can it support a variety of compilers?

Catering to the Debugger

The symbol table is a database, and as with any database, the best organization depends on which queries need to be fast. Unfortunately, queries that are important to the debugger may not occur at all within the compiler. For example, both the debugger and the compiler query variables by name when they process expressions; only the debugger queries them by memory address (for example, when it disassembles a memory-referencing instruction and wishes to print the identifier corresponding to the operand in memory).

The needs of the compiler and debugger also differ because the compiler deals with one compilation at a time, whereas the debugger deals with the entire executable. The debugger may, for example, be confronted with a much larger number of global variables; it may need to acquire (and later discard) additional symbolic information during execution of a program that relies on dynamically linked libraries. We have found that most debuggers have capacity problems due to these issues that must constantly be addressed by the debugger developers.

Dividing the Work

Clearly someone—the linker, on one hand, or the debugger, on the other—must reorganize the data to suit the needs of the debugger.

It might seem best to make the debugger perform all the work: Although the first invocation of the debugger might be slow, the debugger could cache the reorganized data in case it is invoked again before recompilation. Compilation can be fast, and the linker need incur no extra expense at all, provided the debugger can retrieve individual symbol tables from the relocatable object files and resolve relocations itself (a task that it must perform for dynamically linked libraries anyway). Best of all, the debugger may be able to avoid processing some relocatables if the user doesn't refer to them during the debugging session.

Most systems take the opposite approach, however: Linkers combine symbol tables from the relocatable object files and perform at least some reorganization before writing the information to the executable file.

There are several reasons for this:

- Programmers may wish to delete relocatables after linking.

- Binding the symbol table to the executable reduces the chance of losing or mismatching the symbol table.

- The debugger can avoid duplicating work (such as organizing public symbols for rapid access by name) that the linker must perform anyway.

- The linker may reduce the volume of the symbol table dramatically by eliminating duplications.

The last point is probably the strongest argument for involving the linker. The data types, global variables, and procedure definitions that make up the interfaces between separate compilations are defined once by the exporter of the interface and referenced repeatedly by the importers. In a language like Modula-2 - an early object-oriented language used frequently in Europe—which describes the interface via a definition module, it is easy to represent the interface once for the exporter without repeating it for any of the importers. But for languages like C and C++, which rely on textual inclusion, symbol tables can grow explosively. For example, consider that dozens of compilations in a large program may include the same file "stdio.h" or "iostream.h."

Some systems attempt to treat the ".h" file like the Modula-2 definition module; the compiler segregates symbol table information generated by the ".h" file and the linker discards duplicate copies. The linker must ensure that the copies are truly identical, however, because the programmer may have legally used conditional compilation so that the same ".h" file generates different information in different compilations. Other systems require the linker or a post processor to hash or sort all symbols and types in the program to eliminate duplicates (MICROSOFT 1993). These horrendous complications that plague C++—due to header files and executable code in these headers— is one of the major motivating factors behind the design of Java.

Incremental Processing

Reading and processing the entire symbol table for a large program can cause an annoying delay. Fortunately, a typical debugging session exhibits a great deal of locality (LINTON 1986). If the debugger can read the symbol table in a lazy or incremental fashion, it may entirely avoid reading most of the symbol table, and can divide the remaining processing into a number of smaller, less noticeable, delays. Linton's studies showed that most debugging sessions required less than 15 percent of the available symbol table was needed.

Different Target Machines

Obviously different target machines will differ with respect to word size, address range, registers, the use of segments, and so on. Less obviously, there is a trade-off between minimizing the size of the symbol table and supporting a variety of targets. For example, if a target machine has a hardware protocol for saving registers in the prologue of a procedure, or if the debugger can easily infer the identity of saved registers by disassembling code, the symbol table need not list them. But a symbol table that cannot represent the names and locations of saved registers may be unusable on a machine whose protocol is complicated.

Compilers vary in the way they build runtime structures such as dope vectors or C++ virtual function tables. Obviously, different compilers will require different information, and again there is a trade-off between size and generality.

Accessing Symbol Tables

How the debugger accesses the symbol table depends, of course, on which services the debugger provides to the user, but most debuggers have a certain set of queries in common. The following list describes each query and gives one or more examples of its use.

1. *Map instruction address onto the enclosing scope.*

   When the user asks to evaluate an expression, the debugger must use the appropriate scope. When the user asks to trace the stack, the debugger must show the scope or procedure corresponding to each return address on the stack.

2. *Map scope onto statically enclosing parent scope.*

   For statically scoped languages, evaluating an expression often requires searching a hierarchy of scopes. When tracing the stack, the debugger may prefer to show the innermost enclosing function in place of an unnamed lexical scope.

3. *Map scope plus identifier onto type and location.*

   When evaluating an expression, the debugger must search for an identifier within a scope, and then use its type plus its location (which may be a memory address, a register, a constant value, or some combination) to fetch from the child process the number of bits indicated by the data type. This query will need to find functions as well as data and must handle global scope as a special case.

4. *Map instruction address onto source statement.*

   When the program stops, the debugger must show the current source statement.

5. *Map code or data address onto statically allocated variable or procedure.*

   When the debugger disassembles instructions, it may wish to show the names of the variables and procedures to which they refer.

6. *Map source statement onto instruction address range.*

   When the user sets a breakpoint on a source statement, the debugger must find the first instruction of that statement. When the user asks to step through a source statement, the debugger must find the end of the statement.

A Sample Symbol Table: STI

STI, also known as CodeView debug format, illustrates a typical debugging symbol table. It is complicated somewhat by its need to support segmented 16-bit and 32-bit addresses for Intel x86 machines as well as simple 32-bit addresses for non-Intel target machines. It is complicated further because the compiler emits one set of tables, the linker combines these and rewrites them into a different set, and a post-processor called CVPACK transforms that into yet a third set. In the following discussion I'll ignore some of the details required solely for 16-bit machines or for segmentation, I'll concentrate on the third set of tables, and I'll omit some less important details entirely.

The compiler uses two kinds of records to describe most program objects:

$$SYMBOLS	Descriptions of procedures, variables, named constants, and named types
$$TYPES	Descriptions of scalar, array, aggregate, and enumerated types

The $$SYMBOLS section is a series of variable-length records. Each begins with a 2-byte length field, followed by a 2-byte opcode field that indicates the purpose of the record and dictates the set of fields that occupies the remainder of the record.

For example, a record whose opcode is S_GDATA32 describes a 32-bit-addressed global variable and contains the fields listed in Table 8.1.

As a second example, a record whose opcode is S_BPREL32 describes a 32-bit-addressed local variable (Microsoft compilers address these relative to the base pointer register of the Intel 80X86 machine, hence the opcode name), as listed in Table 8.2.

Other record formats include the following:

S_REGISTER	Register variable
S_CONST	Constant
S_UDT	User-defined type
S_LDATA32	C "static" variable
S_LPROC32	C "static" procedure
S_GPROC32	Global procedure
S_THUNK32	Thunk procedure

TABLE 8.1   *Encoding for 32-bit addressed Global Variable*

FIELD	SIZE IN BYTES	PURPOSE
length	2	Number of bytes in the record, excluding the length field itself
S_GDATA32	2	Opcode describes symbol, dictates which additional fields follow
offset	4	Address of the variable (offset part)
segment	2	Address of the variable (segment part)
type	2	Index of the data type within $$TYPES
name	variable	Variable name (length-prefixed string)

TABLE 8.2   *Encoding for 32-bit addressed Local Variable*

FIELD	SIZE IN BYTES	PURPOSE
length	2	Same as above
S_BPREL32	2	
offset	4	Signed offset from BP register
type	2	Index of the data type within $$TYPES
name	variable	Variable name (length-prefixed string)

S_BLOCK32	Nested lexical scope
S_WITH32	Pascal "with" statement
S_END	End of scope of procedure, lexical scope, or "with" statement
S_LABEL32	Statement label
S_VFTPATH32	C++ virtual function table path descriptor

Records describing procedures, nested lexical scopes, and "with" statements are threaded together to describe the scoping structure of the program. In each of these records, one field points to the parent scope and another field points to the next sibling scope within that parent's scope. All records belonging to a scope must appear immediately after the record for the scope itself. A third field within that record points to the last record belonging to it. A record called S_SSEARCH, which must appear at the beginning of the $$SYMBOLS section, points to the procedure at the head of the list.

For example, Figure 8.1 shows the $$SYMBOLS records for the following compilation:

```
procedure outer;
    var outer_var0, outer_var1: integer;
    procedure inner0;
        var inner_var: integer;
        begin
        end;
    procedure inner1;
        begin
        end;
    begin
    end;
```

The structure of individual records within the $$TYPES section is similar to that of the $$SYMBOLS section, except that one record may contain a series of leaf structures, each structure having one opcode and a variable number of fields dictated by the opcode. The 2-byte length at the beginning of the record counts the number of bytes in all the leaf structures.

```
              S_SSEARCH           start
                      |             0
                      |             ^
                      |             |
  S_GPROC32       outer <-+      pParent pEnd            pNext
                        ^  ^        |                      |
  S_BPREL32       outer_var0  |  |        +-------+        v
                        |  |        |       |        0
  S_BPREL32       outer_var1  +-+|                |
                        |  |                       |
  S_SPROC32       inner0      |  pParent pEnd     |      pNext
                        |       |        |        |        |
  S_BPREL32       inner_var    |        |        |      +-------+
                        +-+     |        |        |              |
  S_END                 |      <-+       |              |
                        |                |              |
  S_PROC32        inner1       pParent pEnd     |      pNext <-+
                                            |        |
  S_END                          <-------+       v
                                                  0
```

Figure 8.1

Layout of $$SYMBOLS records in STI graphically.   *The layout and connections of the $$SYMBOLS records for the compilation of a simple pascal procedure and two nested inner procedures.*

For example, this record describes an array with default lower bound and constant upper bound, as shown in Table 8.3.

As a second example (Table 8.4), this record describes a C++ class.

Other opcodes for type records include the following:

`LF_POINTER`	Pointer to type
`LF_ENUM`	Enumerated type
`LF_PROCEDURE`	Procedure type
`LF_METHODLIST`	List of C++ member functions
`LF_FIELDLIST`	List of members of C or C++ struct, union, or class
`LF_BITFIELD`	C bitfield member
`LF_ARGLIST`	List of formal arguments
`LF_VFUNCTAB`	C++ virtual function table

Each record is assigned a number beginning at hexadecimal 1000. When a field points to another record, it uses this number. Numbers below 1000 are reserved for various intrinsic scalar types (such as integer or double-precision real).

STI requires a substantial amount of processing by the linker and the CVPACK post-processor. Some of it makes access more convenient for the debugger. For example, because type records vary in length and use record numbers rather than byte offsets to point to one another, the debugger would have difficulty following these pointers. So CVPACK creates an array that maps type numbers onto offsets relative to the beginning of $$TYPES. In addition, CVPACK separates global symbols from the rest of the symbols and puts them in a separate table, optionally creating hash tables to reduce the cost of searching the globals by name or by address.

Other post-processing is mandated by the design. For example, CVPACK must eliminate redundant $$TYPES records generated by separate compilations because the address of a C++ class method lies in a record separate from the description of the C++ class itself, and it is not generally possible for the debugger to recognize the association between these records unless each data type has a unique index.

When the linker and CVPACK are finished, the executable file has one set of the following tables for each relocatable object:

TABLE 8.3 *Encoding for an array with the Default Lower Bound and Constant Upper Bound*

FIELD	SIZE IN BYTES	PURPOSE
length	2	Number of bytes in the record, excluding the length field itself
LF_DIMCONU	2	Opcode describes type, dictates which additional fields follow
rank	2	Number of dimensions
index	2	Points to record describing the data type of array index
bound	rank * s	Constants specifying upper bound of each dimension; "s" is the number of bytes each constant occupies, dictated by the index type

TABLE 8.4 *Encoding for a C++ Class*

FIELD	SIZE IN BYTES	PURPOSE
length		Same as above
LF_CLASS		
count	2	Number of members
memberlist	2	Pointer to another record listing the members
property	2	Bit mask describing attributes of the class (for example, whether it is packed, whether it has overloaded operators, etc.)
dlist	2	Points to record describing the classes that inherit this class
vshape	2	Points to record describing the virtual function table
length	variable	Size in bytes of the class
name	variable	Class name

sstModule	Address ranges of code and data emitted
sstAlignSym	$$SYMBOLS records for non-globals
sstSrcModule	Mapping from source statements to instructions

The executable has exactly one set of the following tables:

sstGlobalTypes	$$TYPES records for all types
sstGlobalPub	$$SYMBOLS records for public data
sstGlobalSym	$$SYMBOLS records for global procedures

The sstSrcModule table consists of a header followed by an assortment of file-information records and line-information records. The table contains these fields:

cFile	Number of source files contributing code to this compilation
cSeg	Number of segments receiving code from this compilation
baseSrcFile	Array [cFile] of pointers to file information records
start/end	Array [cSeg] of pairs of offsets (giving the range of addresses for each segment)
seg	Array [cSeg] of segment indices, corresponding to the start/end pairs

file-information record for file 0

line-information records for file 0

...

file-information record for file n

line-information records for file n

Each file information record contains these fields:

cSeg	Number of segments receiving code from this file
baseSrcLn	Array [cSeg] of pointers to line information records, one per segment
start/end	Array [cSeg] of pairs of offsets (the range of addresses for each segment)
Name	Length-prefixed file name

Each line information record associates an array of line numbers with a parallel array of segment offsets. It contains these fields:

| Seg | Segment index |
| cPair | Number of source lines |

offset	Array [cPair] of 32-bit segment offsets
linenumber	Array [cPair] of 16-bit line numbers

In addition to $$TYPES records, the sstGlobalTypes subtable contains the vector mentioned before that maps each type index onto the corresponding byte offset.

The optional subtable sstGlobalSym provides hash functions to search the symbols by address or by identifier.

Access Algorithms for STI

With this somewhat abridged description of the STI format, I can describe how to implement an incremental access package for the typical database queries I listed earlier. To simplify, I'll assume there's no need to remove information from memory once we have read it from the file, and I'll assume that procedures and compilations are short enough that linear searching is acceptably fast within any single procedure or compilation.

Our strategy is to establish a number of data structures in memory, each of which is initially empty, but may later contain data read from the executable file. Pointers between data structures indicate whether the target is in memory or the file. Whenever a query needs to use a data structure that is empty, we read just enough information from the file to satisfy the query.

We build the data structures listed in Table 8.5 in a lazy fashion.

In Algorithm 8.2 we use module_map to build module_symbols, and then we use that table to take an address and find the enclosing scope for that address. This is critical as the first step in variable inspection.

Algorithm 8.2 *Map instruction address onto the enclosing scope*

Input	Instruction address
Output	Pointer to $$SYMBOLS record for enclosing scope

    i. If we have not already done so, read sstModules and construct module_map.

    ii. Use module_map plus the input address to find the module.

    iii. If we have not already done so, read the sstAlignSym table for that module and construct the corresponding module_symbols entry.

    iv. Within the module_symbols entry, start with the S_SSEARCH record and traverse the list of scopes to find the one containing the desired address.

Now, given a scope we may need the statically enclosing parent's scope. Again, this is necessary in variable inspection and enables the debugger to eventually get all the way out to global scope. Algorithm 8.3 shows how this is done.

Algorithm 8.3   *Map scope onto statically enclosing parent scope*

Input	Pointer to record in module_symbols for child scope
Output	Pointer to record in module_symbols for parent scope

    i. If scope is "global" then return failure.
   ii. If the "pParent" pointer in the input record is zero, return "global."
  iii. Otherwise, follow the "pParent" pointer.

Then, having a scope and an identifier, Algorithm 8.4 is used to obtain the record describing the type for this identifier as well as its location.

Algorithm 8.4   *Map scope plus identifier onto type and location*

Input	Pointer to record for scope string representing identifier
Output	Pointer to record for type Location

     i. If the input scope is not "global," go to step iv.
    ii. If we have not already done so, read sstGlobalSym and sstGlobalPub and construct address_to_global and name_to_global.
   iii. Use name_to_global to find the appropriate record. Report failure if there is none; otherwise go to step viii.
    iv. Fetch the "pEnd" field of the scope record.
     v. Start with the first record after the scope record.
    vi. If the offset of this record matches the "pEnd" value of the input scope, fail.
   vii. If the name of this record does not match the input identifier, go to step xii.
  viii. If we have not already done so, read the vector at the beginning of sstGlobalTypes and construct type_vector.
    ix. Use type_vector plus the type index within the symbol record to find the appropriate type record.

TABLE 8.5   *Basic Data Structures Built by Debugger for Access to Symbolic Information*

DATA STRUCTURE BUILT	DATA STRUCTURE DESCRIPTION
module_map	Maps any address onto the corresponding module, indicating whether to obtain the symbols for that module from the file or from module_symbols.
module_symbols	For each module, represents the corresponding sstAlignSym information.
type_vector	For each data type index, points to the corresponding record either in the file or in type_records.
type_records	Types records that have been read from the file.
global	Special, reserved pointer indicating global scope.
file_to_module	For each file, gives the set of modules containing code generated from that file. We assume that a particular file is usually associated with only one module, but to handle the more general case we are willing to iterate through a list of modules.
address_to_statement	For each module, provides an array of (address, file, statement) tuples, sorted by address.
statement_to_address	For each module, provides an array of (statement, pointer) tuples, sorted by statement, where each pointer indicates a tuple in the address_to_statement entry for that module. We assume that within a module, all statements usually lie within the same source file, but to handle the general case we are willing to iterate through a list of tuples, selecting the one having the appropriate file. Because the STI format provides only the starting address for a statement, we must infer its ending address from the starting address of the next statement in the symbol table. Thus, instead of storing addresses within this data structure, we store pointers into the address_to_statement data structure, where the addresses appear in order.

address_to_global	Based on sstGlobalSym and sstGlobalPub, maps addresses onto global symbols.
name_to_global	Based on sstGlobalSym and sstGlobalPub, maps identifiers onto global symbols.

    x. If we have not already done so, read the type record from sstGlobalTypes and add an entry to type_records.

   xi. Use the location fields within this symbol record to determine the location and return success.

  xii. If this record is a procedure, scope, or "with" statement, advance past its "pEnd" record; otherwise, merely advance to the next record.

 xiii. Go to step vi.

When a breakpoint fires and whenever we need to map an instruction address onto the correct source statement, Algorithm 8.5 is needed. This algorithm takes the instruction address and, using source line information contained in sstModules, determines the correct file name and line number.

The opposite mapping—from source statement onto instruction address range—is used by the source view to show the breakpointable lines. It is also used whenever the user sets a breakpoint on a source statement. This mapping is shown in Algorithm 8.6.

Algorithm 8.5 *Map instruction address onto source statement*

Input Instruction address
Output Source statement filename and line number

    i. If we have not already done so, read sstModules and construct module_map.

   ii. Use the input address plus module_map to find the appropriate module.

  iii. If we have not already done so, read sstSrcModule for that module and construct address_to_statement and statement_to_address entries for that module.

  iv. Search address_to_statement for the highest address that does not exceed the input address.

Algorithm 8.6 *Map source statement onto instruction address range*

Input   File name and line number
Output   Range of addresses for that statement

    i. If we have not already done so, read the file information records from each sstSrcModule and construct file_to_module.

    ii. Use the file name plus file_to_module to select each module that might contain the desired statement.

    iii. If there are no (more) candidate modules, report failure.

    iv. If we have not already done so, read the sstSrcModule for the candidate and construct statement_to_address and address_to_statement.

    v. Use the line number along with statement_to_address to select all of the tuples having the desired line number. If the set is empty, advance to the next candidate module and go to step iii.

    vi. For each selected tuple, follow its pointer to the corresponding tuple within the address_to_statement table, and compare the file name with our input file name. If no tuple matches, advance to the next candidate module and go to step iii.

    vii. Use the offset from the address_to_statement tuple as the low bound of the range. Return the offset of the next tuple in address_to_statement as the high bound of the range.

Statically allocated variables have a simple mapping from a data address. Statically allocated procedures have the same mapping, shown in Algorithm 8.7.

Algorithm 8.7 *Map code or data address onto statically allocated variable or procedure*

Input   Address
Output   Pointer to record in module_symbols

    i. If we have not already done so, read sstGlobalSym and sstGlobalPub and construct address_to_global and name_to_global.

    ii. Search address_to_global for the highest address that does not exceed the input address.

    iii. Use the data type of the selected symbol to determine the range of addresses it covers. If the input address does not lie within that range, return failure.

Multithreaded Debugging

Some new and difficult issues are starting to become prevalent with multi-threaded applications as threads become mainstream. In this chapter I will discuss debugging issues unique to multithreaded applications. First I will introduce the concepts of threads and processes.

Threads and Processes

Applications will increasingly take advantage of multiple threads as multi-threaded operating systems leave the realms of servers and workstations and land on millions of desktops. With OS/2, NT, Windows 95, and some versions of UNIX, multiple-thread support has now reached the mainstream. The additional complexity that multiple threads add to the programming mix is mind boggling—and very few developers yet realize it. These complexities stem from data sharing between threads in a process and the temporal dependencies inherent in a system where two or more execution paths are operating at times and sequences that are non-deterministic, i.e. controlled by the operating system and other activity in the system.

Even the OS vendors do not seem to fully understand the unique debugging issues brought about by supporting multiple threads, as evidenced by the lack of adequate debugger support for threads in the contemporary mainstream operating systems. In this chapter, I will introduce threads and discuss how they are presented to the programmer, then I will explore the support given to debuggers for thread control, and finally I will explore the unique kinds of bugs that surface in multithreaded applications.

In operating system parlance, the **process** is a unit of resource ownership and of work to be done. In other words, the operating system uses the process as a way of organizing its work and resource allocation. The responsibility of the operating system is to guarantee that processes get a chance to execute in an orderly and timely fashion and that processes are protected from each other—the illusion is that your process is the only process.

The **thread** is the smallest entity within the operating system—on systems that support threads—that is scheduled for execution. As such, the thread is one of many possible subtasks needed to accomplish the overall job of a process. The thread is frequently defined as a single unit of execution. It represents an independent program counter, and it is the unit of execution that is associated with a stack. The operating system *time-slices* between all of the currently runnable threads in the system. A thread can have a priority that promotes it to run more or less often than the default would provide. At any given time, one and only one thread is executing. This gives the operating system a way to synchronize threads entirely in software. Multithreading, by definition, requires multitasking.

Multitasking is the ability of the operating system to run more than one *task* (a process or a thread, depending on the operating system), cycling through all runnable tasks and giving each its small slice of time in which to execute. This gives the appearance of several user-visible processes each making progress "simultaneously." Multitasking operating systems are not necessarily multithreaded. Classic UNIX systems have always been multitasking but did not support threads.

Processes each have private, protected address spaces. One process cannot access directly the data of another process. Only through OS-provided special services like shared memory can one process directly "see" another's address space. Threads are not separate and protected from each other. All threads within a process share the same address space. This is crucial to understand: Threads normally share data with each other, but processes do not. Some thread data is local. Each thread has its own stack and set of processor registers. Heap space is per process normally so all threads within a process share data stored on the heap (that is, its global).

Data shared between threads is a major cause of problems. Because threads are an indivisible unit of execution and form an important execution abstraction for programmers, sharing data between threads seems "unnatural"—and because heap access must be synchronized, more expensive. A special mechanism to give threads local private data that survives across function boundaries exists to keep this execution abstraction pure. It is called **thread local storage**. The stack is the mechanism used to provide this private, non-shared data. This works because each thread has its own copy of the register set and therefore its own private stack. Usually, special facilities are added by the operating system and run-time environment to fully support thread local storage. Debugger must not only understand threads at a fundamental level but must understand thread local storage as well.

DWORD   TlsAlloc(VOID)
> Allocates a thread local storage (TLS) index. Any thread of the process can subsequently use this index to store and retrieve values local to the thread.

BOOL   TlsSetValue(DWORD dwTlsIndex, LPVOID lpTlsValue)
> dwtlsIndex is the index to set value for lpTlsValue is the value to be stored.
> This function stores a value in the calling thread's TLS slot for a specified index. Each thread of a process has its own slot for each TLS index.

LPVOID   TlsGetValue(DWORD dwTlsIndex)
> dwTlsIndex is the index to retrieve value for
> This function retrieves the value in the call thread's TLS for a specified index.

BOOL   TlsFree(DWORD dwTlsIndex)
> Releases a thread local storage index making it available for reuse.

Operating System Thread Control

From the operating system's perspective, every process begins life as a single thread. That thread can create other threads. Once a thread exists it can create as many additional threads as it needs. Usually the operating system has some sort of priority scheme for deciding which thread gets to execute next in the scheduling algorithm.

In addition to the operating system support for thread creation, the operating system must provide many other thread controlling operations. Threads must be able to synchronize with each other to coordinate their activities. There are numerous mechanisms for thread synchronization including events, semaphores, messages, timers, mutexes, critical sections and others.

When a thread wishes to synchronize its activities with another thread, it blocks. This means the thread made a call to an operating system routine that causes the OS to mark the thread as unrunnable until its request is satisfied. A blocked thread does not get scheduled by the operating system. Modern multithreaded operating systems provide these synchronization mechanisms based on special data structure objects, and the threads coordinate with each other through these primitives by *signaling* and *unsignaling* these objects.

A set of basic operating system calls must be provided on any multithreaded system to give programmers access to the system's multithreaded nature. We list and discuss these here. The names happen to be those used in Win32 but are sufficiently generic to be applicable on any multithreaded system.

CreateThread()

```
WinAPI CreateThread( arg arg );
```

This is the call any thread makes to create a new thread within its same address space. The first thread is created by the operating system, but any threads created subsequently are done using this call. There is typically an upper limit on the number of threads that can coexist in a single process, but the unit is high enough to never impose a practical restriction.

ExitThread()

```
WinAPI ExitThread( arg arg );
```

This call is the opposite of CreateThread(). The thread calling this function ceases to exist, and the call itself never returns to the calling process. All resources specifically held by this thread are thereby freed.

SuspendThread()

```
WinAPI SuspendThread( arg arg );
```

When this function is called the thread that is targeted is marked within the OS such that it will never be scheduled to run again. This is, of course, a very dangerous call to make and is usually done only by utility programs and debuggers. This sets up a situation where other threads depend on some resource held by the thread just suspended, which in turn will suspend them. The cascading effect can cause the entire process to become deadlocked.

ResumeThread()

```
WinAPI ResumeThread( arg arg );
```

This is the call to undo the effects of the SuspendThread() call. Again, it is usually programs like debuggers and very specialized utilities that would do this. Users of debuggers may actually have direct access to this call via a "freeze / thaw" capability where specific threads can be suspended and resumed at the programmer's direct request.

TerminateThread()

```
WinAPI TerminateThread( arg arg );
```

More extreme than ExitThread(), this call is not used by normal programs and is provided for OS and system-level utilities (debuggers again, of course) to have complete control over possibly errant threads.

Thread-created Problems (Bugs)

In the previous list of OS thread-control APIs, I hinted that sometimes these APIs themselves cause problems. Even without the ability to suspend and resume threads that can cause total deadlock, programs trying to use threads in a very natural and controlled way can get into a lot of difficulty. This is partly because threads add complexity and that translates into more bugs. Threads represent a completely new paradigm, and that causes a dramatic increase in bugs and confusion. This section discusses typical classes of bugs that occur in multithreaded applications. I will assume throughout this section that the underlying system is a uniprocessor so that only one thread at a time actually is running. All issues I raise here are even more "interesting" on a multi-processor.

Data Corruption

The first class of problems is data corruption. Because each thread operates in the same shared address space of the process, if one thread modifies data that another thread was counting on not changing, this is a bug. Because it is not deterministic which thread runs when, these types of bugs do not happen in the same consistent fashion, which makes them extremely difficult to track down. It is a serious logic and design flaw in the first place for the programmer to allow one thread to assume shared data won't be modified by other threads. In this case, *thread local storage* should be used to ensure that data really is private to a particular thread and no other thread can see this data, much less modify it.

Inadvertent Data Sharing

Because the vast majority of programs and programmers operate—and have operated for decades—in a single threaded environment, it is natural for people to think in these terms. This leads to thinking that the data the program is using now is not going to change in any unpredictable fashion. It also leads to thinking that sequences of steps must be taken one after the other. But once the environment is multithreaded, data is shared; as threads are switched in and out of the processor, steps that seem sequential in the source code are not operated on in that way. Programmers who build or work with operating systems and highly asynchronous event-based systems code learn to deal with this kind of asynchronous behavior—behavior that will become more prevalent in all applications.

Synchronization

Multithreaded applications naturally have synchronization points that force one thread to wait for another thread to finish its task. As described above, numerous types of objects and events are used for synchronization, depending on the application. Special operating system calls are used to force the calling thread to block if the object on which it wants to synchronize is not yet available. The OS call `WaitForSingleObject()` in Win32 is such a call. This call does not return—thus is considered *blocking*—until the object in question is available. The thread on which we are waiting will presumably make the corresponding OS call `SetEvent()` or `ReleaseSemaphore()` to notify the waiting thread that the work on which it depends is complete.

Frequently these kinds of synchronizations are *protection* for shared data that should not be modified until some necessary piece of work is complete. If the *producer* has not yet completed and therefore *signaled* its completion by releasing any waiting threads, but the *consumer* proceeds anyway, a bad situation—a.k.a. a bug—is created because the shared data is now corrupted or has not yet been updated for valid consumption.

Deadlock

The worst situation occurs when two or more threads find themselves in a mutually unsatisfiable situation. To be explicit, if thread A is waiting on thread B and thread B is waiting on thread A, neither thread can ever run again and the application is deadlocked. Unfortunately, because most PC applications grab OS resources that the system itself needs to be freed in a reasonable amount of time, a deadlocked application can and does frequently bring down the entire operating system, requiring a time-consuming (and data-losing) reboot. Fortunately, PC operating systems are getting more robust and with NT, this is no longer the case.

OS Inadequacies

Even with thread-specific execution control, user-accessible thread freeze and thaw, and thread-specific breakpoints there is a lot of complexity (and therefore potential bugs) associated with multithreaded applications that is not supported by debuggers or their host operating systems. One important hole already mentioned is the lack of any debug notification when a thread blocks (that is, becomes unrunnable due to its waiting for some other thread in the same process). This sort of notification would allow the debugger to stop the debuggee definitively and return control to the user with the clear message that the thread he or she is focused on is no longer running. Short of that, some sort of time-out would have to be used, a step that is always fraught with difficulties. Another hole is that there is no clear answer to the user's question "So what is this thread waiting for?" One reason this is such a hard question to answer is that it is not usually possible to obtain a stack-trace for a thread blocked in a system call because no stack frame is generated on a syscall.

In multi-threaded applications synchronization problems will be common. As we gain more experience with multithreaded applications we will find programming and debugging techniques to help avoid and detect these kinds of problems. Debuggers need to provide all the support possible to get started building next-generation multithreaded applications.

Threads Impact on Debugger Architecture

When built for and on a multithreaded system, usually the debugger itself is multithreaded, with one thread dedicated to the execution of the debuggee process and one or more processing all UI-related events. The dedicated debuggee thread spends most of its time in a `WaitForDe-bugEvent()`[1] call that will return only when the debuggee process stops for some reason.

Thread-specific OS Events

There are several possible DEBUG_EVENTs that relate specifically to threads and require that the debugger internally modify its internal thread-related data structures. The following sections will describe them.

EXCEPTION_DEBUG_EVENT

Exceptions can be divide-by-zero, illegal memory reference, hit a breakpoint, complete single-step, or the like. These occur in one and only one thread at a time and cause the entire debuggee to stop. This happens because all threads but one are "suspended" at a given moment of time, and it is the one single

---

[1] Here we will use examples from MS Win32's debug API.

thread currently active on the processor that gets or generates the exception that causes this event.

CREATE_THREAD_DEBUG_EVENT

This event is generated whenever a new thread is created in the process being debugged (due to a call to `CreateThread()`) or once for each thread that already exists when the debugger "attaches" to an existing process. As with `CREATE_PROCESS_DEBUG_EVENT`, this event allows the debugger to set up any thread-specific data structures when the thread is first created but has not yet been allowed to execute even one instruction.

CREATE_PROCESS_DEBUG_EVENT

This event is generated whenever a new process is created in a process being debugged or when the debugger "attaches" to an existing process. This event allows the debugger to initialize its process-specific internal data structures before any further debugging activity occurs.

EXIT_THREAD_DEBUG_EVENT

This event is generated whenever a thread in the process being debugged exits (except for the last thread in a process). This is the inverse of `CRE-ATE_THREAD_DEBUG_EVENT` and allows for cleanup of internal structures as threads are destroyed and can no longer generate any more events or execute any more instructions.

EXIT_PROCESS_DEBUG_EVENT

As with `EXIT_THREAD_DEBUG_EVENT`, this is the inverse of `CREATE_PROCESS_DEBUG_EVENT`. This occurs when the last thread of a process exits or some thread explicitly calls the OS call to terminate a process. The debugger must know when this happens so it knows that there is no longer a debuggee to control.

When a debug event occurs, the debuggee process has all of its threads suspended and the blocked thread of the debugger gets notified of the event through `WaitForDebugEvent()` returning. A specific thread in the debuggee is always identified as being the thread that actually received the event, but all the other threads are suspended as well.

There are, in addition to these debug events, a series of specialized OS APIs related to threads. Here we discuss two of them—`GetThreadContext()`

and `SetThreadContext()`—that are critical to a debugger's getting context information on the stopped thread.[2]

Thread-specific Program Context

When a debug event occurs the debugger is notified of which thread caused the event and the context for that thread is obtained using `GetThreadContext()`. Thread context contains all OS and CPU information about the thread, including its program counter, stack pointer, and the other processor register values. From this information the debugger can show the source or disassembled listing current execution point; it can build the procedure call stack back-trace; it can list the register set current values; and it can know the context for variable and memory inspection. All of this information is thread-specific because it comes directly from the thread context information that applies only to the thread that just caused the most recent debug event.

If the debugger (or the user of the debugger) wants to change any value of a register in the thread context it may do so and write it back to the debuggee using `SetThreadContext()`.

Thread Debugging Model

The addition of threads to the programming arsenal generates tremendous new capabilities and power as well as enormous complexity (HO 1982). This makes it imperative that debuggers are thread-aware; moreover, substantial and powerful new features are needed to deal with complex bugs in multi-threaded programs gone awry.

Isolating a Single Thread

At times, presenting the illusion that the separate threads are really independent is ideal. By this we mean that the user should be able to stop one thread in isolation from all other threads. The user interface should present certain

---

[2] In fact, all applications are assumed to be multithreaded so this is the only way to get debuggee context. The single-threaded application is simply a process that happens to only one thread on which to get context information.

views that are thread-specific and that can be changed to view other threads. This allows the programmer to view two different threads simultaneously, along with all the context of each thread. Included in the context view should be source view, stack, local variables, and thread local storage all nicely tied together. Once viewing two or more threads simultaneously, the user will want to act on one thread and then another independently.

However, since when the process is running, all threads are runnable but only one actually has the CPU and causes the next stop, any thread may be the next to stop. So what does the debugger show in its source view? Does it track one and only one thread or bounce around to that thread that most recently stopped? To provide the illusion of separate independent threads leads to a statement step that applies to one and only one thread in the debuggee. Similarly, a thread-specific run isolates only one thread to run to the next breakpoint or exception. On other occasions, the program needs to run unconstrained by debugger control over individual threads.

User Freeze/Thaw of Threads

The freeze/thaw functionality of the QS needs to be exposed to the user so sometimes all but two threads are frozen, for example. This gives users adequate flexibility over control of their program's threads. Now, a user can step a single thread, run a single thread, control precisely which threads are frozen, and run or step all non-frozen threads.

The debugger controls threads through thread control APIs that typically include a freeze (or suspend) function and the inverse. If the debugger needs to run one thread in isolation, it must make sure all unaffected threads are frozen. Now the debug API to run will only affect the single unfrozen thread. The debug step API always affects only a single thread because at the instruction level executing only a single instruction in a single thread makes sense. When only a single thread is executing it is very likely that this thread will block because it is usually operating in cooperation with the other threads and will probably synchronize with them at some point, which will result in thread blocking. This means that multithreaded debuggers must have a very reliable, user-accessible stop mechanism. A solution to this problem would be for the OS to provide an exception when threads become blocked. However, no OS yet provides this.

Source-Stepping

The non-thread-specific source-step has the debugger freeze no threads and run the source-step algorithm as previously presented. Any thread, at the OS scheduler's control, that stops at a breakpointable statement, user-level breakpoint, or exception will declare the step operation complete. Actually, this changes the meaning of step slightly but significantly. Now, instead of *execute to the next line of source in my textual source view*, it is *execute until some thread hits the next source statement in its context*. Now, due to the nature of thread-switching timing, a debugger is much more intrusive than in other areas.

Breakpointing

Because breakpoints are special instructions placed in the executable text, they are not intrinsically thread-specific. Any thread that executes the breakpoint instruction will get the special breakpoint exception that will stop the current thread as well as all the threads of its process. The illusion that threads are independent is so valuable, however, that providing thread-specific breakpoints may be important. All that is required is a test at the time a breakpoint is hit to see which thread just executed the breakpoint instruction. If it is not the user-specified thread, continue execution via the standard four steps:

1. Replace breakpoint instruction with the original instruction.

2. Machine single-step over that instruction.

3. Re-insert the breakpoint instruction.

4. Continue the debuggee thread that stopped full speed.

Debugging GUI Applications

Graphical User Interface (GUI) Applications

The key to GUI applications is that they are *event-driven*. These events are time-independent *messages*—one for each different event. Mouse-down, mouse-up, keyboard input, focus changes (Z-ordering) are examples of events that each have special messages. There are also dedicated messages for higher level constructs like dialog boxes, combo boxes, edit boxes, menus, and so on. Special procedures written by the user but presented to and called by the *system* get invoked as these events occur. These special procedures are called *window procedures* in Windows and PM-based systems. The same concept exists in X-based UNIX systems as well. GUI applications, including a GUI debugger, are completely dependent on these events (messages) for their correct behavior; if messages are not properly processed bad behavior will result—such as complete unresponsiveness or a "hang." Thus, tracking how these messages get processed is a frequent task for someone debugging a GUI application.

An important distinction should be noted between the operating system and the window manager. The operating system—as with UNIX—may have a robust debugging API in place and yet if the window manager does not allow a context switch to occur from one GUI application to another *at any time*, the user will be unable to debug effectively. As noted earlier, Windows 3.1 and

OS/2 both had these issues making debuggers on these systems more intrusive and much less robust than users find necessary. A well-designed GUI window manager would allow a context switch to occur at any point. But, in practice, all these systems fail in some situations, and the end result is a "hang" that requires a reboot. This makes debugging these types of applications unreliable when the bug involves advanced interactions with the windowing system. It has led some users to opt for a remote dumb terminal to get the debugger out of the way of this kind of complex GUI context switching.

The Heisenberg Principle in GUI Debuggers

The Heisenberg Principle refers to how difficult it is to completely measure and observe a system without the observation itself perturbing the system and changing its behavior. It is an extremely important principle for debuggers to fully understand and be vigilant about. GUI debuggers attempting to debug event-based bugs in GUI applications have enormous problems in this regard. The debugger changes the layout of memory, changes the number of threads and processes in tables in the operating system's data structures, changes the scheduling behavior, and changes the ordering and volume of windows messages traveling through the system. Also, focus issues, repaints and the like change because the debugger windows and the debuggee windows now interact in ways that do not occur when the debuggee is run independently. All of these things and more can affect the debuggee. In the extreme case, a bug can either appear or disappear only when run by the debugger. We work hard to avoid this situation but it is sometimes unavoidable. This is why text-based debuggers that do not use messages are so valuable. A second machine controlling its debuggee can also solve this problem.[1]

Architectural Issues

Single Input Queue

Any GUI application has a message loop, or more than one, that processes GUI events. So does the GUI debugger. Some window systems have only one

---

[1] Remote debugging across the network is the best long-term solution as this prepares the debugger to be used in a distributed application setting, which will be getting more and more common.

input queue shared by all applications. Each message is identified by the window it is destined for unless it is a broadcast message to all windows. Because of this, the GUI debugger and the GUI debuggee will interact sometimes in unfavorable ways. If the application is running and the user clicks the mouse on a GUI debugger window, both the GUI debugger and the debuggee will be affected. The debuggee will be notified that it is losing focus and is having its window(s) Z-order changed. Many Windows messages are simply posted to a queue for the target window, but some messages require the sender to wait for a reply from the recipient. Unfortunately, Windows 3.x contains a major flaw that occurs in this scenario. The click on the GUI debugger window caused a 'reply requested' message to be sent to the debuggee. If a breakpoint stops the debuggee at that precise moment (easy because putting breakpoints on the main event processing functions is common), there is no reply to that 'reply requested' message, which will hang the sender. But the sender is the GUI debugger itself so it and the rest of the system is completely hung by this scenario. Numerous OS issues like this will come up for debugger designers. This may be because OS designers frequently consider debuggers an afterthought.[2] Additionally, there are very few debugger designers relative to the vast majority of OS consumers, so they are not paid much attention. The only workaround for the scenario presented is for the debugger to know very well that it is in trouble (easy because all the information needed is readily available) and that the debuggee must immediately be continued or terminated.

Soft Mode versus Hard Mode

Because the mass market PC window systems have been based on a single input queue system (Windows 3.x and OS/2 2.x), there is an important issue for debugging GUI applications on these less advanced windowing systems. At issue is whether normal processing of messages can proceed when the application is stopped—soft mode—or if the entire system needs to become locked to give exclusive control to the debugger—hard mode. **Soft mode** is a state in which the debugger takes over message processing for the child debuggee but otherwise all message processing for all other processes proceeds normally—the system, except for the debuggee, all appear to operate as they should. **Hard mode** is a special debugging state where only the debugger itself

---

[2] However, the user sees a failure in the debugger when the flaw is actually in the operating system.

gets any messages—all other tasks will be suspended. Hard mode is used whenever the debugger detects that the debuggee has the windowing system in a state that will not allow normal operation. This may happen if the debuggee is in the middle of receiving a Sent as opposed to a Posted message or if the debuggee is using non-reentrant system resources (like system menus). The way hard mode works is that the debugger makes a call to a `LockInput()` function. `LockInput()` does not allow the "locked" debuggee to be switched away from. Thus, once the debugger has locked input onto itself, no other application (notably the debuggee) will have an opportunity to run.

Desirable Features

Specific to GUI debugging, there are several features a debugger can and should provide that specifically aid debugging messages flowing to and from the GUI application.

Messagepoints

One important feature debuggers can provide specifically to aid the GUI application developer is called messagepoints or Windows Message Break-points. These are actually special "smart" breakpoints that are placed on event handlers where window messages are being processed and that know how to "crack" messages. Cracking messages is understanding the type of message being passed and determining the meaning and contents of that message's parameters. Further refinements usually include the ability to select which messages or classes of messages actually trigger the breakpoint to stop the application. Some of the messages may not cause a stop but instead might just be logged to some sort of textual log that records the events received and their time ordering.

Event Logging

Tracing the flow of events is frequently an important clue to erroneous behavior. A convenient mechanism to provide is an event-logging mecha-nism. It may be closely related to the messagepoints feature just mentioned. The debugger may place a special breakpoint at a key message-handling procedure to implement this, or it may "hook" into a system routine if the operating system supports that. In any case, the messages as they flow into and out of the debuggee are captured in some textual log as the application runs so that the user can peruse them later. Figure 10.1 shows a sample of message logging.

Other Desirable Features

A valuable utility called Winsight can and should be integrated into debuggers for GUI applications. The purpose is to discover the application's window tree, the properties of each window, and the message traffic addressed to each window. Additionally, when using a windowing class library such as OWL or MFC, a source of confusion is the control flow path taken when processing a particular message. This is especially confusing because the control flow may shift in and out of user written code. Inherent in the use of a class library is the use of derivation. The natural question the debugger should be able to answer is " what is done at what level of derivation?" A debugger could assist here by logging all entry points associated with the processing of a message for example.

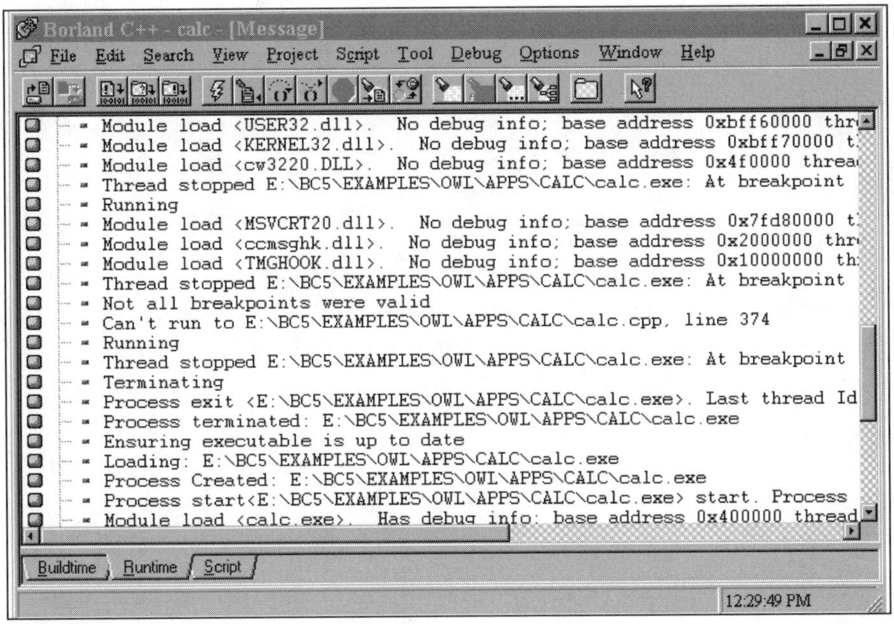

Figure 10.1

Message logging view.   *A list of messages along with their types is shown. User interface controls exist to "filter" down these messages to just the desired type.*

Specialized Debugger Applications

Memory (Heap) Corruption Bugs

One sort of difficult, but common bug is memory overruns. Detection of this sort of bug may occur a long time after and nowhere near its cause. This makes it a very difficult class of bug to track down. And the standard breakpoint/single-step/inspect scenario of debugging will not quickly help find the cause of this type of bug. Instead, some sort of memory view may be needed, especially if it can examine the special portion of memory where the program heap is located. Cooperation from the run-time library may be required to give the debugger a chance to correctly identify used versus free blocks of memory in the heap. And if the debugger knows the format of heap headers it can help detect where in the chain of used or free memory any corruption occurs. Watchpoints placed judiciously may help determine where in the program execution a detected corruption first occurs.

Integrated Memory and Resource Tracking

A tool such as CodeGuard—a debugging tool included with Borland C++
5.0—that is integrated into the compiler and run-time library, can give a very
high degree of run-time debugging and can check for a variety of common
(but usually difficult-to-detect) errors. The kinds of errors that this sort of
tool can automatically detect includes the following:

- Wild pointers, including array bounds and heap corruption

- Stack overflow

- Memory and resource (e.g. file handles, window handles) leaks

- Function call parameter validation

- API return failures (even when not programmatically checked)

- Exceptions

- Uninitialized data access

- Constructor/destructor pairing

For all functions that CodeGuard will support, wrapper functions are created
that serve three purposes: resource leak detection, parameter validation, and
heap protection. These wrapper functions override the original versions. The
new overridden version adds information to the CodeGuard database,
checks passed parameters, and calls the original function. On return, before
the user call-site is given control, error returns from the function are noted.

At run-time, CodeGuard logs and reports any errors detected. If the debugger is present these errors are shown via the debugger; otherwise, the errors
are logged to a file. Resources are tracked in a special-purpose database. It is
the responsibility of the wrapper functions to insert new resources into the
database with an associated handle and owner. As resources are freed the
handle and owner information is checked. And at program termination, all
unfreed resources are reported as "leaks."

Memory regions get special treatment. All allocations and frees of memory
are closely tracked. Any attempts to access memory outside of its designated
boundaries will cause an error that either is logged or will look like an exception within the debugger. In addition, special patterns are written into uninitialized memory blocks so that later as these blocks are used, references
that use this memory as pointers or handles will fail. This is similar to the
strategy in the early 1980s used by Berkeley for UNIX, whereby they forced

a non-zero value into virtual memory location 0 and suddenly masses of programs that had been behaving "correctly" suddenly broke horribly as all the programs that had de-referenced null pointers got a rude surprise.

In order to correctly track accesses into user data areas and to the stack, compiler support is needed. The compiler needs to emit special region information that allows CodeGuard at run-time to verify that all accesses to user data, including stack data, is not misbehaving and causing corruption.

Automatic Memory Corruption Detection

A completely different approach is used in tools like Nu-Mega's Bounds-Checker or a run-time library for error checking. This kind of tool inserts code into the executable and hooks certain critical run-time library calls such as `malloc()` and `free()`. In addition, it inserts special breakpoints in the executable that when hit cause the tool to make a series of special checks on sentinel memory values and other structures that alert the user to memory corruption problems. Unlike CodeGuard, BoundsChecker requires no recompilation or relinking.

Reverse Execution

A user often overshoots the desired position in a program by erroneously invoking the "step" or "continue" command one time too many. The ability to "undo" the most recent command or commands, sometimes described as "executing the program backward," is a seemingly appealing feature. But the cost may not be warranted.

The debugger must either record a trace of the execution of the program or checkpoint it periodically.

One method is to record a trace of each user-level command that alters the state of the child process. By command, I mean a function of the debugger that a user can selet such as "run to next breakpoint." The "undo" command reruns the program from the beginning, re-executing all the saved commands prior to the one the user wishes to stop at. This takes relatively little time during normal execution, but the "undo" operation itself may be very slow if it takes a long time to re-execute the program to the desired point. It may also fail if the program has side effects (such as the deletion of a file) that the debugger cannot reverse; this will cause the program to fail or to execute differently the second time.

Another method is to record a checkpoint of the state of the child process before performing each command that changes that state. The "undo" algorithm then restores the appropriate checkpoint. This may require the debugger to save a large amount of data, and it may make the normal execution of each command much slower. It does allow the program to run at full speed between commands, and it fails only if irreversible side effects occurred after the checkpoint in question.

Still another method is to trace the execution of the program at the machine level, as shown in Algorithm 11.1.

For this algorithm, the "undo" command must read the trace backward, restoring the recorded values as it does so, until it reaches the marker for the desired command. Some optimizations are possible (for example, the trace need only record the first change to a particular register or memory location following the user's command), but potentially it involves a very large

Algorithm 11.1 *Reverse execution*

Input Current instruction address.
Output Adequate state saved to allow reverse execution later.

```
if (a user command alters the child process) then {
    record a marker corresponding to this command;
    if the command modifies a value directly then {
        record the value to be modified;
        proceed with the modification;
    } else if the command causes the child to execute {
        for each instruction to be executed do {
            if this instruction represents an edge of the flow
            graph then
            {
                record its target address;
            } else if this instruction modifies a register or
            memory location then
            {
                record the address of the instruction and the
            value prior to modification;
                allow the instruction to execute normally;
            }
        } // end of do
    }
}
```

---

amount of information and makes normal execution much slower. Like the other methods, it can fail if the program has irreversible side effects, but it is better able to detect these side effects and warn the user about them (for example, by noticing that the program is executing an instruction that traps to the operating system).

Because each method has serious limitations, success in any particular situation depends on whether the user encounters those limitations. The first method works well provided the program has no side effects and does not take long to execute; the third method works well if restricted to situations where the user is stepping the program a single instruction at a time, so that its effect on execution speed is hidden. It's probably wise to let the user disable this feature in any case. In general, I believe this feature is so much work and still fraught with so much error that is not worth the engineering investment. It may be better to build an interpreter and allow a function to be interpreted while the rest of the code is run natively at full speed. Implementing reverse execution is much simpler on an interpreter because the interpreter affords a completely controlled run-time environment where complete state snapshots and checkpoints are feasible.

Remote Debugging

Remote debugging is very useful to avoid the Heisenberg Principle and get the debugger completely separated from the target application. Because no debugger is using resources on the target machine there is almost no effect on the target process that could change its behavior. Additionally, errors in the remote program cannot impact the debugger and confuse it. Finally, using this technique you can debug very large programs and programs that destabilize the operating system. In certain embedded application situations there is no choice but to debug the embedded system remotely from a standard PC. Many commercial debuggers provide some sort of remote debugging capability as do kernel debuggers, as we have just seen.

The remote debugger needs a small proxy debugger on the target machine that has the basic hooks into both the operating system and the application to enable debugging. But it can be kept extremely simple because it needs no user interaction logic and no user interface elements whatsoever. The host debugger, instead of creating a process and expecting the OS to notify it of debugging events, will instead send and receive commands via a serial cable or the network to the target machine. This architecture is very simple, robust, and easy to implement; however, it suffers from poor performance. Everywhere the debugger might initiate an action with the debuggee or wait for an event from the debuggee it simply needs instead to communicate over the serial line to the target stub debugger via an established protocol. And using a language like C++ makes this especially simple because the user needs only to create virtual methods for all the necessary debugger communications and then implement each of them twice, once for the local debugging and once for the remote.

Important tradeoffs must be considered when designing a remote debugging system. Where does the source live? Where does the executable get created on the local or remote system? Where should evaluation be done? And where are symbols managed? These are not easy questions to answer but their answers lead to very different design decisions and debuggee management.

Distributed Object Debugging

Applications constructed out of distributed objects will present new challenges for debuggers. The programmer is thinking in terms of desired behavior and functionality delivered to customers, not about the details of what object resides where. This is similar to the way programmers think about DLLs: There is a moment when the design of what goes in the DLL is important but from then on, the fact that some function is in a DLL is immaterial—the debugger should make this as transparent as possible. The same fact holds for distributed objects. There was a point where the developer made a conscious decision to distribute the application's objects in a certain way but once that decision has been made, the debugger should not make the details of the communication between objects visible—unless this is what is being debugged.

This kind of transparent remote object debugging leads to additional burdens on the debugger. When this application steps into the call to a remote object function invocation, the debugger should stop the remote process, running on a remote server across the network, at the first statement in the remote function call. And when that function returns, the debugger step should next stop back in the calling site on the client side of the network interface.

RPC is one mechanism used to implement distributed objects such as distributed COM objects in Network OLE from Microsoft. Given special notifications that a remote call is about to occur, plus the ability to attach over the network to the remote object, the debugger is able to provide the necessary functionality. Specifically, the debugger is subject to six notifications that occur during the round-trip of one COM RPC call. Three of these occur on the client side, and three occur on the server side. The following is a distillation of information from a specification of Network COM (MICROSOFT 1995).

Distributed object debugging is a much more complex issue and one that is getting to be on the top of the "to do" list for all development tool builders. This is because the era of distributed objects is just about to begin. Several approaches to distributed objects exist. RPC (Remote Procedure Call) was the original approach. Using RPC, calls to functions performed locally are transformed into requests passed over the network to a proxy object on the remote end that reformulates these into the call to the desired function and then captures the result and passes it back to the initiator. The more sophisticated distributed object methods such as DSOM (Distributed System Object Model) and Network OLE (a.k.a. Distributed OLE) use RPC internally so these debugging discussions can focus on RPC and cover all these approaches.

Scenario: Single-step into Remote Function

Assume an application that has some object or objects residing remotely is being debugged. The developer is about to single-step into a function that happens to exist on the remote machine. If this function were not remote, the step would next stop execution at the first source statement inside the function. This is what should happen in the case where it is remote as well. The developer has to assume the infrastructure of the RPC is essentially part of the operating system and is not something to worry about—it should be transparent to the debugging process. Thus, the scenarios that need to be considered are stepping from the client to the server (where there may not yet be a debugger active) and stopping in a breakpoint first in the server and then stepping off the end of a function back to the client (where, again, there may not yet be a debugger active). In both cases, as you can see, it may be necessary to activate a new debugger after the fact. Thus, the architecture must support the messages necessary to activate a new debugger remotely, control that debugger remotely, get all the necessary notifications and data about the process remotely, and be able even to create a new debugger locally if one is not already active.

RPC Debugging Implementation

Both the client and server sides of the RPC implementation must provide hooks for a debugger. Through these hooks, the debugger must be able to get information that a transfer from client to server or vice versa is about to occur. A total of six notifications occur in the round-trip of one RPC call.

When a call to a remote function is made on the client side, the interface proxy is actually executed. This proxy marshals the arguments into a buffer and calls over to the server. As the interface proxy is acquiring the buffer into which it will marshal the function arguments, it checks to see if a debugger is active [*first notification*] and, if so, it calls the first notification function that an RPC transfer is about to happen. The debugger is given a chance to add how much space it wants in the same buffer to be used to control the remote debugger proxy. After the arguments are marshaled into the buffer and as the interface proxy is about to send the buffer, it again checks to see if a debugger is active [*second notification*] and, if so, it allows the debugger now to fill its portion of the buffer with commands to the remote debugger.

Now on the server side where this buffer of marshaled data with debugging commands is being received, if there is a non-zero debug command portion of the buffer or if debugging is already enabled on the server side [*third notification*], then either the debugger is started or the existing one is then notified to process its command. At this point the arguments are unmarshalled and the function is invoked as requested. But the debugger has set special breakpoints that cause the executing function to stop as if it had single-stepped. Still on the server side, the return information is marshalled to be sent back to the client. Again, if there is a debugger active [*fourth notification*] the debugger is given the opportunity to make space in the buffer for its command-response back to the client buffer. And after the return arguments are marshalled, again [*fifth notification*] the debugger places its command-response into the buffer. The buffer now returns to the client side.

Back on the client side, as the RPC mechanism is about to return control to the interface proxy, if a debugger is active or if the returning buffer contains debugger commands [*sixth notification*], the debugger is given control to deal with the command-response from the remote debugger.

Run-time Debugging Aids

In this section, I briefly touch on a specialized type of debugger that is involved at run-time. I describe a type of in-circuit emulator call Soft-ICE, window message monitors called Spy and Winsight and post-mortem analyzers called Dr. Watson and Winspector.

In-circuit Emulators

Soft-ICE uses built-in facilities in the x86 CPUs to provide in-circuit emulation (ICE)-like debugging functionality. To implement memory access breakpoints (which we call watchpoints), Soft-ICE uses the paging and debug registers built in to the 386 processor (which other debuggers use as well). The key to how Soft-ICE works is that it runs before Windows runs—in fact, Enhanced mode Windows runs on top of Soft-ICE. Soft-ICE can set a wide variety of breakpoints, can disassemble code, and can control and inspect programs running on Windows as well as Windows itself [SCHULMAN 1992]. Soft-ICE is a low-level debugging tool very useful for debugging low-level Windows interactions but is much less efficient in tracking down bugs in high-level programs, as compared to the source-level debuggers discussed throughout the rest of this book.

Spy Debuggers

Typical of message or event-based systems such as Windows, OS/2, or Motif is the need to monitor and track all events in the system, especially those relating to the application being debugged. This kind of tool allows one to track all messages and what actions cause which messages. Tools in this category include Spy and Winsight. Figure 11.1 shows the output from Winsight. Messages are usually broken down into categories such as *mouse, keyboard,* and *user-defined*. The benefit of such tools is that in operating systems (or OS-like subsystems like Presentation Manager and Motif) that have graphical user interface systems built-in, messages control all applications, those applications' interactions with the operating system, and those applications'

Figure 11.1

Winsight message spying.

interactions with the user. Given this, and given how difficult event-based programming is to get right, messages frequently go awry in applications and need to be debugged. Being able to monitor all system messages and their handling in the running applications can be critical to solving these kinds of problems. Most modern debuggers include a facility to watch messages interacting with the program or programs that instance of the debugger is currently controlling but do not usually monitor all messages within the entire operating system.

Post-mortem Debuggers

There is a class of diagnostic utilities that allow inspection of program "dumps" after they have crashed. These are called post-mortem debuggers. Dr. Watson and Winspector are diagnostic utilities closely related to debuggers. Unlike standard debuggers, tools like Dr. Watson and Winspector are not tied to one running application. Instead, these kinds of utilities monitor the operating system and its interactions with all running processes. This way, if a failure occurs that affects the operating system, the user can determine which application or combination of applications caused the problem. Winspector is particularly powerful because it provides the call stack, functions, and procedure names within the call stack, CPU register values, disassembly of the instructions, and pertinent Windows information related to the unhandled exception. Because operating systems are getting more robust and protect themselves and other running applications from errant programs, these kinds of tools will have less and less utility.

Parallel Architecture Debugging

Parallel processing uses multiple independent processing units joined together in some network topology to speed execution of a single program (FOX 1987). The push for parallel processing is expected to increase as single-processor computers get more difficult and expensive to build. In some cases we have or will have shortly run into insurmountable physical barriers. Fundamentally diverging architectures—called Single Instruction Multiple Data (SIMD) and Multiple Instruction Multiple Data (MIMD)—exist as ways to provide parallelism. SIMD—also sometimes referred to as massively parallel—has a large number, typically over 1000, relatively simple processors all acting in lock-step on different data but executing the same instruction at the same time on that data. MIMD has a relatively smaller number of more complex, even standard off-the-shelf microprocessors, each operating on independent threads of execution, occasionally synchronizing with each other to complete a single program. Debugging problems on these architectures are numerous and difficult.

Huge Data Inspection Problems

One of the foremost issues facing the debugger designer on parallel architectures, especially massively parallel architectures, is the amount of data involved in typical applications that the user may want to inspect or visualize. Massively parallel machines and particularly, data parallel variants of these, are by nature very data-intensive. Typical data inspection in standard architectures uses a textual display, possibly adding a nice graphical layout, which is completely impractical when the amount of data is 100,000 or even a million times greater. For one thing, responsiveness if using the same approach for data access would be unacceptable. Imagine if, when you go to inspect a variable used as an index into local data stored at each processor, you had 32,000 values displayed for you. At the very least, an incremental approach to data access must be employed. In addition, some sort of graphical form of data inspection is a dramatic improvement to the user because the graphical representation has a much higher information content, pixel for pixel.

A useful SIMD application to illustrate my point is seismic data reduction. Each of 32, 768 processors has 4k of local data storing information about what was recorded abut a unique location in the earth in 3-D space. The data was initially filled in from sonar seismic data sensing (thumping the ground hard and listening to the echo). Now the algorithm starts looking for patterns to determine if there might be a large space containing a valuble resource such as gas or oil. Each processor starts comparing its local data to its neighbors doing smoothing, error correction, noise reduction and the like. But an error in the algorithm corrupts some data and the defect needs to be located and corrected. This is now the task facing the debugger and its user with 32, 768 times 4,000 data locations to examine as the program is break-pointed or single-stepped.

One approach used in massively parallel debuggers is a simple two-dimensional slice through the data where a dot is placed at the x,y position of the data element if the value stored there when applied to a simple user-specified expression resolves to true. The simplest expression might be x == <value>, but thresholding works better for most queries. Color is useful, too. In debugging situations, frequently what is desired is a quick visual inspection for out-of-range values. Values outside some specified range can be displayed in bright red to stand out.

The goal is to present large quantities of data in such a fashion that patterns that point to problems can be discerned and isolated quickly. Arrays in FOR-TRAN and parallel data in MPL are mapped onto the array of SIMD processors by the compilers. There the data elements interact with other data in other processors. Over the course of a computation, the data may form distinct patterns, depending on the algorithms being applied. The user model is to take a snapshot at some critical moment and to view this data to search for patterns or anomalies that point to problems. A simple transformation on the data can allow its presentation graphically as color or gray-scale dots.

And, in the case of FORTRAN arrays, a subselection step can provide a 2D slice of data that is presentable on a bit-mapped screen.

Various ways to subselect huge data sets are needed to make them manageable. FORTRAN programs written for parallel machines tend to use arrays that are extremely large. One obvious way to slice the data is to retrieve only that subset of the data currently viewed and only as the view is moved is more data retrieved—another instance of lazy data retrieval. This is an application of the deferred decision theme that impacts the user by providing better interactive response. Using this technique, scrolling through massively parallel data sets is possible and quite effective. Another technique of subselection is direct use of FORTRAN 90 triplet array slice notation such that the user specifies start, end, and step increment throughout the range to cut down on the amount of data to view.

SIMD Architecture Issues
Multiprocessor Breakpoint Issues

On some multiprocessor architectures, source statements generate code for two or more cooperating processors. An example of this is the MasPar family of SIMD Massively Parallel machines [NICKOLLS 1990, BLANK 1990]. There the scalar front-end and the control unit for the parallel array both receive instructions generated from a single FORTRAN 90 source statement. An issue for a debugger then is the correct handling of a stop at a breakpoint set on such a statement. This may mean that a logical breakpoint may need to be able to refer to two quite different physical breakpoints on two distinctly different processors. Further, it may be necessary for the debugger to individually control the two different processors so that both match up with the specified physical address in a logical breakpoint. And this may imply that when one processor activates its physical breakpoint the logical activation must wait until the second physical activation occurs. Only then, when both sides are stopped at the correct locations, is the breakpoint ready to report a stop to the user.

Multiprocessor Source Stepping

Multiprocessors will be increasingly prevalent in the future. This will complicate many debuggers' algorithms, especially single-step. Loosely cooperating processors can be debugged in a fashion similar to debugging separate processes on today's uniprocessors, albeit with interesting synchronization problems to work out. But it is the very closely cooperating multiprocessors that will provide the most challenge to debuggers. The close level of cooperation I refer to occurs when a single line of source code emits code that will be executed either synchronously or asynchronously on more than one processor. The current and next generations of massively parallel SIMD architectures fall into this category [ROSENBERG 1988]. Execution can be thought of as passing the baton of control from one processor to another. Usually, one processor passes the baton and idles until the other processor passes the baton back (synchronous). The asynchronous case can be simplified to conform to the synchronous one.

Single-step must follow this baton. This is only possible if the single-step algorithm focuses exclusively on the active processor and holds the other processor fixed, unable to execute. Now as the baton is about to be passed from one processor to the other the debugger must be notified. This is called stall detection. The debugger gets a notification that the currently executing processor is about to stall just as it gets notifications about breakpoints. The stalling processor is now stopped so it cannot execute any further, and the single-step algorithm proceeds on the newly activated processor. In other respects the single-step algorithm behaves normally. It still looks at each stopping point to see if execution has advanced to a breakpointable statement. And special breakpoints are still used to proceed rapidly over large blocks of instructions. The MasPar MP-1 and MP-2 debugger utilizes the stall detection built into the firmware of the MasPar architecture to implement this modified single-step algorithm. A FORTRAN 90 compiler generates code simultaneously for a standard workstation front-end and the special SIMD array of processors. Source-level single-step may require stepping through front-end code that switches to SIMD array code and back several times before completing the step.

c h a p t e r 12

Debugging Optimized Code

Much prior work has been done on debugging optimized code on this subject [COPPERMAN 1993; COUTANT 1988; HENNESSEY 1982; ZELWEGGER 1984]. At issue is the importance of compiler optimizations for better performing final applications and how these optimizations are in direct conflict with the goal of a debugger in trying to present as much truthful information about the application as possible back to the developer. In this chapter I will discuss typical and high-impact optimizations and how RISC architectures make these optimizations less and less optional. Then I will discuss the problems these optimizations present for source-level symbolic debuggers. Yet, the goal must be to keep as close to the same optimizations as will be used in the shipping application as possible. I will briefly examine the optimizations that work well with debuggers and finally will discuss the new techniques that must be applied to next-generation debuggers to allow them to handle higher and higher levels of optimizations in applications.

Importance of Optimizations

Optimizations are transformations performed on a program to decrease execution time or, in some cases, to decrease space utilization. These transformations are performed by the compiler or by a related component during the compilation process. Compilation involves transforming human-readable source text into machine-executable binary code. Optimizations can be performed at any of the stages of the overall compilation process. The goal of the optimizations is to create a program that has exactly the same behavior as the un-optimized version but executes faster or takes up less space in memory and on disk, or both.

Optimizations may cause statements to be moved or deleted. Variables may be assigned at different times and may be assigned to registers as opposed to memory as compared to the un-optimized version. The flow of control of the program may be changed from the un-optimized version. Unused variables may be eliminated.

The effects of these kinds of optimizations can be quite significant in performance or space requirements, or both. For example, if a variable assignment located inside a loop is moved outside the loop, the effect will be dramatic because that assignment will not occur for any iterations of the loop. If that assignment is one of only two inside that loop, moving it outside the loop will create a 2× speedup of that loop at run-time.

Impact of RISC on Optimizations

RISC chips have fewer instructions that execute faster. But to get these fixed-size instructions to execute as fast as possible, there must be a minimum of memory accesses. RISC machines tend to have a larger number of registers and tend to have much simpler memory access models, which leads to wanting to keep as much data as possible in the much faster registers. Additionally, RISC machines in use today also employ a variety of other techniques to minimize memory accesses. One of these is branch delay slots, as described earlier in the section on the MIPS architecture.

The RISC architecture requires and benefits from a much higher degree of optimization than non-RISC chips. Optimizations that focus on minimizing memory accesses and maximizing how long crucial variables are kept in registers give the biggest payoff. The performance penalty from not optimizing for register usage is so severe on RISC architectures that users do not want to turn off these optimizations, not even during debugging. Fortunately, these *register allocation optimizations* are among the most straightforward optimizations to handle within the debugger (see "Optimizations Debugged in Practice," later in this chapter).

Difficulty of Debugging Optimized Programs

When statements move during optimization, if the compiler and debugger are not in very close communication about what changed, the debugger will not be prepared to aid the user in setting a breakpoint on that statement. Or worse, the debugger will not be truthful and will actually set the breakpoint at the wrong location. The same issue arises when an exception occurs and the debugger is responsible for reporting the source location for that exception and again, it may not be truthful or be able to track down this moved source statement at all. If variables get moved during optimization, either to new memory locations or to registers, or if they get eliminated completely, the debugger may not be able to report their values when the user needs them.

Why Keep Optimizations during Debugging?

In spite of best efforts, optimizations can and do frequently change the behavior of a program. Performance problems become bugs if they are severe enough. The better the performance of the application during debugging, the faster the debugging process will proceed. These reasons, as well as others, strongly motivate application developers to want to keep the optimizations on during debugging. However, the normal development paradigm has always been to turn off optimizations during debugging; when the application is fully debugged and ready to be deployed, the full optimizations are turned on and the application is shipped to its end users. With the advent of RISC processors the motivation for debuggers that can handle significant compiler optimizations becomes even more compelling. A side benefit of debuggers that can "un-wind" a fairly high degree of optimizations is that users would be more exposed to and would therefore learn more about and appreciate these kinds of optimizations.

Quick Overview of Compiler Optimizations

In this book we will not discuss the details of any particular compiler optimizations—for that treatment refer to either AHO 1986 or FISCHER 1988. In this section we will list some common optimizations and briefly explain what these optimizations do to the code and how that might affect the debugger.

Code Hoisting

If an expression is very busy at a particular point, the expression can be computed and its value saved for subsequent use. This may not save time, but it may by very effective in saving space because an expression that might have been computed many times (but is invariant) is now computed once in a common ancestor basic block. Because this is a form of code motion, the debugger will be fooled into thinking it can present the expression at the point where it was originally computed, but, in fact, its value was precomputed. The debugger would need to be told the new location of the code for this hoisted expression.

Code Motion

An important and very effective optimization is the movement of code that is invariant from within the loop to outside the loop. If an expression will evaluate to the same value no matter how many times the loop is executed, the expression inside the loop is wasted time. A good example of this would be:

```
while ( i <= limit-2 ) // note limit-2 never changes
```

Code motion would instead write this as two statements that would execute much faster and would be especially beneficial if the loop is executed a large number of times.

```
t = limit-2;
while (i <= t )
```

This would be a difficult situation for a debugger because as the user goes to inspect limit at the original location, the expression involving limit is no longer there. However, if the debugger is adequately informed about what happened, this could be debugged correctly.

Constant Folding

The process of deducing at compile time that the value of an expression is a constant and saving that constant for use instead of the expression is called constant folding. This saves both time and space. Because the standard technique for constant folding is to detect the expression is a constant, evaluate the expression by executing the code for it in place within the compiler, and replace uses of it with the result, the debugger will not ever be able to find the code for this expression. This means that the expression cannot be evaluated at debug time and that the components of the expression cannot be examined.

Copy Propagation

We may choose to delay an assignment (or copy) from one variable to another and instead use the right-hand value subsequently wherever the left-hand value had originally been used.

```
A = B;
/* below here everywhere A is used substitute B and
 * try to eliminate the need for this assignment at all
 */
```

The purpose of this is to eliminate the need to make the original assignment at all and thereby eliminate some code we didn't need. The debugger can easily get lost on this optimization because A may have no value in it at all (and may be at risk of being eliminated itself).

Dead Store Elimination

If a variable or expression is stored in either a new variable or a register but is never used again after that, the store was useless and should not occur. Obviously, if the store is eliminated and the debugger is asked to inspect the variable or register where the store was targeted, it will either find the wrong value or won't be able to report at all. This can be handled the same way that standard register allocation optimizations are handled.

Dead Variable Elimination

Similar to dead store elimination—which is about removing unneeded code that modifies either a memory location or a register—dead variable elimination is about removing the use of a variable (and any associated memory assigned to it) that is never used after a certain point. The best that we can hope for from a debugger in this case is that when inspected, the debugger reports a dead variable as being "dead" and perhaps gives us a pointer to where it was last live.

Common Subexpression Elimination

When a series of expressions contains common components or subexpressions, these subexpressions can be combined and not recomputed at runtime, saving both time and space. The issue for the debugger is that when the user goes to examine the components of the expression where the subexpression has been changed by the compiler, unless the compiler went to great lengths to tell the debugger what it should do to compensate, the user will not get truthful results.

Register Allocation

Because the time to store and access variables from registers is a fraction of the time needed for accessing RAM memory (especially on RISC architectures) it is so advantageous to perform this optimization that many compilers do not even have an option of turning it off, as they do for other optimizations. The resulting differences in performance are dramatic. This is a fairly easy optimization on which compiler and debugger can work very effectively together and give the user excellent and truthful results. We will discuss shortly how this optimization is handled in modern compilers and debuggers.

Induction Variable Elimination

An induction variable is a variable within a loop that each time through the loop is modified by a constant amount. This is very common and as with all other analysis of loops, can have big payoffs on loops with very high iteration counts. It is possible in many cases to eliminate one induction variable because it is related to another and one can always be derived from the other. If the induction elimination expression is maintained by the compiler and how to reverse it is made clear to the debugger this type of optimization can be unwound during debugging. I know of no commercial compiler/debugger combination that does so today.

In-line Procedure Expansion

This type of optimization was called "call-by-name" in Algol. The procedure is treated as if it were a macro: Its body is substituted for the call in the caller with the actual parameters literally substituting for the formal parameters. This has become very prevalent with C++ because there are so many small methods that may need very high performance (such as constructors and overloaded operators). There is always a very important (and potentially very expensive) trade-off between speed and space on this type of expansion because an in-line'd procedure may get in-line'd every time it is used. This is a very difficult problem for a debugger. Most debuggers are told nothing by the compiler, and it's left up to the user to figure out how to debug the in-line'd procedure. In most cases, the user sees the call in the source code and the body is invisible; the surprise occurs when trying to "step into" the function body (which does not exist).

Loop Unrolling

Normally we try to move as much code as possible outside of the loop and try to minimize the amount of code executed within the loop. But if the loop iteration count is very low, the computation on the index variable controlling how many times to pass through the loop is actually substantial, and eliminating it becomes the goal. So we may actually see the compiler take the body of the loop and replicate it the number of times we were to pass through the loop—all so that the index variable and the increment and test of it can be eliminated. The debugger can be told by the compiler what has happened and it can fairly easily go to each replicated body of the loop when the loop index variable would have been incremented.

Cross Jumping

This is a control-flow optimization used only to minimize code storage space utilization. It creates a many-to-one mapping between the original source code and the compiler-generated optimized code. In this optimization, the compiler detects that two portions of code share a common tail of execution so that one of the two is eliminated and its execution jumps to the common thread instead of executing in-line as written.

Problems Optimizations Create for Debuggers

If statements move or the program's flow of control changes it is hard to report the correct location of exceptions and for the user to set breakpoints. If variables are eliminated or the same storage location is used by several variables, inspecting a variable may give incorrect results or correct results for the wrong variable. Even single-step may just confuse the user if the ordering of statements is changed sufficiently. Optimizations can sufficiently change things that, if not compensated for by the debugger, will leave the user unable to trust the debugger's context information. This violates the most basic first step in diagnosing a bug: Determine that the program reaches an incorrect state during execution. We now go through several examples of the kinds of symptoms compiler optimizations can have on an unsuspecting debugger (and its user).

Variable Is Unknown to Debugger

Table 12.1 lists three optimizations that can cause the variable to be unknown to the debugger without careful work on the compiler information provided to the debugger.

Reported Variable Value Is Incorrect

A common problem data flow optimizations may cause the debugger is that the variable as presented will actually have an incorrect value. This could be

TABLE 12.1 *Why Variable May Be Unknown in the Face of Three Common Optimizations*

OPTIMIZATION	WHY VARIABLE MAY BE UNKNOWN TO DEBUGGER
Constant propagation	The compiler, when presented with a variable whose value is invariant during its entire scope, may eliminate the variable and instead use the constant value wherever the variable value was used. A debugger presented with this would then report the original variable as unknown, which would be unexpected to the user.
Induction variable elimination	The compiler performing induction variable elimination may combine variables and simplify expressions to improve efficiency. When the debugger attempts to inspect the original variable, again it appears as if this variable is unknown—as if it never existed.
Dead variable elimination	A variable that is still technically in scope but is never referenced again can be eliminated and actually not have valid storage associated with it any longer. Again, the debugger requesting its value after elimination will be presented with information implying the variable is unknown.

caused by having the compiler optimization delay the assignment so that when the debugger inspects that location it has not yet been updated with the actual value of the inspected variable. If an assignment is hoisted to an earlier spot in the computation, the value is available earlier than one would expect from the program as written. Storage allocation optimizations can mean that the variable's value is reported incorrectly because the value is actually being stored somewhere else, such as in a register, at that point in the computation. Some specific optimizations and the ways they make variable values incorrect when inspected are listed in Table 12.2.

No Corresponding Object Code

The most obvious problem caused by eliminated code is that the user cannot place breakpoints on the statement eliminated. Unless the compiler gets the information back to the statement maps, the user will believe this statement is still executable and the breakpoint placed here will actually map to the textually next statement, which may not be a safe assumption. If the statement map is updated correctly, an eliminated statement will look to the user like a comment, which cannot have a breakpoint placed on it. The user may still be quite confused about why this statement suddenly cannot be seen during execution.

One-to-Many and Many-to-One Mapping Problems

Control-flow optimizations can create non-monotonic mappings between the original source code and the optimized code. Many-to-one problems are created in optimizations like cross-jumping, where duplicate code paths are merged into one common tail and the duplicate path is deleted. And one-to-many problems are created in optimizations like in-line procedure expansion (and C++ templates), where a single piece of source code now exists in multiple locations in the final optimizated executable code. Now setting a breakpoint in the original source code can turn into many breakpoints for each place that procedure was in-lined.

Optimizations Debugged in Practice

From the viewpoint of a symbolic debugger, the ideal compiler would generate very straightforward machine code to implement the source program. Every variable would exist in a single location in memory, and every source

TABLE 12.2   *Why Certain Optimizations Cause Variable Values To Be Incorrect*

OPTIMIZATION	WHY VARIABLE VALUES MAY BE INCORRECT
Storage overlaying	If two variables, i and j, are never used at the same point in the computation, the compiler may use the same memory location for them. If the debugger tries to inspect i when that memory location actually is being used by j, the user will not be getting what he or she expected.
Copy propagation	In copy propogation, when two variables have the same value due to an assignment, the assignment can be eliminated and use of the left-hand side variable is replaced by the value of the right-hand side variable. Therefore, inspection of the left-hand side variable will get the wrong result because the assignment never actually occurred.
Global register allocation	As the compiler determines that a variable is in high demand, it places the value of this variable in a faster register and does not force the value to be updated to its permanent memory location until some later time. If during this time, the debugger user inspects this variable, the value will still be the value at the time it was copied to the register, not its current value.
Code motion	Moving code outside of a loop because it is invariant saves a lot of time during computation of long loops, but if the user goes to inspect the result of an assignment hoisted outside of the loop before the loop has actually run, the value is incorrect (it shouldn't have already been saved).

statement would generate a single, contiguous block of instructions. Obviously, the more aggressively a compiler optimizes the code, the further it strays from this "ideal." Unless the debugger can cope with optimizations, it will either fail to help the user examine the program or—even worse—lead the user astray.

The earliest answer to this problem was to tell the user not to turn on compiler optimizations until he or she had finished debugging the program. This is unsatisfactory for two reasons. First, a compiler may perform transformations that look like "optimizations" to the debugger even when its optimization phase is turned off. Second, many bugs manifest themselves only with optimizations enabled. Sometimes these signify bugs in the optimizer; more often, they signify bugs in the source program. For example, consider a program that refers to an uninitialized pointer. If the first reference tests for a non-nil value, the unoptimized version may well proceed harmlessly on many machines because the pointer is allocated to memory that is initially zero; it will fail on the same machines once the pointer is allocated to a register containing a non-zero value left over from the variable that previously occupied that register.

As that example illustrates, there exists a legitimate need to debug optimized code; further, the compiler writer has a vested interest in helping the debugger to do so. That's fortunate because half of the work takes place within the compiler itself, which must give to the debugger a description of the transformations it has made.

The other half of the work takes place inside the debugger itself, which must make use of the compiler's description of these transformations. Sometimes the debugger can use knowledge of the transformations to conceal them from the user entirely. For example, if the debugger knows that a variable has been allocated to a register during part of its lifetime, the debugger can read the value from that register instead of from the usual location in memory.

But it's important to acknowledge at the outset that in many cases, it is impossible to provide transparent debugging of the original source code (except by either de-optimizing the code or providing a duplicate unoptimized version—both of which defeat the intent of debugging the actual optimized code).

For example, consider the "return" statements in this function:

```
float
find_coeff(float f, float x[], float y[])
    {
    for (i = 0; i < (int) f; i++)
        {
        if (f < y[(int) f])
            return x[(int) f];
        if (f == y[(int) f])
            break;
        }
    return x[(int) f];
    }
```

The compiler may emit a single block of code that computes "x[(int) f]" and returns from the function. It then replaces each "return" statement with a jump to that block of code. If the user asks to set a breakpoint at one of these return statements, there is no straightforward way to do so without stopping at both. Even worse, if the program unexpectedly encounters a fault within this block of code, the debugger cannot tell the user which source statement was executing.

As another example, consider a loop containing an invariant assignment:

```
for (i = 0; i < limit; i++)
    {
    j = limit / 2;
    if (x[i] > x[j])
        swap(x, i, j);
    }
```

The compiler may choose to execute the assignment to j before entering the loop. In this case, the debugger can obey the user's request to set a breakpoint on the assignment statement; but if it does so, a user who expects to stop there and print the values of i and x on each iteration will be confused to find that i has not yet been defined and that the loop appears to execute only once.

Two very different approaches have been proposed to deal with the impossible cases:

1. Let the user operate on the source program, but deny requests that have no validity within the transformed program.

2. Let the user operate on the transformed program instead of the source, requiring the user to understand the correspondence.

The first approach would solve our example cases by showing the user a list of source statements with markings to indicate which ones are "safe" for setting breakpoints. The invariant assignment statement would not be "safe." Either the merged "return" statements would be marked unsafe, or the debugger would show the user that setting a breakpoint on one will set breakpoints on the others as well.

The second approach would show the user a set of statements where the loop-invariant assignment actually preceded the loop, and where each return statement was replaced with a goto statement targeting a common expression at the end of the function. The user would compare this with the original program and decide where and how to set breakpoints. Stepping back from the impossible cases for now, let's consider how the compiler can describe to the debugger the transformations it performs, many of which will be more tractable. We will address only a few common ones; there is no limit to the variety of optimizations that might occur, and by their nature, they tend to require multiple, ad hoc solutions.

Register Allocation Optimizations

When a simple-minded compiler generates code for an expression, it loads the value of each variable from its "home" location in memory, performs the computation, and (if the expression is assigned to a target variable) stores the result back into the home location of the target. A good register allocator strives to hold any frequently used value in a register to avoid the cost of loading it from memory prior to each computation and storing it back after each assignment. Thus, the value of a particular variable may live in memory during some portion of its lifetime and in one or more registers during other portions. If the debugger were to look in memory at a point where the value lives in a register, it would obtain at best a "stale" value and at worst an undefined one. The debugging tables can solve the problem by associating with each variable an array of triples, where the first element gives an instruction address, the second element gives a number of instructions, and the third gives a location (a memory address, a register name, or a special value indicating the variable is not live during these instructions). These are sometimes known as "home tables," as shown in Figure 12.1.

These home tables are convenient only for local variables because the linker would need to coalesce tables from multiple compilations to describe global variables. A better approach in this regard is to invert the home tables: For each procedure, emit an array of triples for each register, showing which variable lives in that register during each range of instructions within the procedure. The debugger would then use the home location associated with a given variable unless overridden by the home table for a register within the current function.

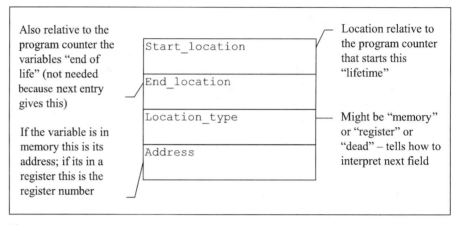

Also relative to the program counter the variables "end of life" (not needed because next entry gives this)

If the variable is in memory this is its address; if its in a register this is the register number

Start_location

End_location

Location_type

Address

Location relative to the program counter that starts this "lifetime"

Might be "memory" or "register" or "dead" – tells how to interpret next field

Figure 12.1

Register allocation "home table."   *Part of a linked list of "home tables" produced by the optimizing compiler when doing register allocation that is placed in the debugging tables to enable the debugger to determine the correct location for a variable.*

Induction Variable Elimination

One can extend the format of home tables to indicate that a value is a function of one or more different variables; then the debugger can evaluate an induction variable by looking up the value of the loop index and performing a computation on that.

Common Subexpression Elimination

As mentioned earlier, the compiler maintains data structures that describe the generated program for use by the optimizer: Several problems can be solved by annotating these data structures and passing them along to the debugger [HENNESSEY 1979].

Typically an optimizer uses a flow graph whose nodes are basic blocks; each basic block describes a series of computations that do not branch, and the edges between basic blocks represent branching. Within each basic block, the optimizer builds a directed acyclic graph (DAG) describing data dependencies. Local optimizations use the DAG to rearrange computations within a basic block; global optimizations move computations between nodes or rearrange the structure of the graph.

Common subexpression elimination and value propagation can cause a value both to be computed "early" and to appear in the "wrong" variable; instruction scheduling can cause it to be computed either early or late. These phenomena cause problems when a fault during the computation requires the debugger to report where the problem occurred, or when the user asks for the value of a variable whose value exists but is in the wrong place. By annotating each node of the DAG with a list of variables and the range of intermediate-code operations over which the node represents each variable, the compiler can tell the debugger where to find the value of a variable (or that the value does not exist) at each point. This information could be presented directly or translated into the home tables described earlier.

Future Trends

Expectations for debugger features are rising at a much faster pace by far than the capability of production debuggers. In some cases, the items discussed in this chapter do exist in some debuggers. However, these items either are just showing up in debuggers (and hence are not well debugged or understood) or are still in the planning stages.

- C/S or distributed or n-tier debugging
- Mixed compiled-interpreted debugging
- Intimate knowledge of object-model and integration into debugging processes
- Ever-tighter integration with other tools such as compilers, editors, browsers, and IDEs in general
- Improvements in thread support
- Profiling and other performance monitoring functions
- More help with the obstreperous bugs such as memory corruption
- Higher levels of optimization thoroughly understood by the debugger and presentation of scrupulously truthful information
- Much faster edit-compile-debug turnaround time (at least 10× faster necessary)
- Completely scriptable debugger that allows users to customize extensively
- True and dependable firewall between the debugger, the application it is debugging, and the operating system

Glossary

/proc   An interface to processes provided on many UNIX systems since about 1988. An alternative to ptrace(), this is a more general process interface that supports debuggers and other utilities needing information or control over running processes.

4GL   Short for fourth-generation language, it groups together a series of languages—usually interpreted—that are used primarily for business types of applications. 3GLs are the standard compiled programming languages like C, C++, Ada. An example of a 4GL is Visual Basic.

activation record   A term used interchangeably with "stack frame." It is the record stored in the per-program memory space called the stack that keeps track of all information necessary during execution of a program about a function as a new function is being called.

algorithms   Structured recipes or formulas for describing a series of steps that must be performed to achieve a desired goal. This book describes numerous algorithms used within debuggers that describe the steps performed by the debugger to accomplish a desired function (e.g., source-level single-step).

animation   In this context, the automatic processing of slowed-down execution of a program showing the results of each step within the current debugger views. All variable views are updated, and the source view shows the current execution point so that the user gets a chance to see execution proceed without continuously requesting single-step operations.

API   Application Program Interface. A collection of function calls to a subsystem (usually a DLL or class library) usually related in some way that a program uses to build up functionality from well-defined, well-tested components. The debug API provided by the operating system is a series of function calls with well-specified parameters giving the debugger writer a solid set of functionality on which a working debugger can be built.

assertion   A programmatic approach to error detection. Typically, a programmer will place assertions within a program to be compiled prior to execution. During execution, usually under the control of some global parameter, the assertions become test code checking for correctness of variable values.

attach   The ability for the debugger to gain control of a running application. Instead of having the debugger create the debuggee process and start its execution, attach allows the debugger to gain complete debugging control of a process started independently and perhaps stopped at a fault.

Basic   A 4GL programming language usually interpreted as opposed to being compiled. Debuggers for Basic therefore are much simpler than for compiled languages because interpreters and debuggers can be tightly integrated with complete control over the execution environment.

BoundsChecker   A production debugging tool from Nu-Mega that checks for memory corruption, overruns, and resource leaks on applications written to run under flavors of the Windows operating system.

branch delay slot   On some RISC processors, in order to optimize speed, the instruction fetched after a jump or branch instruction is actually the instruction that should have logically been executed before the branch, but is instead executed while the processor is fetching the memory addressed by the branch instruction. This feature is a source of complication for debuggers.

branch prediction   Some modern CPUs to optimize performance attempt to predict which of two possible addresses will be the actual target of a branch based on a number of factors determined during execution and prefetch the instructions at the predicted address to save time when the CPU actually gets to computing the branch to take.

breakpoints   Special points in the running code that are to be treated as "probe points" where special debugger-controlled events will occur. Typically this will be a point where the execution of the application is to stop so that the user can look around at context information to determine how the program is behaving. The breakpoints may be actual special instructions placed in the executing code stream, or they may be addresses stored in special registers that the processor checks to see if the current execution point and the value in a debug register are a match.

browsing   An activity related to debugging, browsing is the process of examining the structure and current values of program variables.

bug   A simple, colloquial term for an error or programming defect. The term bug comes from a story that an early tube-based computer contained a moth (which is not actually even a bug) that shorted out two leads and caused the program to behave incorrectly.

C/C++   The most prevalent 3GL (general-purpose programming language) in use today. These are compiled languages in which the compiler translates the program text into native machine instructions. Many of the principles in this book are focused on debugging these types of languages.

callback   A type of function that is passed to a host function as a pointer that the host function calls when certain conditions apply. If the host function has no debug information, most debuggers also lose track of the callback function as it "disappears" inside the host function. Because this style of programming has become prevalent this debugger problem is severe and needs to be addressed broadly.

calling conventions   The specific information and sequencing of that information on the stack as a new function is called must be known to systems that must interact with the compiled code such as debuggers.

child process   A process that is initiated by an already existing process is considered the child of the initiating process, which in turn is known as the parent process. Typical debugging scenarios call for the debugger to be the parent process of the debuggee process it creates, which is then its child.

code hoisting   If an expression is very busy at a particular point, the expression can be computed and its value saved for subsequent use. This may not save time but may by very effective in saving space because an expression that might have been computed many times (but is invariant) is now computed once in a common ancestor basic block.

code motion   An important and very effective optimization is the movement of code that is invariant from within the loop to outside the loop. If an expression will evaluate to the same value no matter how many times the loop is executed, the expression inside the loop is wasted time.

code patching   Breakpoints are also the basis for more extreme code modifications attempted by some debuggers. Instead of inserting a special breakpoint instruction at a given location and saving the original instruction away in debugger memory, any instruction could be inserted into the executable code stream by the debugger. Specifically, a branch or jump instruction could be inserted that jumps to an entire function patched into the program's code space by the debugger to change program behavior in some important way.

CodeGuard   A debugging tool from Borland that, like BoundsChecker, detects memory corruption and resource leaks. In this case, the tool is integrated with a debugger so that detected problems are reported in the same way as standard defects detected by the debugger.

COM   Microsoft's Common Object Model—a standard way in which software is constructed into standard objects that have predictable interfaces. Distributed-COM presents these same standard interfaces across a distributed network. This presents some challenges to debuggers, but the OS vendors are trying to make these remote objects debuggable in the same way as local ones. It remains to be seen how seamless this really is.

common subexpression elimination   When a series of expressions contain common components or subexpressions, these subexpressions can be combined and not recomputed at run-time, saving both time and space. The issue for the debugger is that when the user goes to examine the components of the expression where the subexpression has been changed by the compiler, unless the compiler went to great lengths to tell the debugger what it should do to compensate, the user will not get truthful results.

compiler   The tool that translates human-readable program text into executable code. Typically a compiler directly generates machine-executable code, but it may do so in conjunction with an assembler or it may generate instructions for a "virtual machine." In either case, the debugger is very dependent on the compiler for substantial ancillary information necessary for the debugger to make sense of and perform the necessary mappings during debugging.

conditional breakpoint   A breakpoint that has associated with it an expression that is evaluated by the debugger once the physical breakpoint is activated. If the expression evaluates to true the program will remain stopped and the user will regain control, but if the expression evaluates to false the debuggee is restarted immediately as if the stop never occurred.

constant folding   The process of deducing at compile time that the value of an expression is a constant and saving that constant for use instead of the expression. This saves both time and space. Because the standard technique for constant folding is to detect the expression is a constant, evaluate the expression by executing the code for it in place within the compiler, and replace uses of it with the result, the debugger will not ever be able to find the code for this expression.

context switch   A term from the operating system domain that refers to the events that occur in a multitasking operating system when one task relinquishes control over the CPU to another as directed by the operating system. The debugger is just another process to the operating system so the context switches to the debugger take away from and impede performance of the application being debugged.

copy propagation   We may choose to delay an assignment (or copy) from one variable to another and instead use the right-hand value wherever subsequently the left-hand value had originally been used. The purpose of this is to eliminate the need to make the original assignment at all and thereby eliminate some code we didn't need. The debugger can easily get lost on this optimization because A may have no value in it at all (and may be at risk of itself being eliminated).

CPU   Central Processing Unit—the brain of the computer that controls all execution. Each CPU from each manufacturer is different. The debugger must know in intimate detail about the CPU because it must understand how to set breakpoints, single-step the debuggee, disassemble instructions, display registers, and decode stack frames.

cross jumping   This is a control-flow optimization used only to minimize code storage space utilization. It creates a many-to-one mapping between the original source code and the compiler-generated optimized code. In this optimization, the compiler detects that two portions of code share a common tail of execution so that one of the two is eliminated and its execution jumps to the common thread instead of executing in-line as written.

data breakpoint   A breakpoint that instead of being associated with a particular location in the executing code is associated with a particular variable or data location. Thus, when the specified data location is modified, the breakpoint is triggered and the location in code where that modification is occurring is now easily detectable by the user.

data structure   A well-specified collection of data that is laid out in memory as specified by a "template" that all creators and accessors of this structure follow.

dead store elimination   If a variable or expression is stored in either a new variable or a register but is never used again after that, the store was useless and should not occur. Obviously, if the store is eliminated and the debugger is asked to inspect the variable or register where the store was targeted, it will either find the wrong value or won't be able to report at all.

dead variable elimination   Similar to dead store elimination, dead variable elimination is about removing the use of a variable (and any associated memory assigned to it) that is never used after a certain point.

deadlock   A terrible situation that occurs when two distinct execution units (threads or processes) each are waiting for a resource that the other will not release until its needs are satisfied.

debug API   The application programming interface specifically created by the OS vendors for debuggers and related utilities. These functions for debuggers give special control over other processes to enable all the functionality expected of debuggers.

debug information   Special information generated by the compiler and/or linker to enable the debugger to make the mappings necessary between source code and executable code that will allow the user to maintain the illusion that the original source code is being executed and debugged directly.

debuggee   The program being debugged. The child process of the debugger. Some authors have referred to the debuggee process as the "inferior" process.

debugger   A special program built to control other programs in order to enable programmers to understand, control, and track down defects in their programs efficiently.

debugger kernel   A term some debugger developers use to identify the central core of the debugger. This is a useful abstraction because this is the portion of the debugger that needs to be able to control execution, talks directly to the operating system, and needs to understand not only the debug API but the CPU specifics as well. The other portions of the debugger may be able to be more OS and CPU independent and therefore more portable.

defect   A flaw in an application. A programming error. Also more commonly known as a bug. The raison d'être for debuggers.

Delphi   An application development environment from Borland based on the ObjectPascal programming language. It commonly competes with 4GL-based systems and yet is compiled and therefore has a debugger more like the C/C++ environments.

disassembly   The process of mapping binary machine-level codes back to the textual assembly-language mnemonics used by programmers. A very important process within debuggers both for faster single-step and for the presentation of disassembled instructions in a machine-state debugger view.

distributed objects   A natural evolution of object-oriented programming is the distribution of those objects across a network of computers so that more sharing and better performance are possible. This creates numerous challenges for debuggers.

DLL   Dynamic Link Library—a common way to create shared libraries that present a standard C-style functional interface or API accessible by programs written in any language. The debugger must be aware of when a program loads and starts execution code in a DLL.

dope vectors   A FORTRAN term for an indirection used at run-time to get to the desired functionality. Very similar to virtual function pointers in C++.

DosDebug()   The primary debug interface routine used by the OS/2 operating system.

Dr. Watson   A post-mortem debugging analysis tool from Microsoft. Instead of being tied to one specific application this kind of utility monitors the operating system and its interactions with all running processes. This way, if a failure occurs that affects the operating system, you can determine which application or combination of applications caused the problem.

evaluator   A user interface module and an underlying subsystem of a debugger designed to take a given expression and compute its current value. It does this by passing the typed expression off to the associated compiler and debugger, which use the current values of variables combined as specified by the expression to produce a final value.

event driven   A style of programming prevalent in all GUI-based systems where the behavior of the program is tied to asynchronous actions that occur, usually driven by the user. The events are things such as keyboard activity, mouse activity, or computer peripheral-generated activity.

events, semaphores, messages, timers, mutexes, critical sections   A collection of data structures provided by operating systems as resources to be used by applications for timing and synchronization. These can be used between processes, but they are most commonly used between threads within one process.

exception   A condition generated at run-time that is non-standard in some way and must be handled appropriately. Events that occur within the debuggee that do not allow it to execute unimpeded are exceptions presented by the OS to the debugger. For example, a breakpoint hit by the debuggee becomes an exception for the debugger to handle.

execution control   The process of creating the debuggee process, starting and stopping its execution and terminating it along with all the more fine-grained control performed by a debugger constitutes execution control.

expression evaluation   The process that is performed by the evaluator described above.

file handle   A unique reference to limited resource items. Files have handles. So do Windows, threads, and many other OS-controlled resources.

finish function   A feature of some debuggers that requests the debugger continue execution of the debuggee such that the current function is completed and execution next stops at the point where the current function was originally called. This makes sure all subfunctions of the current function are quickly skipped over.

frame pointer   A real or synthetic pointer to the place in the executing program's stack representing a stack frame or activation record. In most processors a register is dedicated to holding this value, but in some the value must be synthesized from other information and maintained by the debugger itself.

function evaluation   Some debuggers allow expressions that are to be evaluated to contain calls to functions. When these expressions are evaluated, the functions to be called must be executed within the debuggee by having the debugger set up a fake stack frame and causing the debuggee to jump to the specified function.

garbage collection   Many interpreted systems employ a system of regaining unused memory periodically called garbage collection. These systems must take some care to account for interactions between debuggers and garbage collection systems because the debugger may be inspecting variables that the garbage collector wants to eliminate.

GUI   Graphical User Interface—the term used generically to describe the windows, menus, and interaction paradigms used in all mouse-based systems. These are of particular concern to debuggers because these systems present a host of issues for debuggers especially if the debugger itself is GUI-based.

hard mode   Because the mass market PC Window systems have been based on a single input queue system (Windows 3.x and OS/2 2.x), there is an important issue for debugging GUI applications on these less advanced windowing systems. Hard mode requires the entire system become synchronous to give exclusive control to the debugger, usually because of some problem with the way the application and the OS are interacting.

heap   Global, undifferentiated storage allocated and managed at run-time. A source of lots of programming errors, the heap becomes important during debugging, and specialized debugging tools such as CodeGuard and Bounds-Checker have been created to focus on these types of errors.

Heisenberg Principle   Non-intrusiveness in systems being measured or tested has been formally defined by Heisenberg and is called the Heisenberg Principle. It is important that the act of debugging an application does not change the behavior of the application. If this is not the case, the usefulness of the debugger falls into question.

home table   A data structure commonly used to aid debuggers in "unwinding" the register allocation optimizations commonly used even when all other optimizations are turned off. This data structure tells the debugger for any program counter value where is the current "home" for the value now: memory location or register.

hooking   When a function call is replaced with a new call—usually at run-time—the new function has "hooked" into the original. This was the way early PC-based debuggers had to work because there were little or no OS-supplied debugging facilities. This is also a common technique for other types of systems, such as network file systems, printing systems, etc.

ICE   In-Circuit Emulator—a system that takes over the base system's capabilities so that certain measurements or special control can occur. This applies to debugging as seen with Nu-Mega's Soft-ICE product that takes over the system from Windows and then runs Windows on top of Soft-ICE so that the user has complete debugging not over just the application but also over Windows itself and how the two interact.

induction variable elimination   An induction variable is a variable within a loop that each time through the loop is modified by some constant amount. This is very common and as with all other analyses of loops, can have big payoffs on loops with very high iteration counts. It is possible in many cases to eliminate one induction variable because it is related to another and one can always be derived from the other.

in-line procedure expansion   This type of optimization was called "call-by-name" in ALGOL. The procedure is treated as if it were a macro: Its body is substituted for the call in the caller with the actual parameters literally substituting for the formal parameters. This has become very prevalent with C++ because there are so many small methods that may need very high performance.

input queue   This term refers to the first-in first-out data structure maintained by the operating system or GUI framework to handle messages. A windowing system bases its central processing control center on this queue and the messages it contains. Having one queue for the entire system causes deadlocks so the newer systems maintain input queues per process.

inspector   A user interface element and associated debugger subsystem that provides support for inspecting and changing the values of variables in the debuggee's address space. Many debuggers come up with sophisticated syntax for inspectors to allow the user to be specific about the scope for the variable being inspected.

instruction decoding   Emulating the underlying CPU during debugging. This is needed during single-step to determine the minimum number of breakpoints to insert allowing the most high-speed straight-line execution of instructions possible.

instruction pointer   The Intel term for the program counter. A specific register that the debugger must read and write during debugging to control execution.

integrated development environments   A single environment for application development that contains programming editor, project manager, compiler, linker, debugger, and ancillary tools, all operating from within a single environment and interacting with each other as appropriate to maximize the user's productivity. In particular, we see enormous benefits from having the debugger tightly integrated with the editor, compiler, and heap checker.

interpreter   A run-time system associated with a programming language that translates intermediate code into machine-specific code. A debugger for such systems must be tightly integrated into the run-time interpreter, but its job is dramatically simplified compared to fully compiled systems. Basic, Smalltalk, and Java are examples of interpreted systems.

Java   Java is a relatively new programming language evolving from C++ that is interpreted (at least for now) and that runs on many different platforms without programming changes. It has a unique debugging API, and the debugger must be tightly coupled into the Java virtual machine (run-time interpreter).

just-in-time compiler   Java applets and applications are compiled into byte-codes from the user-written textual form. The byte-codes are interpreted into machine executable at run-time by the virtual machine. Attached to the virtual machine is a just-in-time compiler that translates the byte-codes into native instructions on the fly for dramatic speedups.

just-in-time debugging   A program that was running independent of any debugger but whose faults can be just-in-time debugged if the OS catches the fault before releasing the memory and resources for the faulting program and if the OS debug API supports an after-the-fact attach capability.

kernel debugger   Not to be confused with debugger kernel, the kernel debugger is a specialized debugging subsystem provided by the OS vendor to aid in the debugging of components to be added to the operating system such as device drivers.

kernel mode   When the operating system is executing, the processor (if it supports special modes) will frequently be put into a special kernel mode which implies certain special privileges and non-interruptability that can affect debugging.

lazy processing   An approach to gathering large quantities of information in an "defer until we really need it" fashion. This is used typically by debuggers when gathering the large amounts of program symbol table information so that debugger startup time is not terribly long.

leaf routine A routine (or function) that does not call out to any other routines. It is the final destination down that branch of the call tree. This is sometimes noted during compilation so that the calling convention can be simplified and made smaller and faster. The debugger, because it needs to understand the calling conventions used, will need to understand about leaf routines.

linker A critical tool during the compilation process that takes all the object modules and libraries created by the compiler and combines them into a single executable ready to run. A critical job of the linker is to combine and streamline the huge volumes of debugging information generated with each object module by the compiler.

locality The principle that most execution and memory references that will occur close to the current location. This also applies to symbol table information, which can help guide the lazy processing of symbol tables.

LockInput() A function undocumented in Windows 3.1 that was critical to getting a debugger to work on GUI applications. This was part of what was necessary to implement "hard mode."

logical breakpoint The debugger must maintain two distinct sets of breakpoints: physical and logical. The physical correspond one-for-one to physical addresses. The logical breakpoints are associated with source code locations, and there may be more than one at a given source code location.

longjmp An old C-language routine that provided non-local gotos. A very challenging issue for debuggers to deal with effectively.

loop unrolling If the loop iteration count is very low, the computation on the index variable controlling how many times to pass through the loop is actually substantial, and eliminating it becomes the goal. So we may actually see the compiler take the body of the loop and replicate it the number of times we were to pass through the loop so that the index variable and the increment and test of it all can be eliminated.

machine code The actual binary codes that control the execution of the CPU. This is the final output of a compiler.

Mac OS The current operating system running on Macintosh PowerPC computers. It has a debug API similar to TOOLHELP as found on Windows 3.1.

massively parallel When a computer system is built out of a very large number exceeding 1000 distinct processors it is referred to as massively parallel.

memory corruption   When an array is declared to be of length 10 and the program writes at location 11 or when memory is freed and the program continues to use it or a large number of other simple but serious errors occur with memory, corruption ensues that is hard to track down using standard debuggers.

messagepoints   A specialized type of breakpoint that is associated with specific GUI messages. Because these messages drive the core processing loops of all GUI applications it is appropriate to have ways to carefully control execution based on the messages that messagepoints afford.

MIMD   Multiple Instruction Multiple Data—a parallel computer architecture characterized by an array of connected fairly powerful computers, each executing its own individual instruction stream and each working from private data stores.

mnemonic   The textual shorthand used to describe machine instructions. The target format for disassembly views in debuggers.

Motif   The most prevalent windowing system for UNIX. It is based on X-Windows for its basic graphics support and adds a rich powerful set of views and widgets for GUI application construction.

multitasking   An operating system that can switch from one task to another, preserving the complete state of one task so that it can be safely resumed later. Usually the scheduling of these tasks is preemptive.

multithreaded   An operating system that supports the concept of a thread of execution provides the capability to create applications that use multiple threads. Debuggers on such a system need to have extensive and sophisticated support for debugging these kinds of applications.

non-blocking   When a call to an OS API returns immediately it is considered non-blocking. A blocking call will cause the process making the call to hang until its request is satisfied.

nonlocal goto   A programmatic jump to a location up the call stack to an ancestor function from which we ultimately are derived. An example is the (hopefully) now defunct C-based longjmp.

notification   The term used by the OS vendors for getting information to the debugger about how and why the debuggee stopped.

object-oriented A programming concept based on the ideas of inheritance and reuse. Objects created using such an approach are reusable in other contexts because they are general, flexible, and have a well-defined interface whose internals are not important.

off-by-one The classic error of computer science. The cause of a lot of bugs. Common in C and C++ because arrays are numbered starting at 0 but also show up in other contexts.

once only A type of breakpoint that is very useful to debugger users. When a once-only breakpoint is set, the next time execution stops it is removed even if it was not hit. This allows implementation of "run-to-here" where we don't ever get there but instead hit some other exception first.

operating system The base software running on the underlying hardware that provides all the basic capabilities and APIs necessary to build working applications. In particular, the access to the CPU and the debug API are both provided to the debugger by the operating system.

optimizations Techniques applied to the compilation process to try to gain incremental improvements in the execution speed of the compiled program. Optimizations usually work in conflict with debugging because they typically obscure the mapping from source code to machine code so that the debugger can no longer present an accurate picture of the execution to the user.

OS/2 The PC-based operating system currently sold by IBM but that originally was under development by Microsoft. There are many similarities between OS/2 and Windows.

page protection A security scheme implemented in multitasking operating systems to keep one process from accessing a page of memory belonging to another process. Can also be used by the debugger to implement data breakpoints.

parallel architecture A computer construction scheme that arrays multiple separate processors to work on a single problem at the same time.

pass counts A component of conditional breakpoints that is useful in looping constructs. A pass count keeps track of how many times through the loop execution has passed and determines if the requested count has been reached to cause execution to stop.

p-code   Processor independent code that is created by the first level of compiler and then either translated directly into native machine instructions or interpreted at run-time.

physical breakpoint   One of the two levels of breakpoints maintained inside the debugger. The physical level breakpoints map directly one-for-one onto physical memory address locations.

polling   A "waiting" technique when a there is a non-blocking call into the OS but the calling subsystem needs a special condition to exist before it moves on to its next action. Very inefficient.

post-mortem dump   When a process gets an exception and terminates it may produce a complete memory image that can be analyzed with special tools to help determine the cause of the fault.

Presentation Manager   The GUI portion of OS/2.

process   A unit of resource ownership and of work to be done. The operating system uses the process as a way of organizing its work and resource allocation. The responsibility of the operating system is to guarantee that processes get a chance to execute in an orderly and timely fashion and that processes are protected from each other. The focus of a debugging session.

profiling   In some ways related to debugging, profiling is the process of analyzing the performance characteristics of the running program.

profiling registers   Special registers in some CPUs allow profilers to keep track of critical run-time information in these registers. This helps get accurate information about how much time is spent in each routine or within each source line.

program counter   The special register in the CPU that points to the location in memory for the next instruction to be executed. Its value changes after each instruction is executed, either by incrementing by the length of the previous instruction or due to a branch to a new address instruction. Also called instruction pointer by some CPUs.

proxy   An object or function that does something on someone else's behalf. In this context, its usually on behalf of a remote object that we are trying to control or debug.

ptrace()   The older standard UNIX debugging interface function. It was and is used extensively on systems prior to the newer /proc approach.

queues   Data structures that implement a first-in first-out ordering to a list.

register   The hardware storage locations tightly coupled into the CPU and limited in number that are the fastest storage available. A precious commodity that compilers try to optimize their use of.

register allocation optimization   Probably the most important kind of compiler optimization, especially for RISC machines that must maximize their utilization of registers because memory access is so much slower than register access. Can be easily dealt with by the debugger via the use of "home tables."

remote debugging   When debugging an application that is running partially or entirely on a machine connected to but distinct from the machine running the debugger some sort of remote protocol will be used where the local debugger will send messages to a proxy debugger on the remote machine that will actually control the debuggee process.

reverse execution   A much-requested but dubious feature where the debugger would actually back up the program counter and unwind all effects of some number of CPU clicks.

RISC   Reduced Instruction Set Computer—an approach to computer design where simpler constant length instructions are executed much faster than SISC instructions and thereby gain a performance advantage. The chips themselves are smaller and cheaper to build as well.

RPC   Remote Procedure Call—a call to a function is actually translated to a protocol passed over the network to a proxy on a remote machine that translates that protocol back into a function call now made on that remote machine.

run-to-here   A debugger feature where the user can point to a source-code location and request that the debugger run the debuggee up to that point. It does not leave any breakpoint at this location.

scope   The context for validity of a variable. Levels of scope may be global, file, class, function, block.

semaphores   A signaling mechanism used to aid synchronization of distinct program units (processes or threads).

shared memory   A controlled way to have otherwise non-interacting processes be able to share information by using special facilities provided by the operating system.

SIMD   Single Instruction Multiple Data—a computer architecture that is normally also massively parallel (greater than 1000 processors) that all have local data storage but executed the same instruction in lock-step with each other.

single-step   The execution of a single instruction after which the processor will stop and give control back to the debugger.

SISD   Single Instruction Single Data—the standard model for non-parallel processor architectures.

Smalltalk   A programming language that is characterized by its strong object-oriented nature, cross-platform interpreted run-time system, and strong, integrated programming environment.

socket   A mechanism for communication between processes even if those processes are distributed across the network.

soft mode   A state in which the debugger takes over message processing for the child debuggee, but otherwise all message processing for all other processes proceeds normally—the system, except for the debuggee, appears to operate as it should.

Soft-ICE   A debugging tool from Nu-Mega that is an In-circuit Emulator and controls Windows and all applications running on Windows.

source view   An important view within a GUI debugger that gives the programmer a view onto the source code showing breakpoint locations as well as the location of the program counter.

speculative execution   The next generation of CPUs are proposing a new approach to higher performance where several execution units operate in parallel and they each start executing down different paths, one of which will be right and will be used to continue.

Spy   A debugging tool that monitors and reports on all messages flowing through the GUI system of Windows.

stack   The run-time data storage and control flow structure built and maintained through collaboration of the CPU and the compiler.

stack back-traces   The series of activation records created on the stack creates a traceable history of all direct ancestor functions called on the current execution tree. The debugger must unwind this stack and present it as a critical component of current program context.

stall detection   In multiprocessor systems, when one processor stalls waiting for something from another processor, it is important that the debugger can detect and do something about this or the entire system can become hung.

statement step   When single steps are grouped together to implement a step over an entire source statement.

step into   When statement step on a statement containing a function call steps to the first statement within the called function.

step over   When statement step on a statement containing a function call steps completely over the called function and stops at the textually next statement within the current function context.

STI   Symbol Table Information (previously known as CodeView)— Microsoft's debug information standard format. Borland uses an almost identical format as well.

symbol table   The information describing types and locations of symbols generated by the compilation process and consumed by the debugger.

symbolic debugging   Debugging based on user-defined symbol names and source statements as opposed to strictly machine-code and numeric address locations.

synchronization   The process of making two separate threads of execution come together at a specified point for the purposes of making sure a necessary sequencing of events occurs.

system call   A function call to a routine considered to be an operating system facility.

temporary breakpoints   Breakpoints that do not continue to exist past the next stop of execution. These are useful for features like "run-to-here" and "finish function" that go away if a stop occurs for any other reason than hitting the breakpoint.

thread   The thread is the smallest entity within the operating system that is scheduled for execution. The thread is a single unit of execution. It represents an independent program counter, and it is the unit of execution that is associated with a stack. The operating system time-slices between all of the currently runnable threads in the system.

thread local storage   Because threads all share the global per-process data, problems occur when they do so carelessly. To prevent this, stack-based thread local storage is used. Special APIs exist to create and maintain this type of storage.

thunking   The process of passing control from one domain to a very different domain. Usually used for backward compatibility to use older code in a new system. Currently it is most commonly seen in going from 32-bit flat address space code to 16-bit segmented code.

TOOLHELP.DLL   A special auxiliary system to 16-bit Windows to give access to system services not part of the standard Windows API. The focus of this DLL is debugging support.

tracing   Another term for single-step. The single-step bit on the Intel CPUs is called the trace bit.

trap   An operating system term for a condition that occurs that is exceptional and causes execution to take a different course to deal with the trap conditions. The breakpoint instruction on some systems causes an OS trap to occur.

Turbo Debugger   The PC industry's long-standing standard debugger. A text-mode debugger built originally for DOS but now running on all Windows systems and OS/2 as well.

UNIX   The Bell Labs-invented operating system that is now dominated by Sun, HP, and IBM.

variable inspection   A critical feature of debuggers that enables the user to view the values of variables specified symbolically as they were originally defined in the textual program.

VDMDBG   A special debugging subsystem on Windows NT to support 16-bit debugging in the WOW system.

virtual frame pointer   A synthesized frame pointer is needed on some processors (e.g., MIPS) where no hardware register is provided but from the debug information and the stack pointer a virtual frame pointer can be synthesized.

virtual function tables   In C++ and similar compiled object-oriented languages, the way late binding is implemented is that function calls go through a table of pointers to functions so that at run-time the pointers can be changed, changing the function called when that pointer is de-referenced next time.

virtual machine   Similar to an interpreter, it is a run-time system and accepts a stream of bytes that it interprets to the local host native instruction set.

Visual Basic   Microsoft's version of the Basic programming language is a programming environment that is simple to use for simple applications.

watch points   Synonymous with data breakpoints. These breakpoints "watch" a specified variable or memory location and cause a program stop as soon as any instruction tries to access the location.

Win32   The name Microsoft has given to the API it exposes from its 32-bit operating systems. In theory it means applications are portable, but debuggers must still be filled with specialized OS-specific code.

Windows 3.1   The predecessor operating system to Windows 95. It is a 16-bit layer on top of DOS. TOOLHELP.DLL is needed to build a debugger. It uses a completely different debugging approach from that of Win32.

Windows 95   The current mass-market Win32-based operating system for PCs.

Windows NT   Also implements Win32 but in a more robust, secure operating system.

Windows-on-Windows (WOW)   The 16-bit subsystem within Window NT for executing 16-bit applications.

Winsight   Similar tool to Dr. Watson.

References

AHO 1986   AHO, ALFRED V. RAVI SETHI, AND JEFFREY D. ULLMAN. 1986. *Compilers: Principles, Techniques and Tools.* Reading, MA: Addison-Wesley.

BLANK 1990   BLANK, W. TOM. 1990. The MasPar MP-1 architecture. In *Proceedings of the 35th Institute of Electrical and Electronic Engineers Computer Society Compcon Conference.*

CARGILL 1986   CARGILL, T.A., 1986. Pi: A case study in object-oriented programming. In *Proceedings of OOPSLA '86.* Association for Computing Machinery.

CARLE 1987   CARLE, ALAN, KEITH D. COOPER, ROBERT T. HOOD, KEN KENNEDY, LINDA TORCZCON, AND SCOTT K. WARREN. VOL. # 11. 1987. *A practical environment for scientific programming.* Institute of Electrical and Electronic Engineers Computer, Vol. 11:75-89.

COPPERMAN 1993   COPPERMAN, MAX. 1993. *Debugging optimized code without being misled.* PhD Diss. University of California Santa Cruz.

COUTANT 1988   COUTANT, DEBORAH S., SUE MELOY, AND MICHELLE RUSCETTA. 1988. DOC: A practical approach to source-level debugging of globally optimized code. In *Proceedings of the SIGPLAN '88 Conference on Programming Language Design and Implementation.* Association for Computing Machinery

ELLIS 1990   ELLIS, MARGRET AND BARJNE STROUSTROP. *Annotated C++ Reference Manual.* Reading, MA: Addison-Wesley.

FAULKNER 1991   FAULKNER, ROGER AND RON GOMES. 1991. The process file system and process model in UNIX System V. In *Proceedings USENIX.*

FISCHER 1988   FISCHER, CHARLES N. AND RICHERD J. LE BLANC, JR. 1988. *Crafting a Compiler.* Reading, MA: Benjamin Cummings.

FOX 1987   FOX, GEOFFREY C. AND PAUL MESSINA. 1987. Advanced computer architectures. *Scientific American* Vol #66-77.

FYFE 1994   FYFE, ALASTAIR. 1994. C++ Windows Programs. In *Proceedings of the 5th Borland International Conference.* Borland International.

GRAMLICH 1983   GRAMLICH, WAYNE C. 1983. Debugging Methodology. *Session Summary for ACM Workshop on Debugging.* Association for Computing Machinery.

HENNESSEY 1979   HENNESSEY, JOHN. *Symbolic Debugging of Optimized Code,* Association for Computing Machinery Transactions on Programming Languages and Systems, 4(3): 323-344, July 1982.

HO 1982   HO, WINGSHUN WILGON. 1982. *Issues in debugging sequential and concurrent programs: Methods, techniques and implementaions.* Ph.D. diss.,University of California, Davis.

INTEL 1990   INTEL CORPORATION. 1990. *i486 Processor Programmer's Reference Manual.* Santa Clara, CA: Intel Corporation.

INTEL 1994   INTEL CORPORATION. 1994. *Pentium Family User's Manual, Vol. 3.* Santa Clara, CA: Intel Corporation, 1989.

KANE 1989   KANE , GERRY, *MIPS RISC Architecture.* Englewood Cliffs, NJ: Prentice-Hall.

KEMENEY 1985   KEMENEY AND KURTZ. 1985. *Back to Basic.* Reading, MA: Addison-Wesley.

LALONDE 1990   LALONDE, WILF R. AND JOHN R.PUGH, 1990. *Inside*

Smalltalk, Vol. 1. Prentice-Hall, 1990.

LAZZERINI 1992   LAZZERINI, BEATRICE AND LANFRANCO LOPRIORE. 1992. *Progam Debugging Environment: Design and Utilization*. New York: Ellis Horwood.

LEWIS 1995   LEWIS, SIMON. *The Art and Science of Smalltalk*. Englewood Cliffs, NJ: Prentice-Hall/Hewlett-Packard Professional Books, 1995.

LINTON 1986   LINTON, MARK A. 1986. Integrated debugging in a loosely-coupled environment. *SIGPLAN Notices*. Association for Computing Machinery. 1974.

MICROSOFT 1993   MICROSOFT CORP. 1993. *STI-Symbol Table Information specification*. Available from Microsoft's MSDN subscription. Redmond, WA: Microsoft.

MICROSOFT 1995   MICROSOFT CORP. 1995. *The Component Object Model Specification*. Available from Microsoft's MSDN subscription. Redmond, WA: Microsoft.

MIRHO 1993   MIRHO, CHARLES. 1993. It's a raid! Putting four debuggers for Windows through their paces. *Microsoft Systems Journal*. Vol. #4: 35-55.

MOTOROLA 1993   MOTOROLA. PowerPC 601: *RISC Microprocessor User's Manual*. Austin, Texas: Motorola Corporation.

NICKOLLS 1990   NICKOLLS, JOHN R. 1990. The design of the MasPar MP-1: A cost effective massively parallel processor. In *Proceedings of Compcon*. Association for Computing Machinery and Institute of Electrical and Electronic Engineers.

PIETREK 1993   PIETREK, MATT. 1993. Windows NT, OS/2, and debuggers. *BYTE Magazine*.

ROCHESTER 1983   ROCHESTER, JACK B. AND JOHN GANTZ. 1983. The *Naked Computer*. New York: William Morrow.

ROSENBERG 1988   ROSENBERG, JONATHAN B. AND KENT BECK. 1988. *MPPE-The Massively Parallel Programming Environ-*

ment. MasPar Computer Corporation, Technical
Report.

SCHULMAN 1992 SCHULMAN, ANDREW, DAVID MAXEY AND MATT PIETREK.
1992. *Undocumented Windows*. Reading, MA:
Addison-Wesley.

SITES 1992 SITES, RICHARD L. 1992. *Alpha Architecture Reference
Manual*. Maynard, MA: Digital Press.

SUN 1995 SUN MICROSYSTEMS CORP. 1995. *The Java Language
Specification*. Mountain View, CA. Sun Microsystems
Computer Corporation [http://java.sun.com].

ZELLWEGER 1984 ZELLWEGER. POLLE T. 1984. *Interactive source-level
debugging*. Ph.D. Diss, Xerox Parc Palo Alto Research
Center, Technical Report CSL-84-5.

Index